THE IDEA OF THE RENAISSANCE

The Idea of
the Renaissance

WILLIAM KERRIGAN

&

GORDON BRADEN

The Johns Hopkins University Press

BALTIMORE & LONDON

© 1989 The Johns Hopkins University Press
All rights reserved
Printed in the United States of America

The Johns Hopkins University Press
701 West 40th Street
Baltimore, Maryland 21211
The Johns Hopkins Press Ltd., London

The paper used in this publication meets the minimum requirements of
American National Standard for Information Sciences—Permanence of
Paper for Printed Library Materials, ANSI Z 39.48–1984.

Library of Congress Cataloging-in-Publication Data

Kerrigan, William, 1943–
The idea of the Renaissance.

Bibliography: p.
Includes index.
1. Renaissance. 2. Renaissance—Italy. 3. Italy—
Civilization—1268–1559. I. Braden, Gordon, 1947–
II. Title.
CB361.K37 1989   945'.05   88-22983
ISBN 8-8018-3759-6 (alk. paper)

for
Amelia Kerrigan, without whom

Contents

Preface   ix

Part 1. Power
Chapter 1. Burckhardt's Renaissance   3
Chapter 2. Beyond Burckhardt   37
Chapter 3. The Prince and the Playhouse: A Fable   55

Part 2. Thought
Chapter 4. Cassirer's Legacy to the Burckhardt Tradition   73
Chapter 5. Nicolas of Cusa's Symbolic Renaissance   83
Chapter 6. The Neoplatonic Individualism of Marsilio Ficino   101
Chapter 7. Pico della Mirandola and Renaissance Ambition   117
Chapter 8. Descartes's Beginning   135

Part 3. Love
Chapter 9. Petrarch Refracted: 157
    The Evolution of the English Love Lyric
Chapter 10. Lust Captured: 191
    Paradise Lost and Renaissance Love Poetry

Notes   219
Index   255

Preface

This book grew out of a course we taught in the University of Virginia English Department on the period concept of the Renaissance. Although our own training did not include such a course, living memory recalls a time when the idea of the period dominated literary scholarship, and Renaissance studies were indeed *Renaissance* studies.

Consider the work of Douglas Bush, for example. His key notion of "Christian humanism" was meant to rebuke Burckhardt's diagnosis of Renaissance paganism. Yet getting the period concept right was still, in his view, the main business of a Renaissance scholar. New Critics made up the opposition. Almost everyone else agreed that literary history at its most expansive would talk about the period concept. Bush's *The Renaissance and English Humanism* (1939) led E. M. W. Tillyard to confess in *The English Renaissance: Fact or Fiction?* (1952) that his influential *The Elizabethan World Picture* (1943) had dwelled excessively "on the similarities between the epochs" of the Middle Ages and the Renaissance: "There is always the danger of making too much of them."[1] It is true that Bush was offering more than a conception of literary history; the noble alliance of Christianity and classicism in Bush's Renaissance gave him a powerful literary identity, the heroic role of belonging to a later and endangered state of the very tradition he was laboring to understand. Though few claimed the righteous high ground of Bush, scholars of Renaissance literature were engaged in a communal act of retrieval, a renaissance of the Renaissance.

We do not hear very much these days about Christian humanism. Tillyard's alertness to "the danger of making too much" of epochal similarities seems like a remark in a forgotten conversation. Everybody beats the dead horse of the New Criticism, but contemporary opponents of unhistorical approaches to literature often want to dissolve the traditions of the Renaissance rather than continue them. Meanwhile, scholarship of the sort that Bush or Tillyard would have admired has quietly abandoned the period concept. A revolution in critical fashion can be observed in the title of a work manifestly indebted to the Bush tradition, Barbara Kiefer Lewalski's *Protestant Poetics and the Seventeenth-Century Religious Lyric* (1979). In place of "Christian" we find the sectarian precision of "Protestant," and in place of "humanism," with its strong epochal ring, we find the timeless "poetics." Instead of the evocative "Renaissance," we have the flatly denotative "Seventeenth-Century," with which nobody will bother to quarrel. Today's scholars are not so convinced as their teachers that distinguishing the medieval from the Renaissance aspects of a Shakespeare, Donne, or Milton is an important thing to do. The Bush tradition in its current state wants to distinguish Protestant from Catholic things or Anglican from Puritan things. Speculation is more wide-ranging than ever in Renaissance studies today, but, in conventional historical terms, the discourse has contracted to localities, where undoubted refinements in sectarian discrimination have not often led back to the Renaissance at large. "Historical" is something everyone wants to be, yet the contentions provoked by this word no longer center on the period concept.

Doubtless this suspicion has been earned. Period concepts can be static, exclusive, prescriptive, tyrannically obstructing intellectual curiosity. This is especially so in the classroom. Most of us in the academic profession remember times when, burning with some Stevensian idea about Donne's metaphors or some Borgesian nicety in Shakespeare, we eagerly blurted out our thoughts, whereupon the teacher, releasing a deep breath, replied, "Interesting, Miss Hull. But in the Renaissance. . . ." This gambit belongs to the rhetoric of professorial power. Students can verify after a fashion an interpretation of a line or a work; information about a textless entity like the period must simply be taken down. In the higher reaches of scholarly exchange, the period concept has also been employed at times in a regulative manner, to separate possible or learned interpretations from farfetched or ignorant ones. Yet the idea of the period, rather than making us into would-be initiates looking for a few sages able to tell whether we have mastered "the Renaissance," can be treated as an open concept, subject to infinite revision. Perhaps the eclipse of the period concept reflects, like the new sin called "totalizing," a fear that certain kinds of generalization will involve us in untenable metaphysical presumption. But the example of Burckhardt, indeed of Marx, not to mention others, demonstrates the possibility of writing Hegelian history without having much use for Hegelian metaphysics.

The utility of period concepts does not derive from their isolated generality (individualism up, Christianity down). They do their most important work in narratives, where they mingle with fact and coincidence to help us plot the stories of traditions. We probably tend to discard period concepts when the narratives they have mainly served, the traditions they have highlighted, no longer seem crucial to us. It is our contention in this book that the inherited idea of the Renaissance, though it has (at least in literary circles) fallen without uproar into near obsolescence, does propel us into a story that matters today: Burckhardt's story, the history of early modern individualism. About this Renaissance people will indeed bother to quarrel. We believe that this would be, just now, a good debate, clarifying differences and allegiances.[2]

Working through the opening text in our course, *The Civilization of the Renaissance in Italy*, we became convinced that Burckhardt was right in a certain fresh and direct way. Our first part is accordingly an interpretive paraphrase of that famous book, so familiar that its critics do not always appreciate what it is saying. We try to make explicit some of the rigor and connectedness of its argument, and to demonstrate its continuing utility. At several points, especially in chapter 2, we try to coax that argument beyond Burckhardt's own limits, both the ones that he chose—temporal and geographical—and the ones, so familiar from subsequent polemics, that he himself did not recognize. We think that his idea was often wiser than he was, and that it survives a needed purge of the blindnesses and prejudices of post-Romantic German scholarship. In particular, we try to sketch what none of Burckhardt's descendants have managed to supply in comparably decisive form: a picture of how Burckhardt's idea looks, and works, when extended to the general European Renaissance that climaxes a century and a half after the Italian enterprise is effectively ended.

We hope that such a picture, rightly set out, will prompt at least a measure of simple recognition. With all our adjustments, this is still the period that we think and write about. We have tried to mount a Hegelian history of the Renaissance on the pragmatic understanding that ours is only one arrangement of infinitely organizable data, that the concept of the period in some important ways creates, or better, perhaps, calls attention to specific pockets of, the data.[3] The polemical side of our history lies in its assumption that nothing we know today requires us to close down the Burckhardt tradition, though its major theme, the appearance of a newly ambitious individualism, may of course be described in many vocabularies, some of them less respectful than our own, which is not without uneasiness. Burckhardt's thesis receives news like the sea the rain.

Our second part takes its rise from another well-known yet in some ways unassimilated text, Ernst Cassirer's *The Individual and the Cosmos in Renaissance Thought,* which addresses one of Burckhardt's most glaring omissions, Renaissance philosophy. Cassirer demonstrates that there is, in a strong sense, such a thing as "Renaissance philosophy," and that its history may be cast in the terms used by Burckhardt to discuss Italian politics and society. Cassirer's is admittedly a less momentous achievement than Burckhardt's; it owes much of its vitality to the connection with its predecessor. We leave Cassirer behind more quickly than we do Burckhardt. But we take from Cassirer some of his commitment to the autonomy of intellectual history, and set ourselves against the current tendency to deny that ideas have an independent history, being little more than the forms ideology assumes when forgetful of its real purposes. Instead of attempting the blanket coverage of books such as John Herman Randall's *The Career of Philosophy,* which would have been beyond us in any case, we have written chapters about four Renaissance thinkers, and rather than discuss figures representative of widely separate currents in Renaissance thought, our four intellectuals (Nicolas of Cusa, Marsilio Ficino, Pico della Mirandola, and René Descartes) belong more or less directly to the history of Neoplatonism, also the emphasis of Cassirer. Matters of contemporary concern are before us throughout. As shall be evident from the chapters on Pico and Descartes particularly, our various forays into classical, medieval, and Renaissance ideas aim ultimately at elucidating our own sometimes ambivalent, sometimes clandestine inheritance of these philosophical traditions.

The third part is most fully our own. The intention was to give the period concept developed in the first two sections a workout, what for us constitutes a practical application. Renaissance love poetry seems at first glance a massive corpus of uncongenial singlemindedness, and acquaintance does not always contradict that impression. In the terms of Milton's lovely description of Renaissance music, "linkéd sweetness long drawn out," the long drawing out of the Petrarchan tradition appears to exhaust its sweetness and become an independent force, a mysterious yet not very appealing male doggedness. This tradition offers a major challenge to our powers of historical sympathy.

Guided by the period concept, we trace an arc from Petrarch's *Canzoniere* to Milton's *Paradise Lost* and attempt to explain the curve, giving coordinates along the way for some of the age's best, worst, and most peculiar literature. Even in love, especially in love, the male poets of the Renaissance played out the strategic resources of the new individualism.

We hope to be interesting to both specialists and beginning students, and we have tried to bear in mind the separate needs of each. In the end we have produced a denser and more difficult book than we once foresaw, though it remains our belief that spirited undergraduates will profit from this account of Renaissance culture, especially if they have read selections from Burckhardt, Cassirer, and the primary texts. We recognize some of our biases, above all a primary interest in literature. Our omissions are so numerous that we have been unable to find a way of listing them that does not seem impudent or simply ludicrous. An ideal of inclusiveness comes with the very concept of the Renaissance as a period. But no book, and certainly not this one, lives up to that questionable ideal.

ONE

Power

ONE

Burckhardt's Renaissance

It is some consolation that we share the most conspicuous of our omissions with our great original. Jacob Burckhardt announces at the opening of *The Civilization of the Renaissance in Italy* that he will largely pass over art and architecture, and of all the gaps in his coverage this is clearly the one he most regretted. The strongest and most persistent passion in his personal writings—greater than literature, certainly greater than philosophy—is fine arts. He was to become professor of art history as well as history, and he retained the former chair eight years after having resigned the latter. A companion volume to the *Civilization* specifically on art was planned and, by Burckhardt's reckoning, "seven-eighths" finished; the material on architecture was published in 1867 as the Renaissance section of a general *Geschichte der Baukunst.*[1]

Yet what we have of this abandoned completion tends to validate Burckhardt's own sense of its inadequacy. Despite a few specific points of contact, its virtues—detailed research and carefully graded aesthetic judgments—are not the ones that count for the *Civilization.* The art history appropriate to his enterprise would rather be something like that worked out by Heinrich Wölfflin, his pupil and successor at Basel: a canvass of the prevailing stylistic traits of a period with a view to delineating "not the individual products of an age, but the fundamental temper [*Grundstimmung*] which produced them."[2] It was Wölfflin's influential achievement to have demonstrated—largely, indeed, through a contrast between the Renaissance and its successor period, the Baroque—how rigorous a sense of corporate identity can

3

be coaxed from the facts of "pure visibility" in the art of a particular age. Art history had been striving toward such a goal since at least Johann Winckelmann. Where that discipline really tells for Burckhardt's own work is less in anything he says or might have said about it than in the way he allowed comparable ambitions to apply themselves, with unprecedented effect, to other materials: politics, religion, jokes, classical scholarship, cosmetics. Taking up general history with a sensibility nursed in art history, Burckhardt established a mode of *Kulturgeschichte* which set an important standard for seeing the whole range of civilized life as a subtly inclusive whole.

On the intellectual status of what results Burckhardt himself is largely noncommittal. He disowned any serious capacity for abstract argument, and his writings can be maddeningly elliptical. "I have never, as is well known, penetrated into the Temple of genuine thought, but have all my life taken delight in the halls and forecourt of the Peribolos, where the image [*Bildung*], in the widest sense of the word, reigns supreme."³ Wölfflin insists that the unity to be sought in a period's work is not that of "a particular idea or system" ("What has Gothic to do with the feudal system or scholasticism?") but of something vaguer, a *Stimmung*.⁴ Burckhardt himself, in his only serious theoretical statement on the matter,⁵ writes of *Kulturgeschichte* as an attempt to trace, as conventional narrative history does not, the course of *Denkweise* and *Anschauungen,* ways of thinking, points of view— though the term that keeps coming up is, of course, *Geist*. We think "idea" will do, partly because of its looser Anglo-American usage, and also because, as E. H. Gombrich has shown, Burckhardt's own point of reference, despite numerous protestations to the contrary, is Hegel. There are thumbnail pieces of *Kulturgeschichte* throughout Hegel's writing—at least one of which, as we shall see, had a very specific influence on Burckhardt—and the enterprise of the *Civilization* may be described as a subjection of Hegelian idealism to the massive discipline of historical research, a redirection of that idealism to the concrete record of human passage.

That seems to us a wholly proper thing to be doing. We agree with Gombrich that what Burckhardt initiated in historiography is "a succession of attempts to salvage the Hegelian assumption without accepting Hegelian metaphysics,"⁶ but we disagree with his dismayed conclusion that this kind of thing has to stop. It at any rate hasn't. After the positivist critique has had its say, recent years have witnessed a renewed interest in the kind of history that Burckhardt wanted to write. At the leading edge of Renaissance studies in particular a version of Burckhardt's program is frequently reannounced, in an updated idiom: "Cultural systems are manifested in specific forms of expression, such as literature, for example, painting, dress, architecture, music, eating habits, and so on. The totality of such expressions is . . . a complex text consisting of various linguistic and nonlinguistic signs."[7] It is easy enough to suppose that such efforts might profit from being more fully cognizant of their own roots. But Burckhardt is an elusive master. The strength and subtlety of his idea of the Renaissance have to some degree gone unrecognized because of its successful effacement into its examples, its images.

We may begin with the history of that idea, the originality of which has been widely acknowledged but differently defined. It seems most significant to us as a particular devolution of what, on Frank Kermode's prompting, we may call the Western ideal of imperialism.[8]

The contemporary polemical sense of that term is not irrelevant here. Part of the story that any Renaissance historian has to tell is of a multinational enterprise of conquest and colonization by which Western Europe began its transformation from a comparatively inward-looking, self-contained area, peripheral in the global scheme of things, into the indisputable center of the world, the focus of an unprecedented political, economic, and cultural authority. That is not the place to start, however, because the conceiving and analysis of the Renaissance as a period concept does not begin there. For that, rather, we look back to imperialism as a millennial concern—judicial, intellectual, even metaphysical—with the fate and location of the ancient Roman *imperium*.

When Constantine the Great—whose reign forms for Petrarch the beginning of the "modern" age, and is the subject of Burckhardt's first book—establishes Constantinople as the new capital of the empire originally built by the city of Rome, he effects the first *translatio imperii*: a continuity of authority between an old order and a new. With the western lapse of even this restored empire, the political imagination clings to the hope of reestablishing this continuity in some form or other. Reconquered in the sixth century, Italy is technically reintegrated into the old empire for two indecisive centuries; but the Byzantine exarchate at Ravenna is ended for good by the Lombards in 751, and the Roman popes turn to the Franks for protection. After a half-century, it is their momentous joint idea—with some scholarly prompting—to secure this alliance as something more than tribal politics. In 800 the Frankish king is invested at Rome with the putatively greater dignity of emperor of the newly reproclaimed western empire.

We still have Charlemagne's lead signet, with the inscription that announces his program: *Renouatio Romani Imperii*. That motto denotes what becomes, in one manifestation or another, a permanent ambition of our culture:

> Rursus in antiquos mutataque secula mores.
> Aurea Roma iterum renouata renascitur orbi!

> Our times are transformed into the civilization of Antiquity. Golden Rome is reborn and restored anew to the world![9]

The specifically political history of Charlemagne's title is, of course, often a joke and sometimes worse. But the idea behind it gives an astonishing tenacity to the succession, which technically lasts until ended by Napoleon in 1806. Even then theorists could adduce a *translatio*, for Napoleon had crowned himself Emperor of the French two years before, in a ceremony imitating that of Charlemagne. We might even push the descent, in a lurid way, up to 1945; when Hitler called his regime *das dritte Reich*, he was counting the Holy Roman Empire as *das erste Reich*, which lasted just over a thousand years (one of the major scholars of this millennium became official historian to the German High Command).[10]

It is from the thirteenth to the sixteenth centuries, though, that the mythology of the reborn Empire is fullest, most complex, and most urgently hopeful. The Ghibelline cause, given refined form in Dante's *De monarchia*, is the recurrent political fantasy for Italian intellectuals. Even those princes who bring the emperor's efforts to naught are moved to purchase imperial titles from him to establish their own legitimacy. More defiant powers as well envy the emperor's pedigree and, with learned assistance, assert some prior claim of their own. Cola di Rienzi bids to restore the institutions and authority of republican Rome, and wins Petrarch's admiration and support. Florentine writers advance a run of theories by which their city is the proper inheritor of Rome by a previously unrecognized *translatio*. Poliziano argues for the benefit of the Medici that the original arcane name of Rome was in fact Florentia. With the help of Polydore Vergil, Henry VIII avails himself in his own struggle with Rome of the legend that Constantine the Great was of British descent and in turn ancestor of Arthur, so that Henry's own power was lineally imperial. At about the same time, the official crown becomes an object of special desire, actively sought by the kings of France and Spain. And with his success in 1519, the latter suddenly dominates European politics as no previous successor to Charlemagne had, with a realm that stretches not only from the North Sea to the Mediterranean but also to the Atlantic and beyond to the New World. The reign of Charles V calls forth a body of celebratory iconography proclaiming the start of the long-postponed imperial restoration: AVGVSTVS CAESAR DIVVM GENVS AVREA CONDIT SAECVLA, August Caesar, offspring of the gods, founds a golden age.[11] Charles's personal *impresa* is one of the most resonant of the age: two pillars of Hercules, with the motto *plus ultra,* as if in rising to the standards of antiquity he had surpassed them, on terms that antiquity itself would have acknowledged.

Still, the imperial prophecy is a false one, hollow-sounding even in its own time and woefully inaccurate about the future. Charles's empire does not outlast his own weary abdication in 1556, and its like does not rise up elsewhere. It is not for its political history that what we now designate as the Renaissance comes to be called that. More telling in the long run is the cultural program that springs up with the political program but takes on an enduring life of its own. With the Carolingian *translatio imperii ad Francos* comes a related *translatio studii,* a scholarly and pedagogical effort to restore classical Roman literary culture through the systematic collection and copying of its surviving manuscripts and the intensified diffusion of Latin literacy. In crucial ways, the effort was a success. That we have any serious knowledge now of ancient Latin literature we owe almost entirely to the Carolingian scribes; and even as the educational program fades, it sets the pattern for subsequent ambitions: contemporary cultural action through a conscious revival of the antique.

The movement that counts—what we now call humanism—takes decisive form under Petrarch's inspiration and influence in the fourteenth century[12] and is accompanied from the first with propaganda about its historic momentousness. Petrarch's apparently unprecedented division of the past into an *aetas antiqua* and an *aetas noua* at the age of Constantine places his own age at the cultural millennium. His reference to the prior epoch as history's *tenebrae* establishes the "Dark Ages" as a period concept. It is a concept inseparable from the call for a post-new or post-modern age as a regeneration of that finer, earlier dispensation. Petrarch's neo-Vergilian epic on Scipio Africanus contains a heady prophecy of just such a turning point:

> Poterunt discussis forte tenebris
> Ad purum priscumque iubar remeare nepotes.

Tunc Elicona noua reuirentem stirpe uidebis,
Tunc lauros frondere sacras; tunc alta resurgent
Ingenia atque animi dociles, quibus ardor honesti
Pyeridum studii ueterem geminabit amorem.

                    (*Africa* 9.456–61)

Then perhaps, with the darkness dispersed, our descendants will be able
to return to the pure and ancient light. Then you will see Helicon green
again with new growth, then the sacred laurel will flourish; then great
talents will arise again, and receptive spirits whose ardor for the honest
study of the Muses will duplicate the ancient love.

So the conclusion of a poem putatively about a Roman general. The
diversion of political ambition into literary is deeply characteristic of
the movement. In one of the most important humanist works of the
next century, Valla celebrates the Roman Empire as a linguistic empire—"For the Roman *imperium* is wherever the Roman language
rules"—and dramatizes the humanist's task as the restoration of that
empire. He is an avatar of Camillus, who returned the *signa* to the
city, winning a glory second only to that of Romulus as *imperator*.[13]

When in the sixteenth century that effort gains crucial range and
permanence with the help of the printing press, the humanist pub-
lisher Aldo Manuzio takes as his device Augustus Caesar's motto of
Festina lente and the Emperor Titus's emblem—reversed, as on a printing block—of the anchor and dolphin. Erasmus hails an imperial
triumph that mirrors but outdoes that of Charles:

> The man who sets fallen learning on its feet . . . is building up a sacred
> and immortal thing, and serving not one province alone but all peoples
> and all generations. Once this was the task of princes, and it was the great-
> est glory of Ptolemy. But his library was contained between the narrow
> walls of its own house, and Aldus is building up a library which has no
> other limits than the world itself.[14]

It is in passages like these that the Renaissance—"to restore to the
world so divine a thing . . . to call to life what had perished"—most
cogently announces itself.

Humanism becomes the driving force in Renaissance education,
has strong and demonstrable influence in a wide spectrum of Renaissance literature, and keeps a particularly powerful hold on Renaissance
literary criticism. Whatever its disappointments, the movement suc-

cessfully secures the prestige both of the writings of classical antiquity and of the contemporary ambition to imitate them. We should probably regard the political mythology sketched above as largely just the reflection of this far more coherent, persistent, and self-conscious program. Its example irradiates other enterprises as well. Reformation historiographers describe their own time as a *renouatio ecclesiae* that restores the purity of early Christianity. "It has pleased God to renew the world in this past sixty years or so, making the light of his truth to shine beautifully and clearly out of the abyss of ignorance and superstition in which it had long been plunged"—so Théodore de Bèze, whose title page defines his subject as *la renaissance et accroissement* of the church.[15] This rebirth was characteristically linked to renewed attention to Christianity's own ancient texts; Bèze is among several sixteenth-century historians to see this effort as a logical extension of humanism.

The decisive language comes in the comparatively new genre of art history, when Giorgio Vasari reviews the course of painting, sculpture, and architecture in Italy and decides that what begins with Cimabue and Giotto and culminates in his own time is best characterized as a *rinascita dell'arte* superseding a millennial barbarism. It is around the notion of a general rebirth of high culture, *la renaissance des lettres et des beaux arts,* that the notion consolidates in the next two centuries that something novel and important had indeed happened in Europe in the time Vasari was discussing. It is apparently in an early nineteenth-century *Histoire de l'art par les monumens* by Seroux d'Agincourt that *la Renaissance* is first established in print as the general designation for that episode.[16] The scene is then ready for a Burckhardt to add things up.

Yet in doing so, Burckhardt also changes the equation. Here also it is probably significant that the topic reaches him through art history. Erwin Panofsky has shown how even in the Renaissance the understanding of contemporary artistic achievement was complicated because so much less was known about classical sculpture and especially painting than about classical literature. How can one account for the creation of great art, how indeed can one even say it is great art, when the standards are lost?[17] Alberti was going detectably against the grain when—as now seems only sensible—he praised the artists of the quattrocento precisely for their unguided originality: "Our fame ought to be much greater . . . if we discover unheard-of and never-before-seen arts and sciences without teachers or without any model whatsoever."[18] But such fame comes into its own in the nineteenth century, and it is part of Burckhardt's distinction to put forth a general idea of the Renaissance centered not on its links to the past but on its radically innovative character.

Burckhardt is not especially happy with the designation "Renaissance," which he occasionally puts in quotation marks (a nuance lost in available English translations). The section in the *Civilization* on "the influence of antiquity, the 'new birth' of which has been one-sidedly chosen as the name to sum up the whole period," comes not first but third, and it begins with a significant subordination of the whole topic:

> The conditions which have been hitherto described would have sufficed, apart from antiquity, to upturn and to mature the national mind; and most of the intellectual tendencies which yet remain to be noticed would be conceivable without it. . . . We must insist upon it, as one of the chief propositions of this book, that it was not the revival of antiquity alone, but its union with the genius of the Italian people, which achieved the conquest of the Western world. (P. 175)[19]

That subordination has survived subsequent scrutiny. Even in literature, where humanist influence was the strongest, we have come to value the Renaissance precisely for its often exuberant originality, and to see and appreciate that originality in some of the most detailed handling of classical materials (true neoclassical *imitatio* awaits a later age). The general Renaissance quest for classical authority in the most dramatically unprecedented endeavors—Columbus was said to have been inspired to sail west by Aristotle, Seneca, Strabo—now seems in many cases a clearly secondary effort, more strategy or camouflage than source. The nurture or instruction provided by the classics is often less impressive than the unclassical ends to which they and their cachet could be put.

The point of leverage here is not merely the nineteenth-century *Volksgeist* that slips into Burckhardt's language. In the formulation that is the conceptual center of his book, the sense of group identity characterizes the previous age:

> In the Middle Ages both sides of human consciousness—that which was turned within as that which was turned without—lay dreaming or half awake beneath a common veil. The veil was woven of faith, illusion, and childish prepossession, through which the world and history were seen clad in strange hues. Man was conscious of himself only as member of a

race, people, party, family, or corporation—only through some general category.

Such assertions, of course, are a matter of degree, meaningful as one half of a contrast. The completion of this one, in a swift but dense statement, is Burckhardt's idea of the Renaissance:

> In Italy this veil first melted into air; an *objective* treatment and consideration of the State and of all the things of this world became possible. The *subjective* side at the same time asserted itself with corresponding emphasis; man became a spiritual [*geistiges*] *individual,* and recognized himself as such. (P. 143)

This is what Burckhardt puts in place of the rebirth of antiquity as the center around which Renaissance civilization coheres. We are still exploring the usefulness of that change.

By individualism Burckhardt means in part self-conscious uniqueness: "The Italians of the fourteenth century knew little of false modesty or of hypocrisy in any shape; not one of them was afraid of singularity, of being and seeming unlike his neighbors" (p. 144). Burckhardt notes programmatic eccentricities of dress in Florence, and a new use of *singolare* and *unico* as terms of praise. We might add the later, general European taste for heroic tautology in the definition of character: "He will be found like Brutus, like himself"; "paréciste a ti mismo / porque no tienes igual." The idiom of proud reflexivity is indeed a significant part of our Renaissance heritage: "Moi-même je me suis de moi-même assurée"; "Stand like thyself, or like thyself now fall"; "I am that I am, and they that level / At my abuses reckon up their own"; "Yo soy quien soy, / y siendo quien soy, me venzo / a mí mismo con callar." The age was alert to the possibility of self-possession offering itself as its own justification: "Chacun selon son goût s'obstine en son parti"; "like the irregular crab, / Which though 't goes backward, thinks that it goes right, / Because it goes its own way"; "Samson hath quit himself / Like Samson, and heroicly hath finished / A life heroic." [20]

Burckhardt's individualism, however, is not just that. We can be more precise by considering what seems to be the source of his unusually philosophical and abstract language. The definition of Renaissance individualism is a condensation of Hegel's account of classical Hellenism as the culture of *geistige Individualität:* "This is the *elementary character* of the Spirit of the Greeks, implying the origination of their culture from independent individualities;—a condition in which individuals take their own ground, and are not, from the very beginning, patriarchally united by a bond of *Nature*."[21] Burckhardt is thus in a way keeping the classical tradition within his definition of the Renaissance, though the connection now is not a matter of influence (Renaissance humanism was comparatively uninterested in Greek culture, aside from philosophy) but of parallel. Adducing it is helpful because of Hegel's fuller explication of Burckhardt's compactness, the grammar linking his emphasized abstractions. "Subjective" and "objective" here have their technical philosophical weight; what Burckhardt means by "individual" is a certain stance toward reality, a certain relation between subject and object.

The relation is a dynamic one. Objectivity toward the state and all the things of this world involves looking on them without preconception, in particular without the sense of tradition sustained by the continuities of group membership: race, people, party. To behold without expectation is to find things strangely other, objects set apart from us, which we view across a distance, an empty space unmediated by convention. Burckhardt seems to have overestimated the extent to which the Renaissance actually contributed in this regard to the evolution of modern scientific methodology; but his interest is not with achieved knowledge as such but with the psychic reflex to the effort of objectification, which does not straiten the subjective but clarifies it. To become conscious of the empty space between ourselves and external reality is to become newly conscious of the self as its own world, something separate from that reality. Detachment fosters a sense of particularized identity.

In the full context of the *Civilization* another term figures as well, though Burckhardt does not use it here. Hegel is more schematic. He wants to make the point that the individuality of the Greeks is not what he considers the higher kind, "Infinite Subjectivity as pure certainty of itself—the position that the Ego is the ground of all that can lay claim to substantial existence." Greek *Geistigheit* is "not yet absolutely free; not yet absolutely *self*-produced" because it is prompted by an encounter with external reality: "We find its fundamental characteristic to be, that the freedom of Spirit is conditioned by and has an essential relation to some stimulus supplied by Nature. Greek freedom of thought is excited by an alien existence." (*Plus ultra:* something out there.) Nevertheless, "it is free because it transforms and virtually reproduces the stimulus by its own operation. . . . This stamps the Greek character as that of *Individuality conditioned by Beauty* [*schönen Individualität*], which is produced by Spirit, transforming the merely Natural into an expression of its own being." Or, in terms that are most fully Burckhardt's:

> The Greek Spirit is the plastic artist, forming the stone into a work of art. In this formative process the stone does not remain mere stone—the form being only superinduced from without; but it is made an expression of the Spiritual, even contrary to its nature, and thus *trans*formed. Conversely, the artist *needs* for his spiritual conceptions, stone, colors, sensuous forms to express his idea. Without such an element he can no more be conscious of the idea himself, than give it an objective form for the contemplation of others; since it cannot in Thought alone become an object to him.[22]

Here the dispositions of the art historian and the philosopher of history most precisely converge. Hegel is proleptically but accurately glossing the famous metaphor with which Burckhardt strings the various parts of the *Civilization* together: *als Kunstwerk,* as a work of art.

What is un-Hegelian here is Burckhardt's valorization of this mode of individualism above the *unendende Subjectivität* with which it is often confused and toward which, in Hegel's scheme, it is only a phase. Burckhardt's scorn for Hegelian metaphysics entails a scorn for that theoretical goal. As we shall see, Burckhardt's examples of unfettered subjectivity are the villains of his story, and not, as in Hegel, its heroes and inheritors. Even at its most Hegelian moment, Burckhardt's idea of the Renaissance is not born of theory. It is born of irony. But the Hegelian conception of a moment of artful individuality easily survives decontextualization as a compelling account of possible commerce between subject and object across their intervening space. In art objectivity both instructs and serves the needs of subjectivity. Sculptors, say, have to learn a lot about rocks and their make-up, painters have to learn a lot about the chemistry of paints; but they do so in order to make of that studied material something of their own devising, the embodiment of some idea in their own minds. Burckhardt's "*objective* treatment and consideration of the State and of all the things of this world" is essentially the approach of an artist to his medium, generalized to other areas of life. The right look can convert almost anything into a medium. Stand back a little from what others do not notice as they pass by, and you can see a pile of lumber containing all manner of unrealized structural possibilities. And doing so gains you a special edge; detachment earns a new power over the external world. That dynamic is the inner subject of Burckhardt's book.

The political story, told from such a perspective, turns the age's own political mythology almost inside out, to correspond more happily with the historical record. In the temporal boundaries that Burck-hardt gives it, the Italian Renaissance is virtually defined by the ab-sence of the Empire. With the departure of the papacy for Avignon in 1309, the medieval struggle between pope and emperor may have seemed as if it were being settled in favor of the emperor, and the arrival of Henry VII in 1310—what Dante calls his *faustissimus cur-sus*—was hailed by some as the definitive return of imperial authority to Italy. But Henry VII came mainly to raise money by the sale of titles and was back in Germany within a year, and the Empire was a factor of no serious consequence in Italian politics until the rise of Charles V. That rise in turn marks the effective end of the Italian Ren-aissance. The symbolic event is the Sack of Rome in 1527, an ironic version of the long-desired imperial *relatio* that brings Italian political independence to a bitter end. It is between these two events that there flourishes in Italy what Burckhardt calls the "new fact" in history: "The State as the outcome of reflection and calculation, the State as a work of art" (p. 22). Some stimulus here is provided by Henry VII's predecessor Frederick II, but otherwise the new statecraft is both en-abled and necessitated by the lapse of higher legitimacy. In the four-teenth century, Italy is left a patchwork of individual political units "whose existence was founded simply on their power to maintain it" (p. 22). Political authority in such a situation is not an inheritance but a skill, and the next two centuries in the peninsula are given over to exploring, with a new freedom from preconception, what works in politics.

The results are artistic not because they are in any ordinary sense pleasant to behold—criminality and terror form an important part of the lore of the times—but because they exhibit a mastery of the means needed to gain particular ends, to secure a power like that of an artist over his creation. In comparison to the diffused feudal authority else-where in Western Europe, the Italian regimes set a standard for effec-tiveness in the business of government, manifesting "almost absolute power within the limits of the State" (p. 26). The term *state* itself evolves from *lo stato,* the casual designation for the rulers and their dependents. The term "imperial" might also be said to apply, though in a different sense from that discussed so far: an ambition for political canniness and thoroughness analogous to that of the Romans in their prime, without being descended from the feeble end of their specific history. The *renouatio imperii* that takes place in Italy is, as it were, metaphorical rather than metonymic. Humanist usage shows a drift from *imperium* as the specific name for the Roman Empire back, though in an intensified form, to its original meaning as the power to give orders and have them obeyed.[23] Medieval political theory had indeed proposed that "a king is emperor in his own kingdom"—*rex imperator in regno suo*—but it is the Italian Renaissance that first makes good on the pluralization of *imperium* implied by that formula. *Kunst* rather than pedigree, it is available to any state smart enough to size up the situation and do what needs to be done.

There is perhaps less in the *Civilization* than might have been expected about the details of that *Kunst*. There is certainly more to be said about the governmental innovations worked out in the Italian Renaissance—about how the Visconti, for instance, "invented bureaucracy."[24] Burckhardt's main focus is, characteristically, not on the machinery of power as such but on those who developed and exercised it, and most of the space and energy of "The State as a Work of Art" is given over to storytelling about the rulers of the time. It is their aberrant particularity—as of Pandolfo Petrucci of Siena, whose "pastime in the summer months was to roll blocks of stone from the top of Monte Amiata, without caring what or whom they hit" (p. 50)—that gives Burckhardt's book much of its famous flavor. Yet the seasoning is itself rooted in Burckhardt's conception of the political history of the period, which is "imperial" in yet another sense of the term: significantly marked by a shift from oligarchic to one-man rule.

The medieval inheritance for many of the cities in northern Italy is republican, but in the course of the Renaissance almost all of them come under the domination of a new breed of monarchical strongmen. By the mid-fifteenth century, even Florence has submitted to what proves to be the enduring domination of the Medici. The only major exception is Venice, whose culture Burckhardt finds subtly backward or at least anachronistic in other ways as well. Burckhardt's emphasis here has been contested, notably by Hans Baron, who has argued in forceful detail for the vitality and importance of republican culture and "civic humanism" within the overall picture.[25] In the long run, we endorse this correction. But the secretary of the penultimate Florentine republic was a famous admirer of Cesare Borgia, and within his own territory Burckhardt's essential point still holds. Most of the new power that the state gains in Italy is invested in individuals, to make a breathtaking new level of egotism both possible and public. "Do you not know, fool," Bernabò Visconti tells the archbishop in 1360, "that I am pope and emperor and lord in all my territory, and that not even God can do anything except what I want?"[26] The presence and numerousness of such figures in positions of highest visibility broadcast a model that is capable of having a galvanic effect throughout society. The age of the *signori* is the age of heightened individualism passim.

The jump from his long opening section on politics to the short but central section "The Development of the Individual" is perhaps Burckhardt's single most important leap: "In the character of these states, whether republics or despotisms, lies not the only but the chief reason for the early development of the Italian. To this it is due that he was the first-born among the sons of modern Europe" (p. 143). That the larger political arrangements in a culture are of a piece with intimate matters of personal style remains a cogent proposition, vigorously reanimated in recent years by the new historicism and related movements.[27] Burckhardt himself traces several strings of causation.

Within his immediate vicinity, the new ruler attracts and rewards others like himself:

> The illegitimacy of his rule isolated the tyrant and surrounded him with constant danger; the most honorable alliance which he could form was with intellectual merit, without regard to its origin. The liberality of the Northern princes of the thirteenth century was confined to the knights, to the nobility which served and sang. It was otherwise with the Italian despot. With his thirst for fame and his passion for monumental works it was talent, not birth, which he needed. In the company of the poet and the scholar he felt himself in a new position—almost, indeed, in possession of a new legitimacy. (Pp. 27–28)

To the poet and scholar we may add the painter, sculptor, architect. Despotic patronage of the significant arts of Renaissance high culture is a famous, much-studied factor in the growth of that culture. Burckhardt's description of it suggests not the practical bond of employer and employee but subtly parallel enterprise: the ruler makes possible for the artist a career analogous to his own, one enabled not by inherited assignment but by present skill. Worldly success unpredicted by the traditional roles of medieval society, an exemption from the constraints of one's station, can be won by the exercise of the creative imagination.

This generalization of the sense of *Kunst* has historical justification in ideals actually put forward for the princely court. In his influential treatise, Castiglione recommends that all those within the ruler's circle know their arts, both the practical and the fine: "I judge it [the courtier's] first duty to know how to handle every kind of weapon, both on foot and on horse, and know the advantages of each kind. . . . I deem it highly important, moreover, to know how to wrestle." At the same time, "I would have him more than passably learned in letters, at least in those studies which we call the humanities. . . . I am not satisfied . . . unless he be also a musician, and unless, besides understanding and being able to read music, he can play various instruments"; he should also have "a knowledge of how to draw and an acquaintance with the art of painting itself." Such posited omnicompetence almost implies that individual *Künste* are simply applications of some central disposition of artfulness. Attempting a general formulation, Castiglione proposes that the most important art is to make the calculated look natural: "to practice in all things a certain *sprezzatura* [nonchalance], so as to conceal all art and make whatever is done or said appear to be without effort and almost without any thought about it." This performative self-consciousness responds to an edgy social fluidity in which individual style carries new weight, and noble birth is no longer a guarantor of status and power but simply one way among many of making an impression: "Consider . . . how important that first impression is, and how anyone who aspires to have the rank and name of good Courtier must strive from the beginning to make a good impression."[28] The opportunities and dangers of this milieu have attracted much recent scrutiny.[29] They nurture a special kind of personal canniness: "These people were forced to know all the inward resources of their nature, passing or permanent; and their enjoyment of life was enhanced and concentrated by the desire to obtain the greatest satisfaction from a possibly very brief period of power and influence" (*Civilization*, p. 144).

Burckhardt, however, goes on to assert that the new politics stimulates the individuality not only of those it includes but also of those it shuts out:

> For political impotence does not hinder the different tendencies and manifestations of private life from thriving in the fullest vigor and variety. Wealth and culture, so far as display and rivalry were not forbidden to them, a municipal freedom which did not cease to be considerable, and a Church which, unlike that of the Byzantine or of the Mohammedan world, was not identical with the State—all these conditions undoubtedly favored the growth of individual thought, for which the necessary leisure was furnished by the cessation of party conflicts. The private man, indifferent to politics, and busied partly with serious pursuits, partly with the interests of a *dilettante,* seems to have been first fully formed in these despotisms of the fourteenth century. (P. 144)

The disenfranchised discover and exploit a sense of identity independent of civic membership; the loss of communal entanglements can give fresh value and intensity to the cultivation of purely personal territory. The active pursuit of such disengagement is one of the most important themes in the life of Petrarch, who "did not, as Dante for example did, actually take part in the administration of government, did not, for that matter, ever practice a profession or marry or fight a battle."[30] He rejected several lucrative offers of public employment, and he wrote an important treatise on "the right to be alone." Renaissance art and literature are, along with their public functions, the furnishing and often the creation of such well-fortified individual *otium*.

Something is owed here to what is, despite their reputation and capacity for ruthlessness, a certain benignity in the Italian despotisms. Their willingness to let a large part of private life go its own way distinguishes them from later totalitarian regimes. But Burckhardt's generalization holds even for many of those who ran overtly afoul of the new set-up: "Banishment too has this effect above all, that it either wears the exile out or develops what is greatest in him" (p. 145). Expatriation, involuntary and voluntary, is a common and highly visible factor in contemporary life—"The Florentine emigrants at Ferrara and the Lucchese in Venice formed whole colonies by themselves" (p. 145)—and it spawns some brave statements about the self-sufficiency of the individual: "can I not anywhere gaze upon the face of the sun and the stars? can I not under any sky contemplate the most precious truths, without I first return to Florence, disgraced, nay dishonored in the eyes of my fellow-citizens?" (Dante).[31] Against rootedness in one's ancestral *patria* is asserted the autonomy conferred by one's inner resources: "Your virtues can be taken with you to any country" (Pontano).[32]

Such statements are especially common among humanists, for whom they are informed by a reviving interest in Senecan Stoicism, the classical philosophy of private self-respect in imperial times. That becomes the unofficial secular creed of humanism as it blends with a conviction that learning itself is a major source of the needed strength: "Only he who has learned everything is nowhere a stranger; robbed of his fortune and without friends, he is yet the citizen of every country, and can fearlessly despise the changes of fortune" (Ghiberti).[33] The *imperium* of scholarship supplies for the humanist a field in which he can pursue on different terms a goal nevertheless quite similar to that of the *signore*. "Home," Codro Urceo is reported to have said on leaving his native Bologna, "is wherever a learned man fixes his seat"[34]— purposefully transposing a sentiment from Curtius's life of Alexander the Great: "Home is wherever a brave man fixes his seat" (6.4.13). The *uir litteratus* lays claim to the same autarchy as the military *uir fortis*.

Burckhardt himself does not make the connection, but it is the bastard son of a Florentine exile who then provides the major illustration of "The Perfecting of the Individual." Twice estranged from his heritage, Leon Battista Alberti became the classic example of *l'uomo universale:* "assiduous in the science and skill of dealing with arms and horses and musical instruments, as well as in pursuit of letters and the fine arts . . . showing by example that men can do anything with themselves if they will." The lost home can be recuperated, indeed reconquered, by cultural achievement:

> Because of the long exile of the Alberti family he was educated among foreign peoples and did not possess his native tongue, and it was difficult for him to write with elegance and refinement in a language he had not been accustomed to use. But in a short time, thanks to his great zeal and industry, he mastered it, to such an extent that his fellow citizens, eager to be called eloquent in the Council, confessed that for the occasion they took not a few ornaments from his writings to adorn their own orations.

That success, of course, simultaneously reaffirms the exile's continued ties to his homeland, and Alberti's case also makes clear that the heroic self-determination of a life such as his did not disengage from a powerful need for an audience. Alberti's own touchiness about the figure he was cutting could be as fierce as any full-time courtier's: "Art should be added to art lest anything seem to be done artfully when one is walking about in the city, riding a horse, or speaking. For in these things one must watch on all sides in order not to displease anyone greatly." Indeed, the biography we have been quoting is very possibly an autobiography, an intimate but not unique display of the posed illeism so familiar on the Renaissance stage ("Caesar is turned to hear"). It is certainly true that, as the biography relentlessly testifies, Alberti's conscious motive throughout was the cultivating of his reputation: "He embraced with zeal and forethought everything which pertained to fame."[35] That last word has within Renaissance culture the force of a technical term: the "new sort of outward distinction" that provides the "inward development of the individual" with its most exalted goal and passion (*Civilization*, p. 151).[36]

The promulgation of a classicizing cult of fame is among the most important effects of humanism. The study of antiquity brought fresh contact with a generally pagan concept of personal glory—"famam extendere factis, / hoc uirtutis opus" (to broaden fame with actions, this is the task of virtue; *Aeneid* 10.468–69)—and the sheer survival of the classical records of such achievement gave force to the possibility that contemporary efforts might similarly endure. Attempts to secure this kind of memorialization took various forms, such as monumental architecture, but the mainstream was literary: "As far as fame and reputation are concerned the written word is more enduring and influential than anything else" (Vasari).[37] Here is where the humanist could be of most enticing use to the *signore* (or, for that matter, to the republic), and learned panegyric forms a very large current in Renaissance literature. Yet an important part of the cultus was the understanding that fame belongs as much to the recorder as to his subject, if not more so. Ancient writers become the focus of a style of veneration resembling that bestowed on saints, and much of the propagandistic effort of early humanism is devoted to establishing the dignity of letters as a profession within which new genius might gain similar celebrity. The symbolic form of this lure is the public crowning of poets with laurel—a self-consciously classical ceremony revived in the early trecento, most importantly for Petrarch in Rome in 1341. He took the occasion to make what is in effect humanism's first public manifesto, a declaration that poets were now entitled to the same status as imperial conquerors:

> As we consist of both body and spirit, two ways of seeking glory are set before us, namely the way of the body and the way of the spirit. . . . Nor is there any doubt that Caesars strive toward glory by the first of these two ways, and poets by the second. So then, since both Caesars and poets move toward the same goal, though by different paths, it is fitting that one and the same reward be prepared for both, namely, a wreath from a fragrant tree, symbolizing the fragrance of good fame and glory.[38]

We shall return to this ceremony and its ramifications. Its metaphorization of the forms of political ambition sets a durable standard; a mid-seventeenth-century version can be casual in its exaggeration:

> Sleep, ye dull Caesars; Rome will boast in vain
> Your glorious triumphs. One is in my brain
> Great as all yours, and circled with thy bays;
> My thoughts take Empire o'er all land and seas.
> $\qquad$ (James Shirley,
> $\qquad$ "To L. for a Wreath of Bays Sent")

Almost all human endeavor, of course, counts on some kind of acknowledgment. What is special about fame is the extraordinary distance it sets between performer and audience. The spread of humanist literacy—and its eventual alliance with printing—makes it possible to gain and manage a contemporary reputation well beyond the borders of one's immediate community. A developing international republic of letters indeed solicits cosmopolitan celebrity by its very nature. But literature is not merely a pragmatic tool of personal advertising. The separation it sets between writer and reader, one of whom is in all but the most exceptional situations absent in the other's presence, is basic to the nature of writing and most compelling precisely because of its lack of any practical limit. Much of the specific energy of humanism—and part of what sets the Renaissance movement apart from its medieval antecedents—derives from its acute and poignant sense of distance from the classical world it sought to revive: those names survive across a great gulf of time and loss. Reciprocally, the fame toward which one most nobly looks is not to be known or enjoyed in one's own lifetime. "The end of life is the beginning of glory," Petrarch tells an ambitious writer; "cultivate virtue while you are alive and you will find fame after your death." This means, of course, that one's greatest desire must always be, in a sense, frustrated—"one's presence is always an enemy of glory"—but the price can be worth paying. Petrarch's own main point is that a focus on posthumous fame enables one to rise above the competitive malice of the audience to hand:

> While any of your contemporaries survive, you will not fully enjoy what recognition you seek; when a grave encloses all of them, there will come those who judge you without hatred and without envy. Therefore let the present age judge us as it will; if the judgment is just, let us accept it with equanimity; if it is unjust, since we cannot turn to others, let us appeal to the more equitable judges of posterity.[39]

Petrarch's prose autobiography is in the form of a letter to posterity, and his example stimulates similar ambitions. In the next century the spiritual leader of Western Christendom writes the story of his own life, in the third person, for unborn readers: "After his death Envy will be still and when those passions which warp the judgment are no more, true report will rise again and number Pius among the illustrious popes."[40] The unknown future is in many ways the best and proper audience for an ambition to escape the limits of a given social context. The willingness to displease one's contemporaries remains for us an important standard for authorial and indeed personal integrity. In stabilizing such independence with the prospect of eventual acceptance, the cult of fame may be said to provide Renaissance individualism with its most appropriate form of communal belonging.

Yet that is to put a bit too fair a face on it, and we come here to a turning point in Burckhardt's and our argument. The ideal of fame is hardly an untroubled one. It is subject to contaminating calculation— Petrarch's laureation is to a considerable degree prompted and scripted by his own surreptitious efforts—and even in its high-minded form runs foul of the age's Christian conscience. "I greatly fear," Petrarch has the spirit of Augustine say to him, "lest this pursuit of a false immortality of fame may shut for you the way that leads to the true immortality of life."[41] And even on secular grounds there are reasons for unease. Girolamo Cardano, a sixteenth-century Italian describing his own early vow "to perpetuate my name," highlights the joker in the pack: "Did not Caesar, Alexander, Hannibal, Scipio, Curtius, and Herostratus prefer this hope of enduring fame before all others, even at the risk of infamy?"[42]

Herostratus was the destroyer of the Temple of Artemis at Ephesus, which Herodotus had identified as one of the seven wonders of the world. Under torture, he claimed to have done it so that people would remember his name.[43] A governmental attempt to consign him to anonymity was defeated by the ancient media, and he remains as the classical world's clearest exemplar of fame's malevolent secret: an evil and destructive act can be every bit as memorable as one that deserves praise—and possibly even more so.

Burckhardt is sensitive to that potential. He considered his own times disturbingly "Herostratic,"[44] and the section on fame in the *Civilization* ends with some Renaissance avatars of the Ephesian arsonist: "In more than one remarkable and dreadful undertaking the motive assigned by serious writers is the burning desire to achieve something great and memorable. This motive is not a mere extreme case of ordinary vanity, but something demonic, involving a surrender of the will, the use of any means, however atrocious, and even an indifference to success itself" (p. 162). Burckhardt offers illustrations from Renaissance political historians, of whom Machiavelli is particularly lucid; the logic of renown is simply not the logic of morality or even of useful results: "Many who have not had opportunity to gain fame with praiseworthy deeds have striven to gain it with blameworthy actions. . . . Conspicuous actions such as those of government and state, however they are carried on or whatever outcome they have, are always looked upon as bringing their doers honor rather than censure."[45] Renaissance literature becomes fascinated with the perverse side of the cult of fame. Milton characterizes the rebel angel as one that "naught merits but dispraise / And ignominy, yet to glory aspires / Vain glorious, and through infamy seeks fame" (*Paradise Lost* 6.382–84). With an assist from Seneca, the aesthetic of "heroic villainies" becomes particularly well-established on the stage:

> Che temi animo mio? che pur paventi?
> Accogli ogni tua forza a la vendetta,
> E cosa fa sì inusitata e nova,
> Che questa etade l'aborisca, e l'altra
> Ch'avenir dee creder nol possa a pena.
>   (Giraldi Cinthio, *Orbecche* 3.3)

> What do you fear, my soul? Why are you still afraid? Gather all your force for this vendetta, and do a deed so extraordinary and new that this age will shudder at it, and the next to come will scarcely believe it possible.

The speaker of such lines is often a king or prince, but does not have to be. In the most powerful of England's domestic tragedies, the demented provincial father who murders two of his children boasts at his arrest, "My glory is to have my action known" (*Yorkshire Tragedy* 8.31).

Burckhardt's paragraph on *das Herostratische* may be no more than a pendant to the section on fame. But the train of thought that brings him to that topic operates throughout his account of Renaissance selfhood. "The Development of the Individual" goes on to end with an extended portrait of specifically literary infamy—twice as long as the admiring description of Alberti—in the person of Pietro Aretino. Burckhardt is not beyond appreciating Aretino's talent—"a grotesque wit so brilliant that in some cases it does not fall short of that of Rabelais" (p. 172)—but the enveloping response is disgust at the spectacle of a fame so openly degenerate:

> It is probable that he enjoyed special protection as a Spanish agent, as his speech or silence could have no small effect on the smaller Italian Courts and on public opinion in Italy. He affected utterly to despise the Papal Court because he knew it so well; the true reason was that Rome neither could nor would pay him any longer. Venice, which sheltered him, he was wise enough to leave unassailed. The rest of his relations with the great is mere beggary and vulgar extortion. (P. 170)

Aretino is, in more ways than one, Petrarch's sleazy *Doppelgänger* at the far end of the Italian Renaissance. He was born in the same town as Petrarch, where his childhood home acquired something of the same celebrity as Petrarch's birthplace. In exploiting his literary popularity with unprecedentedly effective shamelessness—"in this matter of my being famous," he writes one correspondent, "you don't know the half of it" [46]—he brings to ironic fulfillment the humanist program for establishing the literary profession as a force in public affairs: "Aretino made all his profit out of a complete publicity, and in a certain sense may be considered the father of modern journalism" (p. 171). His dealings with Charles V in particular mark a kind of corrupt consummation of the Ghibelline ideal:

> What then shall I say of the unbelievable, incomprehensible goodness of this illustrious, glorious and blessed follower of Christ? Even though his sovereign mind was still occupied with the revolts in Flanders, the rash conduct of Cleves, the potency of France, and the raids of Barbarossa, he still did not abstain from acknowledging with every possible sign of pleasure my devotions toward his deity. [47]

Literate imperialism finally succeeds as egotistical sycophancy.

The egotism is more authentic than the sycophancy—"I could make even the Emperor a laughing stock if he should make a jest of me" [48]—and what most concerns Burckhardt is not Aretino's obsequiousness but his talent for abuse. Aretino himself saw that talent as the real source of his influence:

> Fa sol che lo Aretino ti sia amico,
> Perchè gli è mal nemico a chi lo acquiste.
> . . . e'l timor se estingua,
> Che egli sol dannarebbe il pater nostro.
> Dio ne guardi ciascun della sua lingua. [49]

> Just be sure that Aretino is your friend, for he is a bad enemy to whoever gets him. . . . May the fear go away that he by himself might destroy the Pope. God save everyone from his tongue.

It is in the business of professional insult—"satire" seems a bit dignified a term—that Aretino's "grotesque wit" finds much of its range. Despite his self-bestowed title Scourge of Princes, he does not restrict his attention to politicians. Burckhardt records his own somewhat appalled admiration for an attack on a contemporary poet:

Bandendo va e la natura, e l'arte,
che il loro culo diventa beato,
quando si netta colle vostre carte.[50]

Nature and art both proclaim that their ass is blessed when wiped with
your pages.

Yet whatever their special sublimity, Aretino's maledictions are most
significant for crowning what was in its own time a highly visible
Renaissance tradition. From the early quattrocento on, Italian literary
life seems unable to conduct its business without the copious assistance of learned invective, almost invariably *ad hominem.* A style of
vituperation established in humanist circles by Valla, Poggio, and Filelfo can be unsettling both for its intensity and for the placidity with
which it was accepted as normal and proper: "Filelfo, on his way
through Rome to Naples, placed his Satires—the most nauseous com-
positions that coarse spite and filthy fancy ever spawned—in the
hands of Nicholas V. The Pope retained them for nine days, read
them, returned them with thanks, and rewarded their author with a
purse of 500 ducats."[51] One book on the topic is called *Les Gladiateurs
de la république des lettres;* the metaphor is Valla's own.[52]

Burckhardt pointedly asserts the contrasting benignity of the artistic community, by way of affirming that "peaceful and friendly competition" can be compatible with the achievements of high culture (p.
168). However, satiric wit can serve an important therapeutic role in a
society such as that of Renaissance Italy, a "corrective not only of this
modern desire for fame, but of all highly developed individuality" (p.
163). Yet as Aretino's case makes abundantly clear, the insulter of the
famous himself aims to become one of them. "Modern Wit and Satire" caps the section "The Development of the Individual" because the
culture of abuse is simply one of the natural products of a large collection of Renaissance men:

> Italy had, in fact, become a school for scandal, the like of which the world
> cannot show, not even in France at the time of Voltaire. In him and his
> comrades there was assuredly no lack of the spirit of negation; but where,
> in the eighteenth century, was to be found the crowd of suitable victims,
> that countless assembly of highly and characteristically developed human
> beings? (P. 168)

If Burckhardt would prefer to sympathize with the targets and blame
"a poisonous brood of impotent wits, of born critics and railers," he

cannot exclude "the envy of famous men among themselves" as an important contributing cause (p. 168).

What works its way through these slight equivocations—we shall see their like again—is a harsh vision of the culture of Renaissance individualism as a zero-sum game, within which it can be achingly difficult to tolerate someone else's presence. The pursuit of a literary career in particular is fueled by and fuels an egotism so fierce that writers can scarcely bear one another's existence. In a letter to Lodovico Dolce, Aretino describes his own encounter with an ambitious poet:

> The wretch, puffed up with a self-esteem that promises him the name of a great poet, spends all his energies in pleasing himself. Having thus gained by his own tributes to himself the praises that he thinks he deserves, he becomes his own adulator, and being delighted only with himself, exalts himself to himself and rewards himself with his own hand as well.

This might pass as a self-portrait, but Venice is not big enough for two such, and the pissant gets on Aretino's nerves. He goes on, not missing the chance for a side-swipe at Dolce:

> As soon as this empty-headed windjammer had convinced himself that he need have no more traffic with dire need, he gave himself over to doing miracles with sonnets, and when he showed me some of them and I told him that four or five were good enough to be yours, his face grew fiery red and he answered me that they were all perfect, and that Petrarch himself would not know enough to pass judgement on their greatness.

Retaliation against such presumption does not have to be merely literary. Aretino gloats when his rival shortly runs into some street justice:

> Anyone who has seen a snake with his back broken who, although he cannot crawl away, still thrusts out his tongue, lifts his head up and spits poison, has seen this tidbit for the gallows trampled underfoot by his own envy and yet snarling like a Cerberus. That was the way the sorry fellow made himself heard when the servant of Signor Giovangioacchino gave him as many drubbings as the shameless rascal had the temerity to pretend that he had written letters to the king of France. God bless Veniero and his friends and the deed their hands did.[53]

Poggio and George of Trebizond are said to have slugged it out publicly in Rome over some translations of Xenophon and Diodorus Siculus. The world of letters was no place for tenderfeet.

In the offing here is one of Burckhardt's most troubled points about the individualism that he is sometimes taken merely to celebrate. Emperors aspire to uniqueness. A private selfhood that adopts in metaphorical form the authority and autonomy of political imperialism will adopt its aggression as well, a chronic irritability in the vicinity of others like itself. Part of what Burckhardt is establishing with his central contrast between the Renaissance and the Middle Ages is that representatives of the former will have a radical difficulty recognizing and working any secure common ground among them. Within the full picture of the period as Burckhardt understands it, that difficulty proves lethal.

The public part of the picture is the story that prompts the first modern political narrative, the story of how Italy lost control of its own destiny to become a battleground for foreign powers. Francesco Guicciardini's *History of Italy* begins with a celebration of the comparative peace achieved among the more important Italian states in the later fifteenth century, though it is not so much a settlement as an edgy balance of power:

> This alliance easily curbed the cupidity of the Venetian Senate, but it did not unite the allies in sincere and faithful friendship, insofar as, full of emulation and jealousy among themselves, they did not cease to assiduously observe what the others were doing, each of them reciprocally aborting all the plans whereby any of the others might become more powerful or renowned.[54]

With the death of Lorenzo de' Medici—replaced by his erratic son Piero—and of Innocent VIII—replaced by the Borgia pope Alexander VI—the "pestiferous thirst for domination" which continues to animate the principals slips once more out of communal control to bring on what becomes known as the *calamità d'Italia.* Lodovico Sforza thinks he is only strengthening his own hand against a perceived détente between Florence and Naples when he invites Charles VIII of France to make good on his claim to the Neapolitan throne. Before events play themselves out, Sforza is dead in a French prison and all of Italy, except a weakened Venice, is under the domination of Emperor Charles V. Guicciardini's political thought generally is much occupied with the ambition of *il particulare,* the political individual, whose drive is both an indispensable resource and a civic menace:

Citizens who seek honor and glory in their city are praiseworthy and useful. . . . Would to God our republic were full of such ambition! But citizens whose only goal is power are dangerous. For men who make power
their idol cannot be restrained by any considerations of honor or justice, and they will step on anything and everything to attain that goal.
(*Ricordi* B1)[55]

The *History* tells how the tragic potential of that drive came to domi-
nate the Italian scene.

In the long view, Burckhardt sees the *calamità* as a greater disaster
than even Guicciardini realized: the effectively suicidal end to the Italian Renaissance. Despite its organization into topics, "The State as a
Work of Art" takes on conventional narrative form as it moves toward
this conclusion, which for Burckhardt is a bitter lesson about the inability of Renaissance Italians to make common cause:

When . . . in the political intercourse of the fifteenth century the common
fatherland is sometimes emphatically named it is done in most cases to
annoy some other Italian state. The first decades of the sixteenth century,
the years when the Renaissance attained its fullest bloom, were not favorable to a revival of patriotism; the enjoyment of intellectual and artistic
pleasures, the comforts and elegancies of life, and the supreme interests of
self-development, destroyed or hampered the love of country. But those
deeply serious and sorrowful appeals to national sentiment were not heard
again till later, when the time for unity had gone by, when the country
was inundated with Frenchmen and Spaniards, and when a German army
had conquered Rome. (P. 142)

Individualism cannot defend its own nest.

This is the story that Burckhardt has to tell, the diachronic dimension recoverable from what is for the most part offered as a synchronic
Bildung. It was the diachronic dimension of Hegel's philosophy that
most directly irritated Burckhardt, and there are good reasons for re-
marking on the general absence from the *Civilization* of any serious
interest in the processes of historical change: "He regarded various
aspects of the Renaissance, from politics to poetry, as objective historical entities whose temporal and spatial boundaries were clearly delim-
ited. He was interested neither in where those entities came from nor
in the directions in which they were tending."[56] Yet we would argue
that in at least one important regard Burckhardt's book is in the grip
of an inclusive narrative, effaced to some degree because it is so painful
a story. Burckhardt's Renaissance destroys itself in following out the

very logic of its own genius. The political fable has roots in received historiographic wisdom, but Burckhardt replicates it with striking originality on other levels, to make it a central part of his idea about the age.

The lengthy third section on "The Revival of Antiquity" ends, unexpectedly, with a section on the "Fall of the Humanists in the Sixteenth Century":

> After a brilliant succession of poet-scholars had . . . filled Italy and the world with the worship of antiquity, had determined the forms of education and culture, had often taken the lead in political affairs, and had, to no small extent, reproduced ancient literature—at length in the sixteenth century . . . the whole class fell into deep and general disgrace. (P. 272)

This is not a standard topic in the study of humanism. It is not there in the work of Burckhardt's contemporary Georg Voigt, and no particular consensus has evolved that any such phenomenon took place, aside from a general sagging of Italian culture under Spanish domination. The early sixteenth century is if anything now remembered as the time when the alliance with printing celebrated and exploited by Erasmus enabled the movement to jump the Alps and achieve a new level of security and influence. Part of what concerns Burckhardt is the inevitably depersonalizing character of this success: "The spread of printed editions of the classics, and of large and well-arranged handbooks and dictionaries, went far to free the people from the necessity of personal intercourse with the humanists" (p. 272). A modern commentator might see no more here than the inevitable obsolescence of a certain style of heroic entrepreneurship. Burckhardt, however, detects something more virulent at work in a few extended attacks on the moral character of humanists as a group. The term *umanista* indeed makes its debut in Italian literature in the satire of Ariosto that Burckhardt cites:

> Senza quel vizio son pochi umanisti
> che fe' a Dio forza, non che persüase,
> di far Gomorra e i suoi vicini tristi . . .
>   Ride il volgo, se sente un ch'abbia vena
> di poesia, e poi dice: —È gran periglio
> a dormir seco e volgierli la schiena.

Few humanists are without that vice which did not so much persuade, as forced, God to render Gomorrah and her neighbor wretched! . . . The vulgar laugh when they hear of someone who possesses a vein of poetry, and then they say, "It is a great peril to turn your back if you sleep next to him."[57]

It is still possible to be unimpressed, especially since the most extensive text Burckhardt has to adduce is labeled by its own author a rhetorical *progymnasma,* or exercise. Burckhardt, however, is alert to a mirroring here of Italy's national fate: the generalized accusations of the sixteenth century merely repeat the *ad hominem* internal polemics of the fifteenth century as a brief against the whole profession. "The first to make these charges were certainly the humanists themselves. Of all men who ever formed a class, they had the least sense of their common interests, and least respected what there was of this sense" (p. 272). Like the *signori,* they are collectively betrayed by their incurable competitiveness.

The point opens onto something less vulnerable than some of the claims that lead up to it. The core of the chapter is Burckhardt's intuitive but compelling delineation of the psychic cost of the typical humanist career:

> For an ambitious youth, the fame and the brilliant position of the humanists were a perilous temptation; it seemed to him that he too "through inborn nobility could no longer regard the low and common things of life."[58] He was thus led to plunge into a life of excitement and vicissitude, in which exhausting studies, tutorships, secretaryships, professorships, offices in princely households, mortal enmities and perils, luxury and beggary, boundless admiration and boundless contempt, followed confusedly one upon the other, and in which the most solid worth and learning were often pushed aside by superficial impudence. But the worst of all was that the position of the humanist was almost incompatible with a fixed home, since it either made frequent changes of dwelling necessary for a livelihood, or so affected the mind of the individual that he could never be happy for long in one place. (Pp. 273–74)

Burckhardt had earlier quoted as if with approval the humanists' own boast about their homeless independence. Here that condition reappears not as a strength but as a curse. Burckhardt is probing a pathology that is built into the very structure of the individualism which he elsewhere praises:

> Such men can hardly be conceived to exist without an inordinate pride. They needed it, if only to keep their heads above water, and were con-

firmed in it by the admiration which alternated with hatred in the treatment they received from the world. They are the most striking examples and victims of an unbridled subjectivity. (P. 274)

The original detachment from group identity that made Renaissance individualism possible comes in the end to a willful and deathly solitude. Burckhardt's revision of Hegel's dialectic issues not in the higher realm of *unendende Subjectivität,* but in an *entfesselte Subjectivität* that is actually a kind of suicide.

This intelligent ambivalence exerts pressure on the rest of Burckhardt's book and indeed much of his historical thought. The theorist of *der Staat als Kunstwerk* is also an impressive prophet of the state's demonic extremity in our own century, from which he recoils in horror: "Power is of its nature evil, whoever wields it. It is not a stability but a lust, and *ipso facto* insatiable, therefore unhappy in itself and doomed to make others unhappy."[59] From his lecture notes we sense a deep pessimism about the modern world that the Renaissance initiates, as well as a strong attraction to the medieval dispensation that he became famous for scorning. Even within the *Civilization* Burckhardt does not imagine Renaissance man merely outgrowing the bonds that obligate him to others like himself. That those bonds become more difficult to recognize and respect was the age's great danger, the problem that most desperately needed to be solved.

The book's last section, "Morality and Religion," takes up directly the means by which combative individualism might be made social and accountable; it proves the most troubled section, awkwardly apologetic at the outset:

> The ultimate truth with respect to the character, the conscience, and the guilt of a people remains for ever a secret. . . . We must leave those who find a pleasure in passing sweeping censures on whole nations to do so as they like. The peoples of Europe can maltreat, but happily not judge, one another. (P. 426)

This is defensive prologue to Burckhardt's concession that the cliché of Italian wickedness in the Renaissance is neither inaccurate nor irrelevant: "It cannot be denied that Italy at the beginning of the sixteenth century found itself in the midst of a grave moral crisis, out of which the best men saw hardly any escape" (p. 427). By the end of the chapter, the formulation has become even more acute: "The fundamental vice of this character was at the same time a condition of its greatness—namely, developed[60] individualism. . . . In face of all objective facts, of laws and restraints of whatever kind, he retains the feeling of his own sovereignty" (p. 442). The health and indeed survival of any individualistic civilization depends upon some external responsibility gaining purchase on that unfriendly surface. But so posed, the need seems almost a contradiction in terms.

Burckhardt himself highlights "the sentiment of honor" as "that moral force which was then the strongest bulwark against evil," and indeed one of the most important legacies of the Renaissance to later times: "This is that enigmatic mixture of conscience and egoism which often survives in modern man after he has lost, whether by his own fault or not, faith, love, and hope. . . . It has become, in a far wider sense than is commonly believed, a decisive test of conduct in the minds of the cultivated Europeans of our own day" (p. 428). Not itself a moral code, honor is a means by which personal pride can be enlisted on the side of morality, protecting that morality against anomie, even to the point of thriving on it. The term indeed has a special aura in Renaissance culture, and it prompts some extravagant language. Burckhardt specifically quotes Rabelais on the Abbey of Thélème:

> In their rules there was only one clause:
> DO WHAT YOU WILL
> because people who are free, well-born, well-bred, and easy in honest company have a natural spur and instinct which drives them to virtuous deeds and deflects them from vice; and this they called honor.[61]

Such honor implants the dictates of conscience so deeply into the individual psyche that no external constraints are necessary. Morality coincides precisely with impulse and desire, so that "Fais ce que voudras" is an injunction that does not threaten the social and civic fabric but is its great source of strength.

The briefness of Burckhardt's discussion of the matter, though, entails a recognition that the ideal is an intrinsically treacherous one. "This sense of honor," he concedes, "is compatible with much selfishness and great vices, and may be the victim of astonishing illusions" (p. 428). The mysterious chemistry that allows egoism to be shaped by conscience also allows conscience to be shaped by egoism. Burckhardt moves on to the most conspicuous specific, the cult of revenge:

> This personal need of vengeance felt by the cultivated and highly placed Italian, resting on the solid basis of an analogous popular custom, naturally displays itself under a thousand different aspects, and receives the unqual-

ified approval of public opinion. . . . Only there must be art in the vengeance, and the satisfaction must be compounded of the material injury and moral humiliation of the offender. A mere brutal, clumsy triumph of force was held by public opinion no satisfaction. The whole man with his sense of fame and of scorn, not only his fist, must be victorious. (P. 431)

Burckhardt gives several vivid examples of the vendetta *als Kunstwerk:* "After dinner he told him whose liver it was" (p. 430). The code is to prove one of Italy's most notorious exports, with private vengeance becoming a major concern for the governments of England, France, and Spain, and a dominant theme on their tragic stages. Burckhardt partly obscures the urgency of his point by ascribing this and other aberrations (such as gambling) to an unusually strong imagination ("the Italian imagination kept the picture of the wrong alive with frightful vividness," p. 430). But the usually invoked motive for vengeance is honor, within whose cultus justice is effectively equated with self-respect. Renaissance literature gives some of its most memorable attention to the Herostratic potential of this noble word:

> —O thou Othello, that was once so good,
>   Fall'n in the practice of a damned slave,
>   What shall be said to thee?
> —   Why, any thing:
>   An honorable murderer, if you will;
>   For nought I did in hate, but all in honor.
>   (*Othello* 5.2.291–95)

Such demeanor had an authority and allure that troubled the very possibility of Renaissance civilization:

When a murder was committed the sympathies of the people, before the circumstances of the case were known, ranged themselves instinctively on the side of the murderer. A proud, manly bearing before and at the execution excited such admiration that the narrator often forgets to tell us for what offence the criminal was put to death. But when we add to this inward contempt of law and to the countless grudges and enmities which called for satisfaction the impunity which crime enjoyed during times of political disturbance we can only wonder that the State and society were not utterly dissolved. (P. 437)

Burckhardt's Italy is a Thélème gone mad, in which "Fais ce que voudras" is, as we would normally expect, a call to anarchy.

Attempts were made in the Renaissance to define honor with enough care to avoid such consequences, primarily by internalizing it and (as Burckhardt does) distinguishing it from fame. But the ethical need it tries to fill finds a more decisive answer outside Burckhardt's territory. Burckhardt himself wonders why Italy did not produce a Reformation, and gives the "plausible answer": "The Italian mind . . . never went farther than the denial of hierarchy, while the origin and vigor of the German Reformation was due to its positive religious doctrines, most of all to the doctrines of justification by faith and of the inefficacy of good works" (p. 444). That is to beg the question of causality, but the contrast is revealing. For it is in Protestant religious experience that conscience and egoism are reconciled by a mystery deeper than that of honor. Luther's account of Christian freedom is boldly paradoxical: "A Christian is a perfectly free lord of all, subject to none. A Christian is a perfectly dutiful servant of all, subject to all." These contrary propositions are interwoven in justification by faith, which begins with the acceptance of the harshest of moral judgments on oneself: "The moment you begin to have faith you learn that all things in you are altogether blameworthy, sinful, and damnable." Yet the certainty of never being able to merit salvation by any action or achievement is met by the promise of salvation *sola fide,* an inward emotional state which is everything: "a splendid privilege and hard to attain, a truly omnipotent power, a spiritual dominion in which there is nothing so good and nothing so evil but that it shall work together for good to me, if only I believe." Humiliation and submission, if sufficiently extreme, recover a primal sense of strength and confidence: "Who then can comprehend the lofty dignity of the Christian? By virtue of his royal power he rules over all things, death, life, and sin, and through his priestly glory is omnipotent with God because he does the things which God asks and desires." [62] Selfishness here is both harshly straitened and grandiosely satisfied. Protestant theologians will develop the traditional Christian attack on individual pride with new force and sophistication; but as they do so, they also intensify the role of the individual conscience, and translate the institutional church into subjective terms that give individualism a new and potent dimension. The Italian project, we might say, was incomplete in subjectivizing only the state. The Reformation, subjectivizing the church as well, in this regard completes the Renaissance.

To put it that way is to gesture toward the *telos* for a general European Renaissance within which Burckhardt's Italy is only the opening chapter:

chiefly thou, O Spirit, that dost prefer
Before all temples the upright heart and pure,
Instruct me . . .

(*Paradise Lost* 1.17–19)

So the invocation of the Muse who finally dictates a Renaissance epic
that can stand comparison with its classical predecessors, in fulfillment of a cultural ambition reaching back to Petrarch's *Africa* and
marked for three centuries mainly by false starts. Milton's righteous
confidence in rewriting Genesis is nurtured by some of the most strin-
gent religious traditions descending from Luther; the result is a major
summing up of Renaissance poetry in some of its most expansive
modes. We think that is neither a problem nor a puzzle: from the point
of view we are trying to establish, Renaissance and Reformation are
antithetical period concepts only within an almost Hegelian dialectic
between individualism and group responsibility by which Burckhardt's idea, now attached to a powerful antithesis, reaches beyond its
Italian closure; and it is only appropriate that the climactic Renaissance
poem should be written in England, the European country for which
the Renaissance and the Reformation are most precisely coextensive.
In history all origins and ends are provisional. Burckhardt's period,
beginning with Petrarch and ending with Aretino and the Sack of
Rome, initiates a fuller version of itself that concludes, in a different
spirit, with the English Civil War and *Paradise Lost*.

T W O

Beyond Burckhardt

The literary history bracketed by Petrarch and Milton will occupy us in the last section of this book. Here we consider the political and social consequences of extending Burckhardt's idea past his own limits, chosen and otherwise. The temporal and geographical limits of the *Civilization* in particular distinguish his Renaissance in important ways from the Renaissance of casual usage—a movement encompassing all of the major nations of Western Europe, proceeding on different schedules in different places, surrounding and somehow including not only the Reformation but also, in some conventions, the Baroque. This Renaissance has never received a definition as decisive as Burckhardt's. Extrapolating from Burckhardt is in some ways easy and obvious, but it requires alertness to difference and change.

In the matter of the state, what transpires in Italy in the fourteenth and fifteenth centuries is only a miniature anticipation of a larger European event that comes into final focus in the seventeenth century. The *signori* reappear in the established monarchies of France, Spain, and England, their power newly and dramatically strengthened in the political arrangement that comes to be known, at the prompting of Jean Bodin, as absolutism. The dispersed authority of feudalism is gradually but decisively centralized along national lines, under the rule of a sovereign possessed of what, measured against medieval standards, seems like "la puissance absolue et perpetuelle."[1] Such language avails itself of some of the starkest precepts of Roman imperial law, with its place for an emperor *a legibus solutus,* freed from the law, since the law is understood to be his own voluntaristic invention: *Quod pla-*

cuit principi legis habet uigorem (What has pleased the *princeps* has the force of law). "We see at the end of edicts and ordinances the words CAR TEL EST NOTRE PLAISIR in order to make clear that the laws of a sovereign prince, though they are established for good and vital reasons, are nevertheless dependent only on his pure and free will." He "must not be at all subject to the commands of others," because "the principal mark of sovereign majesty and absolute power primarily lies in giving the law to subjects generally without their consent." [2] The progress of such governmental ambitions is slower in the rest of Western Europe than in Italy because feudal traditions are more tenacious and the territory and population being brought under the new *imperium* are much greater. But both these retarding forces strengthen the legitimacy and power of the eventual result, to dwarf and indeed doom Italy's achievement as practice catches up to theory. Burckhardt's story continues north and west of the Alps.

The most memorable Renaissance theorist of absolutism takes a step beyond Bodin in seeing that arrangement precisely as the entailment of a social order of radical individualism. Thomas Hobbes's state of nature, in which "there be no propriety, no dominion, no *mine* and *thine* distinct, but only that to be every man's, that he can get, and for so long as he can keep it," could serve as a gloss on Burckhardt's Italy in its darkest potential—even to the malign role of fame:

> Men have no pleasure, but on the contrary a great deal of grief in keeping company, where there is no power able to overawe them all. For every man looketh that his companion should value him at the same rate he sets upon himself; and upon all signs of contempt, or undervaluing, naturally endeavors, as far as he dares (which amongst them that have no common power to keep them in quiet, is far enough to make them destroy each other), to extort a greater value from his contemners by damage, and from others by the example. (*Leviathan,* chap. 13)

Bees and ants may live in natural society with each other, but a creature "continually in competition for honor and dignity . . . whose joy consisteth in comparing himself with other men" (chap. 17) can be made sociable only by the state's arbitrary coercion.

Hobbes is not writing alone; the proverb *Homo homini lupus* (Man is a wolf to man) is widespread in the seventeenth century, and offered by José Antonio Maravall as one of the touchstones of baroque culture.[3] As anthropology Hobbes's thesis no longer carries weight. Primitive societies are in fact intensely social, to the point that their cohesion shows no signs of deriving from any conscious act. What

Hobbes actually describes, harrowingly, is advanced civilization, the civilization of the Renaissance, its iron-willed state a direct deduction from the *entwickelte Individualismus* of its citizenry:

> The only way to erect such a common power as may be able to defend them from the invasion of foreigners and the injuries of one another . . . is to confer all their power and strength upon one man . . . that may reduce all their wills, by plurality of voices, to one will. (Chap. 17)

Modern ears have trouble distinguishing this solution from heroic fascism. We may nevertheless respect the rigor of an argument that effectively replicates at the top of society the imperial ambitions of its constituents. At moments Hobbes almost concedes that the solution may, on another level, be no solution at all:

> In all times, kings and persons of sovereign authority, because of their independency, are in continual jealousies, and in the state and posture of gladiators; having their weapons pointing, and their eyes fixed on one another; that is, their forts, garrisons, and guns upon the frontiers of their kingdoms, and continual spies upon their neighbors—which is a posture of war. (Chap. 13)

This might come from the opening pages of Guicciardini, but it is a fair picture as well of relations between the great powers who eclipse the Italian states. The peace of Spanish dominion in Italy itself is a time of recurring war for the rest of Western Europe, as the new states maneuver for leverage. Spain, France, England, and an Empire aspiring to join their number reenact the struggles of Milan, Florence, Venice, and the papacy. The Reformation effectively contributes to the process by splitting the Church along political lines, subordinating it to the state, and by and large eliminating Christianity as the source of even vestigial international authority. When the Empire's final bid for absolutist coherence lures Europe into the catastrophic Thirty Years' War early in the seventeenth century, the whole situation shows signs of being seriously anarchic, imperial sovereignty once more suicidally unable to tolerate its own kind.

Yet the Thirty Years' War, desolating enough for Germany and the Empire, does not become a *calamità d'Europa* comparable to the Italian disaster. It is if anything a trauma from which Europe almost seems to have learned: the last of the major religious wars, ended by the first general European peace conference. International combat yields at midcentury to domestic interference within the absolutist state itself:

impoverishment and impotence in Spain, aristocratic revolt in France, and in England a civil war whose challenge to the divine right of kings establishes that country as Europe's most advanced polity. The year after the peace of Westphalia, in an act of far-reaching symbolic import, England beheads its sovereign. If we posit that step as the symbolic climax to a general European Renaissance, it constitutes, despite its violence, a denial of Burckhardt's ultimately tragic scenario for the period, since it affirms a serious faith in the social potential of an individualistic ethos. The English left produces some of the age's most explicit programs of every man for himself—"every man by nature being a king, priest, and prophet in his own natural circuit and compass, whereof no second may partake"[4]—but with the conviction that what follows need be neither anarchy nor monarchy. In *Areopagitica* Milton celebrates the schismatic effect of uncensored publication as a source of communal strength; the masonry of the Lord's Temple owes its glory to the lapidary independence of its parts:

> When every stone is laid artfully together, it cannot be united into a continuity, it can but be contiguous in this world; neither can every piece of the building be of one form; nay rather the perfection consists in this, that out of many moderate varieties and brotherly dissimilitudes that are not vastly disproportional, arises the goodly and the graceful symmetry that commends the whole pile and structure. (*Prose Works,* 2:555)

The English monarchy is eventually restored, but it proves definitively compromised by the durability of such ideals; and it is English colonists who eventually codify the individualistic republicanism that proves the most significant political heritage of the Renaissance. The period at its end retrieves the seemingly failed enterprise of the Italian communes: the management of personal ambition as a civic resource.

The language in which such an enterprise is usually praised may obscure the underlying constant. The English disabling of the monarchy is actually not the disabling of the state, but if anything its intensification. By the early eighteenth century England, with the weakest monarchy of any major European nation, is also administratively the tightest ship. "Here," report two impressed Frenchmen in 1713, "everything is under governmental control [*en régie*]"[5]—this from functionaries in the government that advertized its own absolutism most insistently. England is already on its way to becoming the most successfully imperialist country in the modern sense of the term. Its closest competitors for such success, internal and external, are the even more unmonarchical Dutch. The political lesson waiting to be learned is that the absolutist state, all propaganda aside, does not require an absolute ruler.

Hobbes and Bodin, despite their monarchical preferences, concede as much on a theoretical level. Philip II of Spain, determined to read and annotate every royal memorandum, is the last important king to attempt literal personal control of his realm: a heroic effort, but a morose and debilitating one, even a kind of madness. The seventeenth century sees the general institutionalization of the modern European distinction between a ceremonial head of state and an actual head of government, and even in the adamantly royalist regimes historians now tend to locate the enduring gains in state power in the creation of a more or less permanent administrative apparatus that can act in the sovereign's name without his intervention. The "pure et franche volonté" of the monarch increasingly becomes (like Big Brother) a managerial fiction. *Raisons d'État* cannot, in the modern world, be identified with an individual will.

Attempts to have it otherwise in our own time have shown the simple sanity of that depersonalization. If the trans-Alpine states of the Renaissance act in the end less dangerously than the *signori,* that may in part have been because their very size and power make them less responsive to regal whim. The absolutist state, as it were, uses the absolutist monarchy to come into existence, only to dispense with it when it has served its purpose. And though the Renaissance itself is characterized by a potent symbolic homology between the state and the individual, that homology is ultimately best understood as a process, whereby the former symbolism devolves upon the latter. It is Hobbes's evolution in reverse, a passage to the modern condition of competitive individualism within the controlling matrix of a state that seems to do its job by being conspicuously anonymous, acting on behalf of nobody in particular.

Tracing that trajectory is part of what is involved in filling out Burckhardt's picture. More is needed, however, than just completing the story of the state. Burckhardt's emphasis on the state is part of his Rankean heritage as a historian, and many of his strengths are the strengths of that tradition. But it is a tradition that also now seems too subject to the state mythology whose career it chronicles. Absolutism is never really that, and the subsuming of all social relations into those between the individual and the state scants the tenaciously independent life of other factors.[6] Burckhardt now seems to sweep out too much when his definition of the Renaissance effectively dismisses the role of "race, people, party, family, or corporation" in the development of modern individualism. Subsequent study has made us increasingly aware of the continuing force of many such institutions. They all respond to the evolution of the state, and often parallel that evolution with considerable symbolic power. But they can also conflict with the state and sometimes eclipse it, to create a multi-layered context whose subtleties often escaped Burckhardt. We think his central thesis survives, but the cross-currents can be intricate.

Perhaps the largest subject missing from Burckhardt's book is in a way the most surprising, since it is the site of Western Europe's most successful imperial saga. Burckhardt says almost nothing about economics, but it is an important shift in the economic center of gravity that now seems most dramatically to mark the early modern period and to provide the context for writing its "total history." The major contemporary attempt to produce a history of Hegelian inclusiveness is Fernand Braudel's *Civilisation matérielle et capitalisme: Xve-xviiie siècle;* its effort to craft an account that will extend history's reach into the smallest details of everyday life—*les structures du quotidien*—culminates in a picture of the emergence of mercantile capitalism as Western Europe's driving wheel. In that arena competitiveness and cooperation find perhaps their most natural symbiosis, and civilization reaches a unity denied to it politically: "What the Emperor Charles V never achieved—the conquest of Europe—Antwerp managed easily."[7]

To which add, in turn, Venice, Genoa, Amsterdam: the principal diachronic strain of Braudel's account is the shifting locale of Europe's capital city. The financial power so focused is usually undramatic and not quite visible—certainly much less so than state power—but if anything all the more effective for its low profile. From the fifteenth to the seventeenth century the center oscillates between the Mediterranean and the Low Countries; its ultimate destination, by the beginning of the eighteenth century, is of course London, whose reign lasts until living memory. That reign finds its appropriate emblem in the unearthly stability of the English pound, pegged by Elizabeth at four ounces of sterling silver and keeping that exchange value for over 350 years. A unit first created, like the less fortunate Italian *lira,* by the monetary reforms of Charlemagne, the *libra sterlingorum* wins out as the age's most convincing symbol of imperial triumph.

Burckhardt's general disregard of economics deprives his gallery of any full portrait of the Renaissance merchant, who ought to be one of the prime exhibits. Francesco di Marco Datini would do handsomely.[8] Economic historians are incalculably indebted to his unusually pragmatic effort at self-memorialization: he provided that all his correspondence and ledgers—kept "in the name of God and of profit"—be collected and preserved for posterity like some immense literary oeuvre (money is a kind of poetry). The gathering of his wealth required conspicuous versatility among the categories of medieval society. He found it expedient to join no fewer than five different guilds—or, as they were called in Italy, *Arti*. He conducted his business through a complicated system of independently functioning companies in Italy, France, and Spain, whose only official connection was his position as a controlling partner in each of them. As a Pratese he might have been expected to base his activities in the wool trade that was his native city's specialty; but Datini spent most of his working life abroad, and the *Arte della Lana* was only one string in his bow, and not the most important:

> First an armorer and then a mercer in Avignon, he had become a cloth-maker in Prato and was now again a shop-keeper in Florence; next he founded a flourishing import-and-export business, and became the chief partner of a number of different trading companies: he dealt in wool, cloth, veils, wheat, metals, and hides, in spices and pictures and jewels. . . . He even took over, for a short time, the city tolls for meat and wine in Prato; he did some under-writing; and finally (against the advice of all his friends) he set up a bank.[9]

If there is a center to Datini's enterprise, it should probably be located in that late and controversial entry into the activities of the money-changers' guild, the *Arte del Cambio*. It is the growth of instruments of credit that makes diversified careers such as Datini's possible, provides the international grid within which all manner of commodities can be acquired and exchanged through the security and ease of a kind of silent number magic. The merchant capitalist, bound to no particular trade, has command over the whole range of the world's goods, which move as he directs them to his own advantage. He is one of the strongest paradigms for the conversion of external reality into manipulable resource.

Practitioners of commerce at Datini's level—in one distinction, *mercatura* rather than *mercanzia*—are a restricted elite even within the merchant community, and the preindustrial character of capitalism in the Renaissance keeps it, by and large, from taking over the means of production and affecting most of the population as directly as it later will. Agriculture and manufacture, and the lives associated with them, proceed much as before. The expansion of the capitalist marketplace nevertheless touches society as a whole, and on a deep level, with a new sense of the awesomely abstract power of money: *Pecuniae obed-*

iunt omnia (Money controls everything) (Erasmus, *Adages* 1.3.87). Financial savvy offers itself as the model for the triumphant management of the human condition:

> You can be sure that although human life is short, those who know how to make capital of time [*fare capitale del tempo*] and not waste it uselessly will have lots of time to spare. For the nature of man is very capacious, and those who are efficient and resolute will get many things done. (Guicciardini, *Ricordi* C145)[10]

A Marxist definition of the Renaissance can look remarkably like Burckhardt's:

> With the rise of capitalism . . . people begin to live, to produce, to write and read under circumstances which—to a far greater number of individuals—are less "given": conditions are less preordained in the sense that a person's relation to (and his function as a member of) a social conglomerate or community has ceased to be so direct, ineluctable, and transparent. Hence the process of *Aneignung* assumes a more highly dynamic and unpredictable quality; being less predetermined by the given state of natural resources, cultural materials, and literary conventions and traditions, *Aneignung* becomes more and more attached to forms of existence which, far from being presupposed to the individual's activity, appear as its result. . . .
>
> Now the individual tends to confront the conditions and means of production as something alien, as something which he cannot unquestioningly consider as part of the existence of his own self. But as the individual's distance from the means and modes of production . . . grows, there develops new scope for his own choice of productive strategies vis-à-vis the increasing availability of those means, modes, and materials which, practically and imaginatively . . . he can make his own. It is the dynamic quality in the expansion of the scope of the individual's choice and the simultaneity and availability of diverse strategies and objects, that invest the appropriating function with an unforeseen potential of power, energy, and productivity—the more potent and universally usable for having been uprooted from its local and communal predeterminations.[11]

Yet translating Burckhardt's idea into economic terms also makes some of the paradoxes of ambitious individualism clearer. Money is certainly recognized as ambition's least respectable resource, its celebration primarily a topic for satirists:

All this nether world
Is yours. You command it and do sway it,
The honor of it and the honesty,
The reputation, ay, and the religion
(I was about to say and had not err'd)
Is Queen Pecunia's.

(Ben Jonson,
The Staple of News 2.1.38–43)

When Jonson goes on to call Pecunia "The Venus of the time and state" (2.5.34), he skirts an equation of capitalism and prostitution that becomes almost obligatory.[12] What is most generally at stake here is the capacity of the marketplace to act as a universal solvent of all relations to the world: any possession is alienable and its worth unstable, a reflex of how many other people happen to want it that day. An awareness of this state of affairs is widely registered as a recurring shock at the thought that worth is something not intrinsic and constant. "What's aught but as 'tis valued?" asks Shakespeare's Troilus (*Troilus and Cressida* 2.2.52), in a cynical play that moves toward a vision of universal whoredom. Hobbes, whose "natural condition of mankind" in many ways resembles a Bourse more than a battlefield, is as harshly lucid as usual. The marketplace may be individualism's field of play, but it is simultaneously the corrosion of any secure self-respect:

The value or worth of a man is as of all other things his price—that is to say, so much as would be given for the use of his power—and therefore is not absolute, but a thing dependent on the need and judgment of another. . . . And as in other things, so in men, not the seller but the buyer determines the price. For let a man (as most men do) rate themselves at the highest value they can, yet their true value is no more than it is esteemed by others. (Chap. 10)

Hobbes's specific subject is social hierarchy, the age's most visible standard of evaluation. Talk of buying and selling gains much of its disturbing power from the acute pressure that the new economy exerts on that structure. The best known speech from *Troilus and Cressida* concerns a threat to the established rankings of "degree": "Degree being vizarded, / Th' unworthiest shows as fairly in the mask" (1.3.83–84). The increasing translation of wealth into monetary terms makes a fortune (as it's called) much easier to win and lose, and gives the edge to skills other than those traditionally cultivated by the upper classes. The age is shot through with a potential for social mobility, both upward and downward, that occasions much comment—again, usually from satirists.

The unease with which such mobility is characteristically viewed should warn us against extrapolating it too quickly. Burckhardt on this point is atypically naïve: "The main current of the time went steadily toward the fusion of classes in the modern sense of the phrase" (p. 353). That is to posit an ideal which the age neither attained nor desired. Whatever Renaissance individualism was, it was not egalitarian:

> In London, the rich disdain the poor. The courtier the citizen. The citizen the country man. One occupation disdaineth another. The merchant the retailer. The retailer the craftsman. The better sort of craftsman the baser. The shoemaker the cobbler. The cobbler the carman. One nice dame disdains her next neighbor should have that furniture to her home, or dainty dish or device, which she wants. She will not go to church, because she disdains to mix herself with base company, and cannot have her close pew by herself. She disdains to wear that everyone wears, or hear that preacher which everyone hears.[13]

Since Marx, our eyes cannot miss the patent obsession of Renaissance culture throughout the period with social status and its insignia. What now seems remarkable is the social conservatism that in the end triumphs over economic dislocation and leaves the traditional strata substantially intact. The notion of a classless society is promulgated in certain Reformation sects, but gains no official sanction in the dominant Protestant churches or republican theory. Luther himself vehemently denounces the peasant revolt conducted partly in his name. The utopian democrat James Harrington feels no evident contradiction writing an economically based class division—"horse" (yearly income over £100), "foot," and "servants" (disenfranchised)—into the constitution of Oceana, his "equal commonwealth."[14] The spread between the social orders if anything widens during the Renaissance. Peasants and artisans, whipsawed by the inflation that is a dramatic feature of the new economy,[15] are often worse off than they had been before, and their occasional acts of rebellion—never sufficiently coordinated to be a major historical force—are usually conservative efforts to repair the erosion of their medieval standing. At best the lower ranks fight simply to stay in place.

A class struggle of more effect takes place further up the scale, between the new monarchies and the feudal aristocracy. The establishment of absolutism involves undermining baronial independence, especially the military capability that is the original purpose of the medieval warrior caste; this political stress combines with economic pressure to make the Renaissance, in Lawrence Stone's famous phrase, an extended crisis of the aristocracy. Marxist historians have seen this crisis as an important opening for the bourgeoisie, and replaced Burckhardt's formulation with a picture of the Renaissance as a *bürgerliche Revolution* in which the state and the mercantile middle class make common cause against the nobility. Again, though, the model has come to seem significantly anachronistic. A bourgeois-state alliance has proved difficult to document, and it is not entirely clear that the Renaissance middle class had a class consciousness, or at least a class allegiance, sufficient to carry out such a program. For the characteristic act of the successful bourgeois is to use his new money to buy land and set himself up with the traditional accoutrements of aristocracy. "Chi ha danari compre feudi ed è barone" (He who has money buys a fief and he is a baron).[16] Land so acquired is not necessarily run more profitably than before. It is purchased not as a capitalist investment but as the site for an aristocratic way of life. Middle class values—a parsimonious work ethic, scrupulous self-denial in the interests of profit—tend to stay where they are, unenvied by the other orders.

The other major route for upward mobility is attendance at the absolutist court, where something like Burckhardt's mixing of social backgrounds does take place; but success there is even more individualistic and even more self-consciously aristocratic in its dress. Noble birth is the first requirement Castiglione postulates for his ideal courtier, and the social code he goes on to present falls under that sign: all courtiers should act like true aristocrats. Monarchs frequently find it expedient to reward such aspiration with the reassignment of old titles or the creation of new ones, since doing so helps ratify their own authority. New nobles indeed more than compensate for any thinning of the ranks; the inflation of aristocratic currency is a much noted matter, and often denounced as a major scandal. But it is a scandal precisely because nobility remains the money of account, recognized as such by both the state and society at large. For all its strains, the demilitarized aristocracy keeps a lock on the social imagination, and by the end of the Renaissance, even in England, the class has not withered but simply had its function and membership adjusted within the new political framework. A later time, finding the outcome hard to distinguish from a feudalism whose categories it retains, will take to calling the seventeenth-century arrangement the *ancien régime*.

The result is thus to some extent a circular course that changes nothing. It does, nevertheless, manage to irradiate the lives even of the unsuccessful with a sense of possibility. Social dislocation, however temporary, is also metaphorical opportunity, permanently expanding the idiom of self-representation on all levels. Psychic empire shares space in the Renaissance mind with psychic nobility—in many ways the more successful figure of speech, to the point where we may no longer recognize it as such. Once more classical Stoicism helps negotiate the process, making aristocratic prestige the product of individual resource: "It is the soul which ennobles, and it can rise from any man's station and above his fortune" (Seneca, *Epistles* 44.5). Poggio, who cites this passage, meditates on the history of the term "noble" to assimilate it partly to fame—"the ancients called a man noble (*nobilis*) if he was known (*notus*) in some special way, be he notorious or admired"—but then tops this etymology with another: "We call men *noble* for their own upright deeds and for the glory and fame they win by their own character. We seem to derive the word from ourselves (*nobismet ipsis*), not from others." The pressure here is to convert nobility into an inner state prior to any outward certification—"Nobility is not externally derived but springs from one's own virtue"[17]—a meaning which we instinctively now register as the primary one. So also *dignitas,* the Roman term for the rank that comes with the holding of a particular office, promulgated by humanism in a wider sense. We will be giving special weight in our next section to a famous Renaissance text that asserts the inclusive dignity of man, defined as humanity's lack of ties to any preexisting function in the cosmos. Such usage enfolds upper-class identity into the individual spirit as mysterious strength of character.

The code of honor occupies just this terrain. The term's original civic meaning, similar to that of "dignity," persists in the Renaissance; but Alberti, for one, specifically devalues it as secondary.[18] True honor is not the result of social success but its interior cause, Rabelais's "natural spur and instinct." In *Gargantua,* this disposition leads the Thelemites to re-create the cultured leisure of feudal aristocracy as though spontaneously, on impulse. For Alberti, "satisfying the standards of honor, we shall grow rich and well praised, admired and esteemed among men."[19] The term bears traces of the class struggle between the aristocracy and the state; Castiglione cites it as a reason for not obeying one's prince: "In dishonorable things we are not bound to obey anyone."[20]

Honor's vengeful imperatives are an especially acute case. Private justice is one of the baronial rights most urgently interdicted by the new order, but tenaciously a part of the image of elite self-regard. Often, especially in English revenge plays, the exercise of that right is presented as tragic, but it is not uniformly so. Lope de Vega's peasant hero Peribáñez, having killed the local Comendador in revenge for an affront, earns from the king not anger but admiration: "¡Cosa estraña! / ¡Que un labrador tan humilde / estime tanto su fama!" (A strange thing, that such a lowly laborer should value his reputation so highly! *Peribáñez*, ll. 3105–7). Punishment is out of the question; rather,

> a un hombre deste valor
> le quiero en esta jornada
> por capitán de la gente
> misma que sacó de Ocaña.
> (3112–15)

A man of such valor I want to have in this campaign as captain of the same company that I have raised in Ocaña.

With this comes the medieval privilege of rank:

> para la defensa y guarda
> de su persona, le doy
> licencia de traer armas
> defensivas y ofensivas.
> (3119–22)

For the defense and protection of his person, I give him the right to bear arms defensive and offensive.

The rarity of such advancement in the real life of the Renaissance does not compromise its power or accessibility as fantasy. *Tanti eris aliis quanti tibi fueris* (You are valued by others as you value yourself).[21]

The specific affront for which Peribáñez retaliates is sexual, the Comendador's attempt to seduce his wife. Cuckoldry, actual, possible, or imagined, figures prominently in Renaissance lore as a prime occasion for revenge, the result of a special twist in the conception of honor. The medieval heritage gives that conception a significant asymmetry by gender. For women, honor refers to sexual virtue, the form of social dignity most widely available to them. That usage survives almost unchallenged in the Renaissance, but given a new torsion: a woman's honor is a crucial part of her husband's honor. Behind male touchiness about that possession we may sense a movement that looms more and more in recent social history, the creation of the modern nuclear family. *La famiglia* is already a sufficiently important focus in Italy that Burckhardt might have given it more notice. It is an enduring middle term between the individual and the state, and the subject of the treatise in which Alberti's remarks about honor occur. With the Reformation and the further devaluing of celibacy, marriage rises in dignity while the family unit sheds some of its extensions and shrinks toward its present size.

The accompanying theory of this unit is rigorously patriarchal; the family and the absolutist state are very frequently likened to each other as institutions that both require strong paternal control.[22] Burckhardt wrote incautiously of Renaissance women standing "on a footing of perfect equality with men" (p. 389); the cultural innovation of the period is probably better located in the grandeur of the rhetoric with which women are persuaded to monogamous submission: "Such a duty as the subject owes his prince, / Even such a woman oweth to her husband" (*Taming of the Shrew* 5.2.155–56). The Marquis of Montrose is particularly, breathtakingly unguarded:

> My dear and only love, I pray
> >This noble world of thee
> Be governed by no other sway
> >But purest monarchy . . . .
> But I must rule and govern still,
> >And always give the law,
> And have each subject at my will,
> >And all to stand in awe.
> But 'gainst my battery, if I find
> >Thou shunn'st the prize so sore
> As that thou sett'st me up a blind,
> >I'll never love thee more.

He compares himself to Alexander the Great, ruling with noble jealousy "the empire of thy heart."[23]

Female acceptance of such demands is nevertheless imagined as gaining some of ambition's characteristic rewards. Montrose, in a tactic that shall concern us more fully in our final section, promises the woman fame in return for fidelity:

> >if thou wilt be constant then,
> >And faithful of the word,
> >I'll make thee glorious by my pen

> And famous by my sword:
> I'll serve thee in such noble ways
> Was never heard before;
> I'll crown and deck thee all with bays,
> And love thee evermore.

At least as significant, however, is the investment of the family unit itself with some of the structure and goals of Burckhardtian individualism. The Italian treatises stress the lure of genteel autonomy—"self-sufficiency, a worthy resolve and proper to a princely spirit"[24]—possible to a well-run household. "I do not have to send to the city for anything that is necessary or fitting for the life of a poor gentleman," claims Tasso's *padre di famiglia,* boastfully modest.[25] But the grandest aspirations are dynastic.

Gargantua makes the classic statement in his famous letter to his son, Pantagruel:

> Among the gifts, graces, and prerogatives with which the Sovereign Creator, God Almighty, endowed and embellished human nature in the beginning, one seems to me to stand alone, and to excel all others; that is the one by which we can, in this mortal state, acquire a kind of immortality and, in the course of this transitory life, perpetuate our name and seed; which we do by lineage sprung from us in lawful marriage. . . . I offer thanks to God, my Preserver, for permitting me to see my grey-haired age blossom afresh in your youth. When, at the will of Him who rules and governs all things, my soul shall leave this mortal habitation, I shall not now account myself to be absolutely dying, but to be passing from one place to another, since in you, and by you, I shall remain in visible form here in this world, visiting and conversing with men of honor and my friends as I used to do.[26]

The letter passes on to a program of humanist learning that has been called "the most ardent conceivable hymn to the glory of the Renaissance."[27] That enterprise of piety to the past is here presented as a means to the end of securing the survival of the parent in the child: "If the qualities of my soul did not abide in you as does my visible form, men would not consider you the guardian and treasure-house of the immortality of our name."[28] The fashioning of children is assimilated to the humanist cult of literary immortality. Ben Jonson, in an epithalamium, goes so far as to suggest that nexus as the sexual turn-on of chaste love, the libidinal motor of modern marriage:

Haste, haste, officious Sun, and send them night
    Some hours before it should, that these may know
All that their fathers, and their mothers might
    Of nuptial sweets, at such a season, owe,
        To propagate their names,
        And keep their fames
      Alive, which else would die,
For fame keeps virtue up, and it posterity.
        (*Underwood* 75.145–52)[29]

Our offspring are, in effect, the works of art that we can hope will survive our own death.

The themes of art and procreation are memorably twined in Shakespeare's sonnets: "You must live, drawn by your own sweet skill" (16). Jonson movingly calls his own dead son his "best piece of poetry" (*Epigrams* 45). A rural clergyman, similarly bereaved, is more direct: "He was my hope."[30] For a father without the resources of art, the loss of an heir, especially a male heir, was an occasion of particular pain, a loss of prospects. It is in the future of his family that his own aspirations are likely to be most powerfully invested: "The bringing up and marriage of his eldest son is an ambition which afflicts him as soon as the boy is born, and the hope to see his son superior, or placed above him, drives him to dote upon the boy in his cradle."[31] Social mobility is in practice something usually achieved across generations. Able yeomen, in a scenario that Sir Thomas Smith offers as typical for sixteenth-century England, "daily do buy the lands of unthrifty gentlemen, and after setting their son to the school at the universities, to the law of the realm, or otherwise leaving them sufficient lands whereon they may live without labor, do make their said sons by these means gentlemen."[32] The institution of *mariage légitime* serves these ambitions by guaranteeing the bloodlines and giving the middle- or lower-class family the lineal definition of a noble house. Shakespeare's life records testify with particular strength to his own commitment to such an effort, winning the coat of arms that his father had been denied, losing his only son, dying in the hope that, like the English king who was the subject of his last play, he had established his succession through his daughters. It is very possible that knowledge of his extravagant immortalization through his works would not have consoled him for the fact that his line proved no more durable than that of the Tudors.[33]

The Renaissance fear of cuckoldry and fascination with bastards are testimony to the vulnerability of such plans to other, more insidious threats. The unifying plot that Rabelais introduces into his saga in its third book is Panurge's quandary over whether to get married: "There's no other way of getting legitimate sons and daughters, by whom I can hope to perpetuate my name and armorial bearings, and to whom I can leave my inheritances and acquisitions." But: "If . . . my wife were to make me a cuckold—and you know this is a great year for cuckolds—that would be enough to make me fly off the hinges of patience. I like cuckolds all right. They seem good fellows to me, and I like visiting their houses. But I'd rather die than be one of them." [34] A lengthy succession of divinations and experts cannot get around the proposition that the only secure way to avoid being cuckolded is to avoid marrying. The final oracle recommends having a drink. George Chapman ends one of his plays with a virtuoso oration on the present time as "the horned age," succeeding those of gold, silver, brass, iron, lead, and wood (*All Fools* 5.2.231ff.). Shakespeare can be comparably jaunty in the endless horn jokes that salt his comedies; but he also puts some of his greatest art into showing what going off the hinges of patience in this matter can be like in its most terrifying forms:

> Had it pleas'd heaven
> To try me with affliction, had they rain'd
> All kind of sores and shames on my bare head,
> Steep'd me in poverty to the very lips,
> Given to captivity me and my utmost hopes,
> I should have found in some place of my soul
> A drop of patience; but, alas, to make me
> The fixed figure for the time of scorn
> To point his slow unmoving finger at!
> Yet could I bear that too, well, very well;
> But there, where I have garner'd up my heart,
> Where either I must live or bear no life;
> The fountain from the which my current runs
> Or else dries up: to be discarded thence!
> Or keep it as a cestern for foul toads
> To knot and gender in!
>
> (*Othello* 4.2.47–62)

We know of no critic who does justice to the compressed specificity of this passage. "There" in line 57 points not to Desdemona's vagina but to her womb, from which should run the current of Othello's lineage, part of his life that will triumph over his mortality. That is why the pollution of that place is a pollution of Othello's own self. His irrational fury is the terror of the individual will confronting intractable uncertainty in its bid for self-preservation. *Othello* is not about jealousy in general. It is about a specific Renaissance pathology, the self-poisoning jealousy that can arise in a man in whom the fame-lust of the period and the desire to propagate have fused.

Human biology mandates an ambiguity in any claim to fatherhood, an ambiguity that leaves any paternal aspiration at the mercy of wills not its own. The never fully dominable woman can always admit a competitor into what the imperial self conceives as one of its most intimate resources.[35] The prospect of cuckoldry is thus one of the points at which that self is most acutely at risk, and as such gears with the age's highest tragic themes. The cuckolded husband is a potential Macbeth to his rival's Banquo:

> They hail'd him father to a line of kings.
> Upon my head they plac'd a fruitless crown,
> And put a barren sceptre in my gripe,
> Thence to be wrench'd with an unlineal hand,
> No son of mine succeeding. If't be so,
> For Banquo's issue have I fil'd my mind,
> For them the gracious Duncan have I murther'd,
> Put rancors in the vessel of my peace
> Only for them, and mine eternal jewel
> Given to the common enemy of man,
> To make them kings—the seeds of Banquo kings!
> (*Macbeth* 3.1.60–69)

THREE

The Prince and the Playhouse: A Fable

It is not only dynastic ambition that brings individualism to such a crisis. We end this part with a further illustration, in a parable drawn from some of the most familiar Renaissance texts.

Machiavelli's *The Prince* is not extensively cited in Burckhardt, but that seems largely because its presence is taken for granted. Perhaps no other single Renaissance writer so powerfully validates Burckhardt's own emphases. As the first major theorist of the modern secular state, Machiavelli is the ultimate source for Burckhardt's opening thesis; and in his most famous work, he provides the document to clinch that thesis: a handbook for the practicing *signore*. Written in direct response to the *calamità d'Italia*, *The Prince* is the age's most influential attempt to formulate Italy's political testament. The more extensive republican theorizing of the *Discorsi* on Livy pales beside the swift, indelible analysis of the opportunities and demands of one-man rule. Within that category, Machiavelli bores in on rule that makes a decisive break with tradition, on "principalities that are completely new in respect to their prince and composition [*stato*]," and on rulers with no hereditary legitimacy, who go "from ordinary citizen [*privato*] to prince" (chap. 6).[1] Machiavelli codifies not merely the practical politics of these new men, but also much of what becomes the standard lore about their style: their studied ruthlessness, their thirst for fame and glory, even their patronage of high culture ("a prince should show that he is an admirer of *virtù* by giving recognition to talented men, and honoring those who excel in a particular art"; chap.

21). And Machiavelli's text also contains the germ of the famous trope that unifies Burckhardt's book:

> To come to those who, by means of their own *virtù* and not by fortune, have become princes, let me say that the most outstanding are Moses, Cyrus, Romulus, Theseus and the like. . . . And examining their actions and lives, we see that from fortune they received nothing but the occasion; which in turn offered them the material they could then shape into whatever form they pleased. (Chap. 6)

Forma and *materia* turn up again so paired in the concluding exhortation to Lorenzo de' Medici: "In Italy there is no lack of material to be given form" (chap. 26). Machiavelli's central subject is individualistic political success *als Kunstwerk*.

So conceived, the political topic opens itself to Burckhardtian generalization. The Machiavellian Prince is Renaissance man, addressing his surroundings with a new freedom from preconception, and exploiting that freedom to secure for himself a new level of power over his world. Machiavelli supplies some of the generalization himself in his running opposition of *virtù* and *fortuna,* the first being the resource that most concerns him. In his penultimate chapter, he locates his own novelty in a claim for the power of human virtuosity within the scheme of things:

> I am not unaware that many have been and still are of the opinion that worldly affairs are in a way governed by fortune and by God, that men with their wisdom are not able to control them, indeed, that men can do nothing about them. . . . When I think about this sometimes, I am to some extent inclined toward their opinion. Nevertheless, so that our free choice may not be obliterated, I hold that it could be true that fortune is the arbiter of half our actions, but that she still leaves the other half, or close to it, to be governed by us. (Chap. 25)

However concessive, the rejection of the conventional wisdom is a significant first stroke in Burckhardt's period concept, the affirming of a new dispensation against the strictures of the medieval moral heritage.[2] The prescripts of Machiavelli's treatise enable their practitioner to take control of his earthly destiny.

Yet it is also Machiavelli's distinction to make evident just what that control can cost. He coolly follows the logic of *imperium* to some Tacitean extremities: "The Romans, to hold on to Capua, Carthage and Numantia, destroyed them, and did not lose them. . . . For the truth is that there is no sure way of keeping possession of [free cities], except by demolishing them" (chap. 5). Even the more ordinary course of business can be programmatically brutal: "Of all princes, it is the new prince that finds it impossible to avoid the reputation of being cruel, since new states are full of dangers" (chap. 17). And if the successful new prince may expect the need for deliberate acts of cruelty to fade with time, the underlying principle does not, and is no less chilling. Machiavelli is here weighing the question of "whether it is better to be loved than feared," and the conclusion is relentless: "Since men love at their own pleasure, and fear at the pleasure of the prince, a wise prince should build his foundation on what is his own, not on what belongs to others" (chap. 17). Love is an inferior bond because it is so difficult to exact, and the Prince's emotional universe is kept systematically bleak by his rigorous calculus of power: I can make you fear me much more reliably than I can make you love me. One may perhaps aspire to the fusion imagined in classical imperial panegyric: "Ipse metus te noster amat" (Even our fear loves you).[3]

Tradition, however, has been most unnerved by the terms in which Machiavelli recommends behavior that in itself would be perfectly worthy of affection and loyalty: "A prince . . . should appear, when seen and heard, to be all compassion, all faithfulness, all integrity, all kindness, all religion. And nothing is more essential than to appear to have this last quality" (chap. 18). In this way, he can avoid being hated—as much a desideratum as being feared. But the operative word is of course "appear":

> It is not necessary . . . for a prince to have all of the qualities mentioned above, but it is certainly necessary that he appear to have them. In fact, I would go so far as to say this, that having them and observing them at all times, they are harmful; and appearing to have them, they are useful; for example, appearing to be compassionate, faithful, humane, upright, religious, and being so; but his mind should be disposed in such a way that should it become necessary not to be so, he will be able and know how to change to the contrary.

Politics in Machiavellian practice is preeminently a matter of the impression one makes on others, and the Prince's central resource—more fundamental than physical prowess or mastery at arms—is his ability to manage that impression at will: "Those princes who have accomplished great things are the ones . . . who knew how to manipulate the minds of men with shrewdness." The key is that all the Prince's *personae* be just that; he must not be bound by principle or habit to a particular style of action, because events may always call for something different. He must know when to be a lion and when to be a fox: "A fox in order to know the traps, and a lion to frighten the wolves. Those who live by the lion alone do not understand matters." Detached and versatile, the Prince must be a *gran simulatore e dissimulatore*.

That is to say, a good actor. Machiavelli does not put it that way himself, but his discussion verges on identifying the Prince's essential *Kunst* as the art of theatrical performance, the ability to be wholly convincing in any number of assumed roles. It is an art that has become central to our picture of the Renaissance, whose later phases are a momentous time in the history of the drama. Burckhardt gives over several pages in the *Civilization* to wondering why the Italian Renaissance had so little to show for itself in this area (pp. 312–16). His theory virtually requires that it should have had its Shakespeare, or Lope, or Corneille. Even before the rise of the great theaters in England, Spain, and France, the likening of life to a play becomes established as one of the age's signature tropes.[4] In a famous humanist document of the early sixteenth century, the metaphor helps define a heroic sense of human potential, as man the performer displays his protean abilities before an audience of the gods: "As he of gods the greatest, embracing all things in his might, is all things, they saw man, Jupiter's mime, be all things also."[5] A repertoire of masks, which includes the "angry and raging lion" and the "cunning little fox," climaxes with a dead-perfect replica of Jupiter himself. The divine spectators are so awed that man wins a place at their table. Machiavelli's hero takes a recognizable version—less elevated, more bluntly effective—of that route to self-deification:

> [Cesare Borgia] had [Remirro de Orca] placed one morning in Cesena on the piazza in two pieces with a piece of wood and a bloodstained knife alongside him. The atrocity of such a spectacle left those people at one and the same time satisfied and stupefied. (Chap. 7)

The Prince makes himself a god on earth by grasping the basic theatricality of politics.

Yet the very terms of that success are insidious. The theatrical trope gains much of its staying power from its ability to cut more than one way. It is not merely exhilarating: "When we are born, we cry that we are come / To this great stage of fools" (*King Lear* 4.6.182–83). Machiavelli is not merely debasing a noble metaphor; to see politics as theater is also to trouble political power itself in profound ways. For theatrical success is also a form of enslavement; "the artist-performer," as Kenneth Burke puts it, "is the servant of the very despot-audience he seeks to fascinate."[6] As any performer knows, power so won is relentlessly and mysteriously vulnerable, capable of reverting to its hostile source swiftly and without warning. And when, as in the political arena, the audience is made up in great part of other, highly competitive performers, whose impressionability is never ingenuous or without strategic purpose, the insecurity increases exponentially. Politics becomes, in other words, a Hobbesian marketplace in which everyone's political stock is priced by actual and potential enemies. Individual ambition so pursued threatens to corrode its own base. It is one measure of Hobbes's lucidity about the role of reputation as it factors into the competitive milieu that he insists that his autocrat must be put in place by an extraordinary covenant. No single contestant will be able to fight his way to the top and overawe his fellows with any permanence. In the *Discorsi* (1.2) Machiavelli sketches such a covenant at the primeval origins of monarchy, but it is merely a way to get started on a cycle of governmental experiment and change and carries no transcendent legitimacy; and no comparable sanction is imagined for the new Prince in the modern world. Yet without it his authority is forever open to an unaccountable failure to convince.[7]

Machiavelli himself, of course, does not say as much. We guess at his attunement to the problems involved through what seem slips in his own argument. An unexpected gesture toward a sanction transcending the political Bourse comes at the end of his discussion of Agathocles the Sicilian:

> It cannot be called *virtù* to kill one's fellow citizens, betray friends, be without faith, without pity, without religion; all of these may bring one to power [*imperio*], but not to glory. . . . his vicious cruelty and inhumanity, together with his infinite iniquitous deeds, do not allow him to be counted among the most outstanding famous men. (Chap. 8)

Power is here subordinated to an uncharacteristically austere standard of fame, both posthumous and non-Herostratic. Machiavelli briefly seems to embrace the humanist hope that fame could be the new basis for stable political morality—precisely the hope in which he is elsewhere notoriously uninterested. Agathocles here perhaps takes the hit for Cesare Borgia, the closest thing to a hero in Machiavelli's book, but one guilty at least in reputation of all the crimes here charged to the Sicilian. We might well have expected Borgia's story to be told here, in the chapter "on those who have become princes through iniquity"; but it is slotted instead, not altogether convincingly, into the previous chapter, "on new principalities acquired with the arms and fortunes of others," as though to evade the Herostratic potential that nevertheless shapes both Machiavelli's and Borgia's *Nachleben*.

There are other, subtler lapses of Machiavellian rigor as well, the most telling of them masquerading as the book's most confident moment. The line of argument that converges on the mythic victory of *virtù* over *fortuna* imposes as a condition of success a calculus of self-denial whose final term is so harrowing that Machiavelli himself tries to obscure it.

We encounter fairly early in the book a distinct note of asceticism in the Prince's career. In order to avoid being hated, he must refrain from some of the traditional perquisites of absolute power. "What makes him hated above all . . . is being rapacious and a usurper of the property and the women belonging to his subjects: he must abstain from this" (chap. 19). That is an astringency admirable in itself, a fairly straightforward application of the humanist principle that control over others must be earned by self-control. But the reasoning is of course not moral but strategic, and it can censor any unguarded emotion. Guicciardini is usefully explicit on just what being Machiavellian means in more ordinary matters of human behavior: "Though few men can do it, it is very wise to hide your displeasure with others, so long as it does you no shame or harm. For it often happens that later you will need the help of these people, and you can hardly get it if they already know you dislike them" (*Ricordi* C133). The power attained this way might enable one eventually to take postponed revenge on the object of one's displeasure, but, within the complex network of opportunity and need, that satisfaction is hardly guaranteed, and probably a dangerous and distracting hope. One should simply swallow the animosity at the stern insistence of cunning. Taken with full seriousness, the Machiavellian career imposes an emotional discipline that is almost saintly.

Machiavelli is clearest about this when he returns to the theme of versatility in his concluding discussion of *fortuna* and *virtù*. Wanting to be specific about the potential of the latter, he works out a contrast between natural inclinations of *respetto* and *impeto*:

> Men can be seen . . . to proceed in different ways: one with cautiousness, another with impetuousness; one by violence, another with strategy; one by patience, another by way of its contrary; and each one by these diverse

methods can arrive at his goal. Moreover, in the case of two cautious men, we can see one carry out his plan, the other not; and likewise two men prospering equally well by means of two different methods, one being cautious and the other impetuous: which stems from nothing else if not from the conditions of the times that do or do not conform to their course of action. . . . For, if a man governs himself with caution and patience, and the times and circumstances are in accord so that his course of procedure is good, he will go along prospering; but, if times and circumstances change, he is ruined, because he does not change his course of action. Nor does one find a man wise enough to know how to adapt himself to this. (Chap. 25)

Still, Machiavelli can now imagine a wisdom that would make a man invulnerable; it is the ability to "deviate from that to which he is naturally inclined":

The cautious man, when it is time for him to act with impetuousness, does not know how; and so he is ruined; for, if he were to change his nature with the times and the circumstances, his fortune would not change.

In a contemporary letter on the same subject, Machiavelli is more expansive:

Certainly anybody wise enough to understand the times and the types of affairs and to adapt himself to them would have always good fortune, or he would protect himself always from bad, and it would come to be true that the wise man would rule the stars and the Fates.[8]

Thus one of the age's strongest affirmations of the power of the individual to master his condition. But the very acuity of the formulation makes specially evident how demanding a lesson must be learned to gain that end. Consistent personality is a luxury the Prince cannot afford; among the things he must be prepared to sacrifice is his own nature.

At such moments, the implicit theatrical trope seems in touch with the actor's psychic vertigo, his experience of having, in the very exercise of his skills of self-creation, lost any sense of a real or natural self underlying his roles:

Who, in his life flattering his senseless pride
By being known to all the world beside,

Does not himself, when he is dying, know,
Nor what he is, nor whither he's to go.[9]

That vertigo accompanies Renaissance individualism as one of its logical possibilities, a terrifying inward rebound from the self's attempt
at dominance over others. It is a glimpse from which Machiavelli
quickly averts his argument. He offers the example of Julius II, who
"in all his dealings acted impetuously" and succeeded in everything he
did. Machiavelli keeps temporary faith with his own thesis by sup-
posing that "if such times had come that might have required him to
act with caution, his ruin would have followed from it"; but that is a
weak concession and the reasoning has been skewed. For in the famous last paragraph Machiavelli denies his own insight with a celebration of *impeto* as intrinsically the better way:

> I am certainly convinced of this: that it is better to be impetuous than
> cautious, because fortune is a woman, and it is necessary, if one wishes to
> hold her down, to beat her and fight with her. And we see that she allows
> herself to be taken over more by these men than by those who make cold
> advances; and then, being a woman, she is always the young man's friend,
> because they are less cautious, more reckless and with greater audacity
> command her.

Machiavelli reverts to a metaphorical version of an image he had earlier rejected, the Prince as the peremptory taker of women. It is an
image of heroic confidence that symbolizes Renaissance selfhood in
one of its least constrained postures, but its immediate purpose seems
to be to distract us from where we were heading: toward a recognition
that self-possession is also, on a deep level, a form of self-alienation.

Following through on that recognition, the age's greatest literary
career finds its take-off point.

Not the least reason for introducing the theatrical trope into analysis of *The Prince* is the subsequent importance of that book, read and
unread, to the Renaissance stage, especially in England. Machiavelli
himself delivers the prologue to Marlowe's *The Jew of Malta*—"Albeit
the world think Machevil is dead, / Yet was his soul but flown beyond
the Alps"—and provides a compact and brutal statement of the doctrine of the new prince:

> Many will talk of title to a crown:
> What right had Caesar to the empery?

Might first made kings, and laws were then most sure
When like the Draco's they were writ in blood.

There are some plays, such as Marlowe's own *Tamburlaine*, that
dramatize the direct seizing of such power through force and intimi-
dation; but the main tradition of Renaissance political drama centers
on the more richly theatrical aspirations of the Machiavellian schemer,
manipulating others with his changeable masks. The example in
Shakespeare's early work is his first major character. A lengthy, di-
gressive series of plays on the reign of Henry VI unpredictably, unmistakably shifts gears in the middle of the third installment when
Richard, Duke of Gloucester, remains on stage to deliver Shakespeare's first great soliloquy, in which he details the "soul's desire" not
satisfied by the recent victory of his house in the civil wars and the
crowning of his brother as Edward IV. Richard is driven by individualistic ambitions unprecedented in the trilogy and unsuspected by his
own kin. He locates their origin in a primal lovelessness linked to his
physical deformity:

Why, love foreswore me in my mother's womb;
And for I should not deal in her soft laws,
She did corrupt frail nature with some bribe,
To shrink mine arm up like a wither'd shrub,
To make an envious mountain on my back . . .
And am I then a man to be belov'd?
(*3 Henry VI* 3.2.153–57, 163)

From this he deduces an uncompromising formulation of the imperial
theme:

since this earth affords no joy to me
But to command, to check, to o'erbear such
As are of better person than myself,
I'll make my heaven to dream upon the crown,
And whiles I live, t' account this world but hell,
Until my misshap'd trunk that bears this head
Be round impaled with a glorious crown.
(165–71)

He emphasizes the improbability of his success—"yet I know not how
to get the crown, / For many lives stand between me and home" (172–
73)—and imagining his frustration rouses him to defiant violence:

"from that torment I will free myself, / Or hew my way out with a bloody axe" (180–81). Yet as he immediately makes clear, he knows that his greatest resource is not physical strength but his capacity for Machiavellian deceit:

> Why, I can smile, and murther whiles I smile,
> And cry "Content" to that which grieves my heart,
> And wet my cheeks with artificial tears,
> And frame my face to all occasions.
>
> (182–85)

Reminding himself of this gives Richard a propulsive confidence that leads him through a catalogue of treacherous versatility to a climactic invocation of the master's name:

> I'll drown more sailors than the mermaid shall,
> I'll slay more gazers than the basilisk,
> I'll play the orator as well as Nestor,
> Deceive more slily than Ulysses could,
> And like a Sinon, take another Troy.
> I can add colors to the chameleon,
> Change shapes with Proteus for advantages,
> And set the murtherous Machevil to school.
>
> (186–93)

It is one of the definitive assimilations of Machiavellian politics to theatrical role-playing. Richard ends with a cocky affirmation of the power of *virtù* centered on just that skill:

> Can I do this, and cannot get a crown?
> Tut, were it farther off, I'll pluck it down.
>
> (194–95)

Murdering the recrowned Henry VI two acts later, Richard identifies himself with remarkable precision as a Burckhardtian individual:

> I have no brother, I am like no brother;
> And this word "love," which greybeards call divine,
> Be resident in men like one another,
> And not in me: I am myself alone.
>
> (5.6.80–83)

Shortly thereafter, he gets his own play. *Richard III* begins with a re-
prise of the earlier soliloquy, a resentful contemplation of his ugliness,
until it generates a political program:

> Why, I, in this weak piping time of peace,
> Have no delight to pass away the time,
> Unless to see my shadow in the sun
> And descant on mine own deformity.
> And therefore, since I cannot prove a lover
> To entertain these fair well-spoken days,
> I am determined to prove a villain
> And hate the idle pleasures of these days.
>
> (1.1.24–31)

We may divine by now that the bitterness is itself something of an act.
It is being cultivated as a resource. Richard's divorce from love is the
detachment of Renaissance individualism, aware of its unlikeness to
others as it sizes them up with exploitative intent. Machiavellian role-
playing is the relevant art for such a medium; Richard is simply back-
ing off to give it room to work.

He is also fleshing out in remarkable ways the gender conflict
staged in Machiavelli's fable of *fortuna* and *virtù*.[10] Shakespeare's dire
amplification of this figure for Renaissance success lies in Richard's
lifelong antagonism with the womb; another self-fashioner in his tradition, Milton's Satan, will also turn against the idea of his own creation, symbolized by the abused womb of his consort Sin. Richard bids
to avoid the dependence on women that is the consequence of male
dynastic ambition. His destruction of all those who stand between
him and the crown is an outrage to the womb-work of legitimate
succession; the curses of mothers, including his own, bombard him
throughout the play. His sublimely daring retaliation is to perform
precisely the action whose impossibility he announces at the start: se-
ducing the widow of one of his victims, winning entrance to the inner
court of his archenemy. Doing so almost wins him over to more conventional styles of narcissism:

> I do mistake my person all this while! . . .
> Shine out, fair sun, till I have bought a glass,
> That I may see my shadow as I pass.
>
> (1.2.252, 262–63)

But Richard's career as a lover is not, as he had it in the opening solil-oquy, an alternative to his career of villainy, but one of its forms. Anne's yielding spells her doom: "I'll have her, but I will not keep her long" (229). Richard pursues the rigor of his imperial solitude to an inverse of the dynastic hope: not an alliance with the womb but its submission and humiliation.[11]

Such lovelessness is a requirement of Richard's career as well as its cause. By not loving, Richard gains an edge on everyone else in the court, one that allows him to obtain for himself any particular thing that he wants. In that condition he does not sorrow but frisks:

> He cannot live, I hope, and must not die
> Till George be pack'd with post-horse up to heaven.
> I'll in, to urge his hatred more to Clarence
> With lies well steel'd with weighty arguments,
> And if I fail not in my deep intent,
> Clarence hath not another day to live.
> Which done, God take King Edward to his mercy,
> And leave the world for me to bustle in!
>
> (1.1.145–52)

This, of course, about his two brothers. The crisp cheerfulness of such deliberations gives the early acts of the play its unforgettable spirit. Richard is an unholy illustration in political terms of Alberti's dictum: "Man is by nature suited and able to make good use of the world, and he is born to be happy."[12]

The ultimate business of the play, however, is to bring Richard to account. His ascent to the throne is quickly followed by the unraveling of his power and his death at the hands of his own subjects. And his fall is not cautionary in the way it would be as an exemplum in *The Prince*. We are not to try to figure out where Richard made the wrong move he might have avoided, but to recognize in him an offense to a fundamental moral order:

> A base foul stone, made precious by the foil
> Of England's chair, where he is falsely set;
> One that hath ever been God's enemy.
>
> (5.3.250–52)

God eventually punishes such offenses. At least in art, the schemers inspired by Machiavelli's treatise characteristically find themselves fac-ing such a force and finally destroyed by it. English writers in particular show the influence of a long line of legitimate succession in their national monarchy (its rescue dramatized in *Richard III*) and of the new moral stringency brought by the Reformation. Their shared imaginative field circumscribes Machiavellian politics with an un-Machiavellian expectation of divine vengeance almost never unsatisfied on the stage or in print. This retribution in time acquires the status of a mere convention and can in context seem feeble and unearned. Certainly none of the "answers" to *The Prince* have achieved the classic status of the book they seem to refute; in performance, similarly, it is hard not to make Shakespeare's Richard more compelling and interesting than any of his adversaries. Yet we have argued that English moralism stands in important dialectical relation to Italian individualism, is effectively entailed by it even within Burckhardt's account; and Shakespeare's play takes its boldest leap when it dramatizes Richard's destruction not as a contingent assertion of superhuman will but as an inward collapse brought on by the very nature of Richard's art.

On the night before the final battle, the ghosts of Richard's victims appear in dreams to him and to his adversary. Their message to Richard is "Despair and die!" The terror with which he wakes is a note unsounded before:

> O coward conscience, how dost thou afflict me!
> The lights burn blue. It is now dead midnight.
> Cold fearful drops stand on my trembling flesh.
> $\qquad$ (5.3.179–81)

Richard, it turns out, has an unexpected conscience, almost Protestant in its tenacious inwardness. He is, to our surprise, capable of feeling guilt and fearing punishment. But the subsequent effect is even more remarkable:

> What do I fear? Myself? There's none else by.
> Richard loves Richard, that is, I am I.
> Is there a murtherer here? No. Yes, I am.
> Then fly. What, from myself? Great reason why—
> Lest I revenge. What, myself upon myself?
> $\qquad$ (182–86)

The speech becomes a soliloquy with two speakers, interrupting and arguing with each other. We guess at Richard's uncanny sense that there is someone else in the tent with him. Conscience here merges

67

into self-consciousness become almost psychotic in its separation of performing and observing selves, no longer held together by the bond that had seemed as secure as a tautology:

> Alack, I love myself. Wherefore? For any good
> That I myself have done unto myself?
> O no! Alas, I rather hate myself
> For hateful deeds committed by myself.
>
> (187–90)

This is Richard's detachment come home. The coolness with which he had chosen and crafted his role reappears as a dizzying cleavage in the self. He now spins in that void: "I am a villain; yet I lie, I am not. / Fool, of thyself speak well; fool do not flatter" (191–92). But what is most terrifying is not confusion of identity but the objective clarity of the self he has made. For toward that self he now finds he has no more affection than he had for any of his victims:

> I shall despair; there is no creature loves me,
> And if I die no soul will pity me.
> And wherefore should they, since that I myself
> Find in myself no pity to myself?
>
> (200–203)

The ostensible self-hatred of the opening soliloquy here returns with new conviction and forcefulness, as the unreckoned consequence of his victory over the womb: he has lost the ability to mother himself. The career of victimization becomes at the end self-reflexive; the loveless manipulation of others is ultimately a lovelessness in the manipulation of the self.

The ghosts thus figure in supernatural terms an event that makes sense in other ways as well. We may call it the revenge of the audience. The performer exposes himself to it in the very process of gaining power over them. What he does to them is revisited upon himself, and they are always with him.

The impact of that realization is not wholly dispersed by Richard's recovery the next morning. The classic expression of that recovery—"Conscience avaunt! Richard's himself again"—is not Shakespeare's but an eighteenth-century addition, and defines precisely what has become impossible. In its original context, Richard's restored will to fight looks less like resilience than a bravura acceptance of damnation: "March on, join bravely, let us to it pell-mell; / If not to heaven, then hand in hand to hell" (5.3.312–13).[13] The prospect of damnation gnaws at the theatrical trope in much of its later life in Shakespeare's work:

> Life's but a walking shadow, a poor player,
> That struts and frets his hour upon the stage,
> And then is heard no more. It is a tale
> Told by an idiot, full of sound and fury,
> Signifying nothing.
>
> *(Macbeth* 5.5.24–28)

Such motiveless despair is a recurring descant on the imperial theme.

Against this background we gauge the force of the famous valedictory speech of Shakespeare's career, in which his most successful metatheatrical figure begs for forgiveness in arrestingly inclusive terms:

> Gentle breath of yours my sails
> Must fill, or else my project fails,
> Which was to please. Now I want
> Spirits to enforce, art to enchant,
> And my ending is despair,
> Unless I be reliev'd by prayer,
> Which pierces so, that it assaults
> Mercy itself, and frees all faults.
>> As you from crimes would pardon'd be,
>> Let your indulgence set me free.
>>
>> *(Tempest* Ep. 11–20)

The actor's traditional appeal for applause is translated into a prayer for the state of his soul, in a way that does not distinguish him very clearly from either the character (duke of the most implacably despotic of the Italian principalities) or the author (the age's consummate man of the stage). Their joint surrender gives Renaissance individualism its unexpected *telos* in seeking peace and comfort in submission to powers they had striven to awe. The logic of self-deification uncovers a countervailing proposition. God is other people.

TWO

Thought

FOUR

Cassirer's Legacy to the Burckhardt Tradition

Fresh intelligence and great erudition, which often dwell apart, merged authoritatively in the books of Ernst Cassirer. He was one of the few men of this century who could presume to pose for himself, and to answer without crippling reliance on secondary works, the largest questions of Western intellectual history. Though the label "Neo-Kantian" accurately designates his grounding assumptions about philosophy, his fascination for the Renaissance behind the Enlightenment was deep and tenacious. His early work on Descartes and Leibniz, along with the first volume of his *Erkenntnisproblem,* was already immersed in Renaissance thought, which must account in part for the eerie belongingness Cassirer experienced when, in 1920, he first visited the Warburg Library in Hamburg. His guide on that occasion, Fritz Saxl, remembered his parting comment: "This library is dangerous. I shall either have to avoid it altogether or imprison myself here for years."[1]

During the next decade he returned whenever possible to this vast and idiosyncratic collection. One fruit of the association was *Individuum und Kosmos in der Philosophie der Renaissance* (1927), a landmark contribution to intellectual history and the single most important supplement to Burckhardt's Renaissance. This study covers the fifteenth and sixteenth centuries, primarily, after a long opening section on Nicolas of Cusa, in Italy. *Die platonische Renaissance in England und die Schule von Cambridge* (1932), though focused on the Cambridge Platonists, widens his portrait gallery of Renaissance minds to include Montaigne and Shakespeare, and it may be viewed as a continuation

of his earlier book into the seventeenth century. Some of his final ar-
ticles were on Burckhardt, Pico, and Ficino.[2]

The Individual and the Cosmos in Renaissance Thought is not only a
remarkable book about Renaissance ideas, extending Burckhardt's
concepts of subject, object, and individuality from culture to thought,
or rather returning them, with their new Burckhardtian inflections,
to the Hegelian realms in which Burckhardt found them in the first
place. It is remarkable simply in being about the Renaissance. Since
the Enlightenment, the thought of this period has not interested many
important philosophers. To Leibniz the work of Ficino and Pico already seemed as quaint and contorted as metaphysical poetry would
seem to Samuel Johnson: "We cannot judge Plato's teachings by Plotinus or Marsilio Ficino, for they have perverted his fundamental doctrine in their scurryings after the miraculous and the mystical. One
cannot but be astonished at human short-sightedness when one ob-
serves how the later Platonists leave in the dark the excellent and profound teachings of the master regarding virtue, justice, and the state,
and on the art of definition and classification of concepts, the knowledge of the eternal verities, and the innate ideas of the mind."[3] At last
the Platonists, for centuries lagging behind the Aristotelians in the
practical matters of textual transmission and responsible commentary,
had put their house in order. On the surface at least, Kant has lost
touch with around two-thirds of the intellectual *dramatis personae* in
Cassirer's book. Today, despite what Cassirer and others have accomplished in the way of rehabilitation, our best philosophers appear to
know little or nothing about major Renaissance thinkers, with the
exception of culminating figures like Bacon, Descartes, and Hobbes.

The attitude persists that Renaissance philosophy, being in fact, as
the name implies, a series of revivals of the classical schools (Neoplatonism, Neostoicism, Neoskepticism, etc.), is a redundance doomed
to be forgotten sooner or later by a cultural memory in which space
is getting dearer all the time. The impetus to delineate the period came
late, and not from philosophers; as we have seen, Burckhardt drew
his major concepts from Hegel's treatment of the Hellenic age in a
mood of ironic contempt for the age of pure subjectivity, the age of
philosophy, that caps the *Phenomenology.* We still, by and large, study
Renaissance thought because it rubbed off on things we find more
interesting. Contemporary art historians and literary scholars probably know the intellectual history of the period better than trained
philosophers, which is also to say that, more than sixty years after its
publication, Cassirer's remains the finest book in the field. With all

due respect to the competition, his is the best philosophical mind ever to have surveyed Renaissance thought.[4]

Of course there have been cavils and qualifications. John Herman Randall complained of the Neoplatonic bias in Cassirer's account of the growth of scientific epistemology.[5] No scholar today would accept Cassirer's insistence that Nicolas actually inspired the thinkers of Italy. Some of his assumptions about individual figures, particularly Nicolas, have dated. But probably the worst that can be said is that Cassirer, ever alert to the antecedents of future philosophies, especially that of Kant, writes a constructivist and teleological history, not a contextual one. It is certainly true, to give the objection its weight, that if we were to come to Renaissance thought with other questions in mind than "How did all of this in time produce the three Critiques?" we might discover that some of its apparent unoriginality snapped to life.

Stoicism, say. Cassirer recognizes the prevalence of Stoicism, yet this matter is kept way off on the periphery of his vision. Why is no mystery: because in one conception of philosophy—Cassirer's—Stoicism just isn't interesting, even, pretty much, in its classical state. F. M. Cornford once remarked that if archaeologists were to unearth the 750 lost books of Chrysippus, "any student would cheerfully exchange them for a single roll of Heracleitus."[6] Yes, but the students have to have been fed from their earliest courses a certain line on the history of philosophy. Its central ambition is metaphysics, and metaphysics, as Aristotle said (*Metaphysics* 982B), starts in the mood of wonder (*to thaumazein*), with minds freed from creaturely distress and open to a purer appetite: wonder is the happy pang of speculative hunger. Stoicism was never wonderful in this way. In its vision of human perfection, it was as practical as other philosophy was reflective. It began in the expectation of catastrophe, thwarted will. Its characteristic problem was not what reason can reliably ascertain, but how in this disappointing world we can master our frustrated passions. Cassirer, relatively uninterested (at least at this point in his career) in agonistics, prefers the blue skies of epistemology. The result is a history without serious emergency.

In obvious ways *The Individual and the Cosmos* is a thoroughly old-fashioned book. Cassirer writes the birth narrative of the metaphysical subject attacked with such ferocity by Nietzsche, Heidegger, and Derrida, to name only three of its more influential opponents. This subject conceives of itself without biographical or political urgencies. It is not hungry, bored, bereft, envious, frightened, vain, or oppressed. It stands in the presence of an object and reflects upon the security of its conceptual mastery over this object. By the end of the Renaissance, it may know that the seeming integrity of objects dissolves into minute particles—the world, as Donne wrote, "crumbled out again to his atomies"—but that is an understood difference between objects and subjects. Cassirer tells the story heroically. Indeed, comparing his work to Burckhardt, one notes first of all the complete disappearance of moral suspicions about Renaissance individualism. The ambition to conquer self and world through knowledge is, for Cassirer, morally untroubled.[7] From the confines of the medieval distinction between soul and body, which was vertical, hierarchical, and moral, the Renaissance split between subject and object, which is horizontal, participatory, and epistemological, gradually emerges, and Cassirer orchestrates with considerable feeling those moments when the mind surveys a new empire of self-knowledge won during its investigation of objects.

The tale has Kant in mind. The supreme irony in the course of Western thought occurs when Renaissance empiricism reverses the Platonic expectation: certain truth, not unstable opinion, can be enjoyed in the realm of particulate nature; motion itself obeys mathematical laws. In philosophy this achievement is accompanied by increasingly convincing indictments of the frailty of subjectivity, which requires rigorous method to keep its wayward speculations on track, and in the extreme is no longer thought to correspond to, or somehow merge with, the object known. Mind, not temporality or materiality, is the source of appearance and error. Kant dispels irony from this subversion of Plato, and in his prearranged marriage of subject and object consummated in the fact of objective knowledge, allows the plot of Renaissance thought to end like a romance in reunion. Because subjectivity works that way, we have objectivity.

Thus Burckhardt's contention that "an *objective* treatment and consideration of the State and of all the things of this world became possible" as the "*subjective* side at the same time asserted itself" (p. 143) becomes in Cassirer's companion piece Renaissance foreshadowing of the Kantian revolution:

As science and art become more and more *conscious* that their primary function is to give form, they conceive of the law to which they are subject more and more as the expression of their essential freedom. And with that, the concept of nature and, indeed, the whole world of objects, takes on a new significance. The "object" is now something other than the mere opposite, the—so to speak—*ob-jectum* of the Ego. It is that towards which all the productive, all the genuinely creative forces of the Ego are directed and wherein they first find their genuine and concrete realization. The Ego recognizes itself in the necessity of the object; it recognizes the force and the direction of its spontaneity. (P. 143)

The law the object obeys is our law, mind's lawgiving spontaneity, and its regulation is therefore our freedom. With Kantian realizations of this kind, the intellectual conflicts of the Renaissance achieve resolution for Cassirer.

A new distinctness waits at the end of the story. The "Neo-Kantian" element consists in expanding the model of Kant's epistemology into a theory of culture. Implicitly in *The Individual and the Cosmos,* and more openly in the second volume of *The Philosophy of Symbolic Forms,* Cassirer's Renaissance is unconsciously sorting out intuitions bundled together long before in primitive myth and ordering them in their modern forms. Art, science, religion, and philosophy, interfused throughout the Renaissance, move toward a great differentiation, eventually taking their places as relatively autonomous sectors of Enlightenment culture—in Cassirer's estimation, the mind's systematic clarification of its own productive powers. Less positive attitudes toward this culture, such as those found in Heidegger, Derrida, or Rorty, would obviously produce an importantly revised history of Renaissance thought.[8]

When, for example, Cassirer states in his introduction that he "intends to remain within the realm of the history of philosophical problems" (p. 6), it can be objected that there were no "philosophical problems" for the Renaissance figures he studies most thoroughly. "Problems" in his sense of the term, such as the apportionment of responsibility for the fact of knowledge to subject and object, require an academic tradition tight enough to agree upon the presuppositions out of which problematics arise. Scholasticism had philosophical problems in this sense, such as the status of universals, and so did the academic aftermath of Kant, from which Cassirer's problems are drawn. But the academic philosophy of the Renaissance has been largely forgotten. Most of the thinkers in the standard histories have about them a touch of the cranky amateur or inspired hobbyist. Nicolas, Pico, Machiavelli, Montaigne, Bruno, Bacon, Hobbes, and Descartes never taught in a university; few of their works were taught in universities. It is a mistake to approach them as if they were, like the intellectuals of today, professionals making sense within institutional traditions. Cassirer's Kantian teleology sacrifices the unacademic, individualistic messiness of Renaissance thought.

Of its kind, the book has exceptional strengths. Cassirer ranges widely through Renaissance culture, as good at noticing as he is at

abstracting, frequently brilliant on (what are for him) peripheral subjects; the two pages devoted to Petrarch's lyrics (143–45) are richer
than many longer discussions. Again and again he moves chunks of
philosophical history into suggestive designs: "The Platonic category
of transcendence and the Aristotelian category of development mate
to produce the bastard concept of 'emanation'" (p. 18). Some of the
cases where we have good reason to believe that Cassirer is wrong or
partial do not especially damage his argument. That Cusanus, for instance, should have so much in common with Italian Neoplatonism
without having influenced it may be thought to strengthen the explan-
atory power of the period concept.

Nor, finally, is the Neo-Kantian program of his history so great a
handicap. Most histories of philosophy, even the new antirationalist
ones, aim toward Kant, if not as the place where jumbles got clarified,
then as the place where errors got enshrined most seductively. The
subject/object philosophy did, after all, carry the Western world by
the end of the Renaissance, and Kant was its premier tactician. What
to think of science, how its successes change the rest of thought: these
were pressing questions for the seventeenth and eighteenth centuries,
however we may now regard Kant's assumption that philosophy, in
the name of an inclusive rationalism, was best equipped to answer
them.

To our knowledge, the only history of Renaissance thought to rival
Cassirer's in learning and intellectual authority is Hans Blumenberg's
The Legitimacy of the Modern Age, especially its dense concluding chapters on Cusanus and Giordano Bruno.[9] This writer is more conscious
of periodization, more acute about the decisions endemic to intellectual history. Cassirer tries to steer clear of "the dispute concerning the
content and the legitimacy of those historical concepts 'Renaissance'
and 'Middle Ages'" (p. 5), which is precisely what Blumenberg wants
to clarify. But here, too, the question is how to position Renaissance
science in relation to the finite world of medieval Christianity, and
Nicolas of Cusa is still the first figure to be reckoned with.

Justifications for epochs are not of a piece. About some of them we
can offer fairly "realistic" descriptions (the Middle Ages, the Renaissance); others we define for more heuristic reasons (Romanticism,
Modernism). On both ends of the spectrum periods are usually
marked at the beginning by what Blumenberg terms a "new seriousness" (pp. 473–76). This nascent self-periodization is generally re-
proachful. Thus a catholic Christianity indicting the worldliness of
antiquity, its forgetfulness of transcendence, launches the Middle Ages
as an epoch whose seriousness will not depend on worldly confirma-

tion. In the Renaissance a new seriousness reproaches the Middle Ages for exactly this commitment, its fruitless and unclassical seriousness. Burckhardt once maintained that branding Arianism a heresy was decisive for the epoch of the Middle Ages.[10] In this spirit, Blumenberg concludes his study with the Renaissance pantheism of Bruno, whose infinite God so perfectly transferred himself to the universe at its creation that the local event of the incarnation was squeezed out of history.

We have no idea what Cassirer would have made of this powerful vision of Christianity destroyed from within by its own fascination with the new greatness of the universe. But it seems to us not altogether unrelated to his own concluding pages, which also follow a discussion of Bruno:

> But all these predicates claimed by the *divinity* are now equally attributable to the human *soul*. . . . The Ego can face the infinite cosmos inasmuch as it finds within itself the principles by which it *knows* that the cosmos is infinite. . . . The philosophy of the Renaissance never resolved the dialectical antinomy that is enclosed in this double relationship. But it has the indisputable merit of having determined the problem and handed it down in a new form to the following centuries, the centuries of exact science and systematic philosophy. (P. 191)

The two major histories of Renaissance thought end similarly, with a dizzy convulsion in the face of infinity, a delirious and uncertain calculation of what has become of God, that looks ahead to the drier business to come.

One of Blumenberg's key ideas for understanding change in intellectual history is curiosity, which he traces from Augustine's vice to science's virtue. Whenever there is a sense that limits have been placed on knowledge, whenever intellectuals suspect that beyond these limits, *plus ultra,* exist things unknown yet in principle knowable, a will to theoretical success tends to assert itself; the great dream of modern knowledge born in the Renaissance is to leave *nothing unsuspected.* Cassirer, we believe, would have welcomed Blumenberg's importation of desire or self-interested rational magnificence into the equations of intellectual history. His own teleology actually invites it:

> In Franciscan mysticism the medieval mind begins the great work of redeeming nature and liberating it from the stain of sin and sensuality. But there is still lacking a knowledge corresponding to this love and capable of

justifying it. We saw that this knowledge begins with Cusanus, who also began as a mystic, but who now requires and seeks the *speculative* justification of nature. And for this, of course, another path had to be taken. (P. 52)

There is already a roll cleared in metaphor for a will to theoretical success in the way locutions such as "is still lacking," "requires and seeks," and "had to be taken" supply the drive in Cassirer's history.

The continuing vitality of Cassirer's book for students of Renaissance culture stems from his departure in Burckhardt, and the extraordinary degree to which this history of ideas chimes with the ambitions released in Burckhardt's Italy. Cassirer assumes that Burckhardt omitted philosophy because, to all appearances, "The fundamental drive of the age, which is the impulse to clear delimitation and articulation, to distinction and individuation, seems to be not yet active in philosophy—or to founder in the first attempt" (p. 3). He sets out to demonstrate that, on the contrary, "the new universal life sought by the Renaissance leads to the demand for a new cosmos of *thought*" (p. 6). Although Cassirer shuns the subject of period concepts in *The Individual and the Cosmos,* the book is informed by sophisticated views on this issue that would not be embarrassed, at least not much, under Blumenberg's scrutiny. Cassirer understands that the Renaissance cannot be given the unity of a state or configuration, but must be conceived dynamically as *something changing,* an ongoing to-and-fro of conservation and innovation. Toward the end of his life, he warns against the familiar assumption that, to subvert the period concept, the telling procedure is to take allegedly Renaissance ideas and adduce their pre-Renaissance pedigrees:

Whenever . . . we make any comparison between the Middle Ages and the Renaissance, it is never enough to single out particular ideas or concepts. What we want to know is not the particular idea as such, but the importance it possesses, and the strength with which it is acting in the whole structure. . . . But the historian of ideas is not asking primarily what the *substance* is of particular ideas. He is asking what their *function* is. What he is studying—or should be studying—is less the *content* of ideas than their *dynamics.* To continue the figure, we could say that he is not trying to analyze the drops of water in the river, but that he is seeking to measure its width and depth and to ascertain the force and velocity of the current. It is all *these* factors that are fundamentally altered in the Renaissance: the dynamics of ideas has changed.[11]

The unity of the period concept in this dynamic structuralism would appear to be, even more than in Burckhardt, a narrative one. To this extent, readers need not swallow Cassirer's teleology to profit from his history. It can be taken as the drift of the story. We are free, as in the forthcoming chapters of this book, to question, temper, or reverse the heroic tone of his narrative. But after Cassirer, there can be no doubt that ideas answerable to Burckhardtian individualism did indeed sweep through Renaissance thought.

In its strongest and unmistakable formulation, the idea of the Renaissance is an idea of history's tripartite periodization: a "classical age" of original purity, a "Renaissance" seeking to regain those excellences, and a "middle age" that divides them. This clear humanist idea of the Renaissance, familiar in literary, scientific, and political contexts, is often vestigial in the philosophy of the period. Thus, for example, Bacon's attack on medieval thought extends as well to the philosophies of antiquity, and in the place occupied by the classical age in the humanist paradigm, we find only the lark of *De sapientia ueterum,* where Bacon half-heartedly "discovers" his civil and natural philosophy in classical myth, or a more serious biblical appeal to the heritage of Adam's dominion over nature.[12] The figure that we, like Cassirer, begin with, Nicolas of Cusa, has almost no trace of the Renaissance schema. There are no reproaches toward the Middle Ages in his philosophy, for they do not exist for him. If the Renaissance had not occurred, his work would seem an eccentric passage in the stream of medieval thought. As it happens, he is the riverhead to a new age in intellectual history.

FIVE

Nicolas of Cusa's Symbolic Renaissance

Nicolas Krebs (1401–64), the son of a boatman, was born in the village of Cues on the Moselle River. Cassirer and other writers present his educational journey almost emblematically, as the medieval world pours into the mind of a single student those elements of its culture destined for transformation in the forthcoming Renaissance. We no longer believe in the first leg of this journey, his supposed training at Deventer by the Brethren of the Common Life. But he studied for over a year at Heidelberg, where he was exposed to the nominalism of Marsilius of Inghen. At Padua he read canon law, and after a stay in Rome, he completed a year in theology at Cologne. His training in canon law was put into practice at the Council of Basel, where he switched from the conciliarist party to the defenders of papal supremacy. Pope Nicholas V made him cardinal in 1448, and Bishop of Brixen in 1450. Various disputes with Archduke Sigismund led to his exile from his native region in 1460. Just after the ban was lifted, in 1464, Cardinal Nicolas died at Todi in Umbria.

His interests included mathematics, astronomy, cartography, printing, calendar reform, statics, and dynamics. He collected manuscripts, first for Italian acquaintances, later for the library at a hospice he had established in his hometown of Cues. Among his early discoveries was a manuscript he brought to Rome in 1429, containing twelve unknown plays by Plautus. He left sermons and mathematical writings. But his reputation rests on twenty-five philosophical texts, all of them in Latin, about half of them in the genre of the dialogue. Often the meditations circle about "enigmas," symbols that convey divine mysteries, or man's relationship to divine mysteries—geometrical forms blown open to infinity, the nexus of slanting lights in a gem, the negating Latin prefix "in," the portmanteau Latin word *possest* (*posse* + *esse*), the metaphor of hunting for God, an ominivoyant portrait, a game of bowls. To discover an announcement of the Renaissance in these works, we must lift parts of his discourse out of context. But the future is also a context.

Historiography as we know it requires at least two characters: one naïve enough to call something new, and one who knows better. As can be expected when a thinker is offered as a threshold figure, especially between the Middle Ages and the Renaissance, skeptical scholarship has chipped away at the burden of originality imposed on Nicolas by periodizing commentators. To cite one instance only, Nicolas probably found his antithesis of *complicatio* (enfolding) and *explicatio* (unfolding) in Thierry of Chartres, who himself found it in Boethius.[1]

Yet an increasingly chastened sense of his originality and influence has not really threatened his position at the beginning of histories of Renaissance thought. For a good threshold figure ought to be anamorphic. Our feeling that Nicolas invites us to spin out the future, that we can craft a more shapely story line if we bear him in mind as a point of reference when we write the final chapters, seems all the better justified in the face of evidence that would make him a fitting conclusion for the previous story. A familiar rhetorical scheme in Cusan studies is to pile qualification on qualification, medieval allegiance on medieval allegiance, then proceed with the same act of dilation performed by Cassirer. His "real intention," Pauline Moffitt Watts has written, "is to work out a synthesis of those traditions to which he found himself heir." Nicolas tried to comprehend his education, in effect to summarize medieval thought. Within a few sentences, however, retrospect becomes prospect, and the effort at synthesis now affords "a new vision of man for his contemporaries," which in grasping, "we will progress greatly in our attempts to understand the anthropology of the Renaissance and its historical implications."[2] If they do begin with Nicolas, histories of Renaissance thought will move toward more clamorous intellectuals, alert to crisis. Blumenberg contends that Nicolas attempted to forestall the secular invitation implicit in late medieval nominalism, which by exaggerating God's transcendence, and taking salvation out of our hands, made it likely that we curious human beings would eventually get around to figuring out the world as best we could in our limited, infinitely revisable fashion. Opposing this thesis, Hans-Georg Gadamer declares that the "magnificent ease" of the Cusan is not the tone of someone saving the

Middle Ages.[3] In a lengthy critique of *The Legitimacy of the Modern Age,* Jasper Hopkins casts doubt on Blumenberg's grasp of Cusan subtleties, though he is unable to do much damage to the assumption, shared by Cassirer as well, that Nicolas figures prominently in the historical process whereby traditional predicates for God, such as infinity and endlessness, get transferred to the world and man's projects in the world, at the same time that traditional predicates for man and the world, such as change, get invested with an aura of quasi-divinity.[4] Yet he, too, like Gadamer, denounces the idea that Nicolas, foreseeing the internal collapse of medieval Christianity, made one last effort to buttress the strained arches of the cathedral. The Cusan has every characteristic we expect in a threshold figure, save agitation.

The stakes seem high to us. But game is the Cusan genre. We nowhere glimpse the melancholy of Ficino, the exertion of Pico.[5] A highly intellectual wonder (*admiratio*) over Christianity's alignment of God, man, and world is both his departure and his effect. He never doubts God. The divine attributes, especially the Trinity, infuse his symbolism. Here and there he maintains that immortality befits the human mind, but he does not really argue for it in the manner of Ficino, Descartes, and the Cambridge Platonists.[6] Though he shares their view of the contingency of reason, Nicolas is untouched by the resignation of the scholastic nominalists. For he transvalues weaknesses: the key gesture of *docta ignorantia* (learned ignorance) is the dialectical turn by which a limit to our knowledge can be surpassed through our knowledge of this limit. With knowing folded back on its own boundary, an apparent rebuke to our intellectual aspirations becomes a tribute.

We shall encounter other maneuvers of this kind in subsequent chapters. *Plus ultra* is a recurrent motif of the age. Renaissance intellectuals made strife, the overcoming of various finitudes, into a programmatic virtue, and frequently these philosophical schemes for overcoming limitation reflect the personal competitiveness of the thinkers themselves. In the last paragraph of his *Natural History,* Francis Bacon connects some of the Renaissance preoccupations treated in part I of our book—fame, honor, tyranny, godlike magnificence—to ambitious styles of thought:

> The delight which men have in popularity, fame, honor, submission and subjection of other men's minds, wills, or affections (although these things may be desired for other ends), seemeth to be a thing in itself, without contemplation of consequence, grateful and agreeable to the nature of man. This thing (surely) is not without some signification, as if all spirits

and souls of men came forth out of one divine limbus; else why be men so much affected with that which others think or say? The best temper of minds desireth good name and true honor: the lighter, popularity and applause: the more depraved, subjection and tyranny; as is seen in great conquerors and troublers of the world; and yet more in arch-heretics; for the introducing of new doctrines is likewise an affectation of tyranny over the understandings and beliefs of men.[7]

Nicolas lacks this fervid rivalrousness. He is not intent on demonstrating that the alternatives to his view of things are barren, corrupt, wrong in ways that are seriously consequential. The unconverted participants in his dialogues are not ridiculed, as they are in Cusa's major Renaissance disciple, Giordano Bruno, whose philosophy has welcomed the new styles in satiric aggression. Nicolas indicts the pretenses of university disciplines such as logic or cosmology. Yet whatever he says about the feebleness of Christian theorizing counts in the end as its excellence, since the religion is uniquely a *docta ignorantia*.

While Nicolas seems at times to sever the thought of a precursor like Pseudo-Dionysius, turning the negative theology against its long-standing ally, hierarchical gradation, those strings are still in tune and can be asked to play whenever the consequences of their silence might be ominous. He is a Christian Neoplatonist, in the tradition of Plotinus and Proclus as Christianized by Pseudo-Dionysius and Erigena. The pulse of a Neoplatonic emanation beats in his thought: ventures into rupture and negation come out of unity, and into unity they return. The final devotional aim of his *coincidentia oppositorum* is to reduce to zero the antagonism between antitheses, really to intuit their impossible unity, that we may behold a God who lies "beyond the coincidence of contradictories."[8]

In the *De li non aliud* he asserts that the principle of identity, logic's foundational claim that A is A, and not not-A, conceals a negative moment. "You are you" is a pallid way of saying "You are not other than you": identicals come together through the negation of difference. Insofar as all things receive their identity from the creator, God is the bestower of *non aliud* (not other). The Bible's familiar tautology of the divine, "I am that I am," becomes Nicolas's strange "The not-other is not other than the not-other." It is difficult to know what to make of this argument, if it is an argument. Certainly Nicolas wants us to feel that positive identity, the is-ness of things, colludes with negation and difference—that "are" and "are not" do not contradict each other, but coincide. From the postmodernism of our own age, we are familiar with attacks on identity and the instabilities to which they can lead. But Nicolas's *non aliud* performs the same duty identity always has: keeping things distinct, as they were created distinct. His play with the difference in identity symbolically enhances the negative, elevating it to equality with (which is to say, identity with) positive determinateness. Tradition wished to praise the mind for seeing what is. Nicolas, asserting that only a human being senses "not cold," wishes to praise the mind for noting what is not. It comes to the same thing.

Nicolas's famous discussions of individual perspective have not broken so cleanly with harmony and community as we sometimes imagine. The universe is centerless, or all centers; earthly perceivers solipsistically imagine that other bodies orbit about their planet. But this is a long way from saying that we do not have one world in common, that there is no singular world, just a plurality of world views.[9]

In the *De uisione dei* Nicolas sends the monks of Tegernsee an omnivoyant portrait, probably of Christ. As they stand at different points about this portrait, each monk will see its face staring back at him. All are singled out. When the monks realize this, they are able to pierce what Nicolas calls "the wall of paradise." The icon is a figure for how the selfsame God can be given to each individual, not as a comprehensible entity, but in a unique vision:

> Man can only judge with human judgment. When a man attributeth a face unto Thee, he doth not seek it beyond the human species, because his judgment, bound up with human nature, in judging transcendeth not its limitation and passivity. In like manner, if a lion were to attribute a face unto Thee, he would think of it as a lion's; an ox, as an ox's; and an eagle, as an eagle's.
>
> O Lord, how marvellous is Thy face, which a young man, if he strove to imagine it, would conceive as a youth's; a full-grown man, as manly; an aged man, as an aged man's![10]

Each beholder in his distinct individuality is the unfolded image of Christ; therefore the self-knowledge of each must include a unique relation to Christ. "Each face, then, that can look upon Thy face beholdeth naught other or differing from itself, because it beholdeth its own true type."[11] The initial lesson of the omnivoyant portrait verges on radical solipsism. Ultimately it is a Christian emblem of the Many regathered in the One. Borges cites Nicolas in the first paragraph of "Avatars of the Tortoise" (and elsewhere), but modern readers should be warned that in Borges the games of infinite regress, cracking open "crevices of unreason" in the rational edifice of our reality, have a monstrous destructiveness they either lack, or possess only momentarily, in the serene play of Nicolas.[12]

The clearest example of rupture's retreat to unity occurs in Nicolas's political thought. In the conciliarist view of church government
Nicolas defended in *De concordantia,* the authority of the pope derives
from the consent of the faithful passed up through the structure of the
church. The pope, as a delegate of the faithful, is subject to correction
or replacement. Nicolas stated his preference for elective monarchy in
the secular *imperium.* The two orders should remain relatively autonomous, and, in urging their separation, Nicolas damaged the ecclesiastical version of *translatio imperii.* Though his arguments were not
grounded in historical linguistics, he proclaimed the fraudulence of
the Donation of Constantine seven years before Lorenzo Valla's humanist classic *De falso credita et ementita Constantini donatione.*

As Paul Sigmund has shown, however, the liberal sympathies in
Nicolas's treatise, reflecting the traditions of canon law he studied at
Padua, coexist with absolutist tendencies drawn from Neoplatonic hierarchy. At times, abandoning the theory of delegation, Nicolas offered a competing theory of rule by personification, in which the pope
is by ontological fiat, councils and consent aside, the *figura ecclesiae.*
Moreover, the hallmark of properly representative councils is their
unanimity; they must after deliberation act as one, *per inspirationem,*
proving by their unity the continued presence of the Holy Spirit.

The main goal of the conciliarist movement was to allow cardinals
to solve the problem of the divided papacy. When that problem was
solved in another quarter, and the Council of Basel deteriorated into
interminable bickering, the erstwhile defender of rule by consent became, in Sigmund's words, "an exponent of papal monarchy in the
church," championing the hierarchical supremacy of the pope and disparaging the authority of councils.[13] The abiding factor in Nicolas's
inconstant political thought was a concern for preserving harmony.
Ultimately, to sanction a unified church, the Neoplatonic recesses of
his theory overwhelmed its conciliarism. The example of his political
philosophy suggests that the liberal, subversive side of Nicolas, his
ludic attraction to *nihil* and *infinitum,* owes some of its serenity to a
deep predilection for order.

We have begun by emphasizing the devotion to hierarchical unity
in Nicolas because, like Cassirer, we intend to present him as the *complicatio* of certain trends in the Renaissance to come. The relationship
is largely symbolic rather than developmental, which is not to say that
the role of symbolic beginning casts Nicolas in an alien and unearned
part. For once we have observed the poverty of apparently novel ar

guments, such as negation's intrusion into unity in *De li non aliud,* we must then take account of their appearance. The modernity of Nicolas may be a half-truth, but half-truths are not lies. He stirs, in Cassirer's phrase, the "thought-mass" of scholasticism.[14] He can be read as a daring symbolist of the secondary, suppressed, or mysterious terms in the great dualities of Western thought, among which, in a prominent position, stands infinity.

Finiti et infiniti nulla proportio, there is no proportion between the finite and the infinite. All attempts to know God, even those of the negative theology, are disproportionate. As the creation of an infinite God, our universe possesses an infinity of its own—not *infinitum positum* (being of all that could be), but *infinitum priuatum* (limitlessness of a particular world system). We cannot know God absolutely, as God knows himself, and we cannot know "the quiddity of things" in this world as they are known by God. Our knowledge rests on comparison and degree. It cannot be definitive. Thought is like a polygon that keeps multiplying the number of its sides, striving to become a true circle.[15] Mathematics does not give us access to a supersensible realm of absolute Ideas. It is a creation of the human mind, or so Nicolas came to believe: our best image of the face of thought (*De beryllo* 32).

Nicolas's incision between the finite and the infinite appears to have been superimposed on nominalism's distinction between the divine *potentia ordinata* (ordained power of God, at work in this creation) and *potentia absoluta* (absolute power of God, which might have made any number of universes).[16] But the nominalists received the limitedness of actuality with injunctions to intellectual modesty. Our concepts are provisional, like the world they hope to exhibit; in the advice that has come to be known as Occam's razor, our fiction-making should be kept to a minimum. But Nicolas infuses his quasi-nominalist dualism with different attitudes. The *nulla proportio* does not imply that creation has been severed from an acosmic God, for there *is* a relationship between the finite and the infinite, that of being without proportion; most of Nicolas's energies as a philosophical symbolist are devoted to creating metaphors for this negative relatedness. In practice he uses the dichotomy of *complicatio* and *explicatio* to supply the infinite with worldly content. Eternity, we are told in *De uisione dei,* is the concept of a clock, the *complicatio* of time in its specific succession.[17] He also stresses that the human creation we think of as intelligibility serves us perfectly well within the sphere of our ordinary activities. Objects get weighed, if only by means of the comparative systems we invent. Coins get minted, and, although none of them is round in an ideal

Euclidean sense, and their value is conventional rather than inherent, they get spent. Theologically, Christ is the splice, union of the finite and the infinite.

With regard to the Renaissance, the most important channel between the two terms of the dualism lies in the idea that the human mind is the image and likeness of God. What limitless creation is to deity, conjectures and approximations are to man. Our very inability to grip things as they are, to arrest thought in secure truths wholly adequated to reality, constitutes our analogue to the infinite plenitude of God. Like infinity, thought is self-surpassing. Here Nicolas prefigures Italian Renaissance treatises on the godlike dignity of man.[18] The simultaneous appeal to the limitedness or humanness of knowledge and the serviceability or deformity of knowledge reminds Cassirer of Kant. "In Kantian language, it [the disproportion between the finite and the infinite] shows that our knowledge, to be sure, is bounded by insurmountable limits; but that within the domain assigned to knowledge there are no limits placed upon it."[19] *Plus ultra:* something out there that can never be in here. When Nicolas writes of the perfect circle that an ambitious polygon can never quite become, of the God known to us only through a delineated face, of the imageless infinite, Cassirer reads anticipations of the thing-in-itself. The pragmatic thrust of Cusa's work will eventually become embodied in scientific method; his perspectival metaphysics of knowledge will be resumed in a more skeptical fashion by Hobbes, Locke, and Hume. Nicolas thus contains, for Cassirer, embryonic versions of the traditions inherited by Kant, who like Nicolas himself will seek to resolve them in a single philosophy. He is the Kant on the other side of the Renaissance.

We can thicken the line from Nicolas to Kant by noting that motion or incompletion is among the traditionally subordinate terms quickened in his philosophical symbolism.

By the seventeenth century, science had posited its own incompletion in the famous "idea of progress," which can be viewed as the idea of the Renaissance turned inside out. The classical was now ahead of us: instead of there being an excellence in the past man could labor nostalgically to regain, there was an excellence in the future he could strive hopefully to reach. Some of the more enthusiastic assessments of man's deformity treated in our next two chapters were now adjusted downward or, as in the case of Descartes, fitted out in new rationalist disguises. Confidence in progress stemmed, not from the natural divinity of the human intellect, but from its submission to the self-restraint of method, one of the great rallying cries of the age as a whole.[20] The various intellectual machines that went under the name of method promised the discipline necessary to replace the old ideal of knowing things as God knows them with a human, cumulative, ever-productive ideal of knowledge, to be fulfilled in the largeness of history by the human species. Mankind took the place of the godlike individual. Leveling the difference between uncommon and ordinary minds, scientific method would protect the future against great but eccentric geniuses, and the cowering idolatry of followers willing to waste centuries spinning out their mistakes. History was now foolproof against middle ages. All would be judged alike, by method. Knowledge would proceed methodically.

An ancient assumption that stood in the way of this alliance between rational ambition and the idea of progress was the belief that time, motion, and change were essentially defective, the source or consequence of error. For Plato and Christianity alike, mutability was reason's foe. But as the heroes of Renaissance science accomplished the stunning irony mentioned in the last chapter, gaining certainty in the realm Plato consigned to opinion, motion was redeemed. Euclidean geometry became analytic geometry; mathematics assimilated the Δt of calculus. The nascent empiricism found its most telling examples of lawful regulation in projectiles, pendulums, magnets, planetary orbits, circulating blood, interacting gases, falling bodies. Clockmaking was elevated from an eccentric hobby to a fine art.

The long association between stillness and perfection continued to bedevil Enlightenment utopianism, especially in literature. To us, the inhabitants of these end-point societies seem tepid, complacent, and often tyrannical in their devotion to their own stasis; by showing utopia in its familiar guise, yet indicting its motionlessness, modern writers like Zamiatin have created the ironic, cautionary genre of dystopian fiction. "Life it self is but motion," as Hobbes declared in *Leviathan* (chap. 6). But our very receptiveness to dystopian irony— we are familiar almost to the point of cliché with the sentiment that, because man lives amid contraries, and thrives on the energy of division, he could not endure insipid lutes where the ripe fruits never fall—is a sign of how completely successful the redemption of motion has been. When Leopold Damrosch, Jr., tells us that Blake's "profoundest insight was that there can be no heaven without energy and life, intensified and purified perhaps but certainly not bleached away in endless repose," it requires an act of historical imagination to realize that such a truth had to be discovered.[21] Yet it did, and the further purgation of stasis from our cultural heritage remains a passion of contemporary intellectuals. For centuries thought projected its perfection as rest, stillness, eternity. "Thinking," Aristotle wrote in *De anima*, "has more resemblance to a coming to rest or arrest than to movement" (407A). Blake's discovery was, of course, central to the thematics of romanticism. The usual Renaissance assumption, even among the empiricists, was that man longs for rest above all. Hobbes was not denying that we desire tranquillity, just that we can find it in this world. But Renaissance science cleared the way for an emotional renovation. What it discovered about the compatibility of reason and motion, romanticism explored in religious, spiritual, and political terms.

Sometimes Nicolas activates the old symbolism of restful perfection.[22] Yet our dominant impression is that movement—the quest, the hunt, the bowling game of *De ludo globi*—excited him as much as, maybe more than, the ideal of stillness. By introducing movement into the immutable order of Platonic geometry, he produces his famous "enigmas" about infinity. He asks us to picture circles inflating to such a size that an arc coincides with a straight line, or shrinking until the pressure of diminishment bends the diameter into the circumference. The circularity of the medieval cosmos seems to explode and implode before us in these thought-experiments. However easeful the tone of the philosopher, his symbols are tinged with delirium. Bruno felt the rush.

Nicolas presents an intriguing variation on scholasticism's unmoved mover in *De possest*. Just as identity is canceled difference, so stillness is infinite, and therefore canceled, swiftness:

> I will take the example of boys playing with a top—a game known to us all, even in practical terms. A boy pitches out a top; and as he does so, he pulls it back with the string which is wound around it. The greater the strength of his arm, the faster the top is made to rotate—until it seems (when it is moving at the faster speed) to be motionless and at rest. Indeed, boys speak of it then at rest.[23]

Driven at an infinite speed, every point on the circumference of the top would be simultaneously present at every point on the ground beneath its rim. In the context of the dialogue, this infinitizing of "boys playing with a toy" shows how the eternal God, reconciling motion and rest, can be simultaneously present at every instant of time—a temporal complement to the spatial simultaneity enfolded in the omnivoyant portrait of *De uisione dei*. Yet this enigma seems also to carry a foretaste of our beatitude. Thought moving at an infinite velocity introduces a novel dizziness into the idea of rest.

In *De docta ignorantia*, Nicolas asserts that our identification with Christ will deepen infinitely in the life to come. We must have something to do, a propulsion, in the hereafter, and, to evoke this unmedieval beatitude, Nicolas adopts the metaphor of unappeased appetite:

> Now, our intellectual desire is to live intellectually—i.e., to enter further and further into life and joy. And since that life is infinite, the blessed, still desirous, are brought further and further into it. And so, they are filled—being, so to speak, thirsty ones drinking from the Fount of life. And because this drinking does not pass away into a past (since it is within eternity), the blessed are ever drinking and ever filled; and yet, they have never drunk and have never been filled.
>
> . . . [The situation is] as if—to use an illustration from the body—someone hungry were seated at the table of a great king, where he was supplied with the food he desired, so that he did not seek any other food. The nature of this food would be such that in filling him up it would also whet his appetite. If this food were never deplenished, it is obvious that the perpetual consumer would always be filled, would always desire this same food, and would always willingly be brought to the food. And so, he would always be able to eat; and, after having eaten, he would still be able to be led to the food with whetted appetite.[24]

Tantalus, his appetite intact, but now compatible with satisfaction, has gone to heaven. A positive interest in unnaturally prolonged appetite does not appear until the late hours of classical literature. In Homer, when warriors eat and drink, they do so explicitly to kill their longing. But in Nonnus, when Dionysus invents wine, the gods set up a contest between the new taste and the old favorite, honey. Honey cloys. With wine, however, "they became always more thirsty, and again wanted more" (*Dionysiaca* 19.257–58).[25] The sober inebriation of Nicolas's heaven looks forward to the revival of a more truly Dionysian appetite in figures like Pico della Mirandola.

He also has literary affinities with the Renaissance. One of the authors of this book, a longtime student of Milton, is struck that this foreconceiver of so many Renaissance pursuits should have begun his career with *De concordantia catholica*, whereas the first book of the author whom we generally place at the end of the English Renaissance was *The Reason of Church Government*. Transposed from Catholicism to Anglicanism, the issues were pretty much the same, as were the solutions, though of course Milton would remain loyal throughout his career to the consequences of government by free consent. Many have noted similarities between Cusan enigmas and metaphysical poetry; extended discussions of the matter usually run aground in the absence of real historical connection. But, in the spirit of anticipation, it does seem just to say that Nicolas is to metaphysical verse approximately what Ficino is to Spenserian romance. Ficino decodes fragments of classical myth, repetitively extracting his Neoplatonism from a series of figurations, whereas Nicolas enfolds his ideas in dense symbols rendering the familiar weird.

In making such pronouncements we are not thrown back on the dubious procedure of imagining a Cusan literature, then claiming that somewhere down the line a school of Renaissance poets borrowed our thought. For the metaphysical art is there in Nicolas himself, who exploits, sparingly but magnificently, the symbolic opportunities afforded by the genre of the philosophical dialogue. The quiet minimalism of these moments *is* their magnificence; Nicolas achieves effects of transcendental simplicity comparable to the severest masters of the cinema, directors such as Carl Dreyer, Kenji Mizoguchi, and Robert Bresson, who will risk everything on a single unemphatic camera placement.[26]

De possest, for example, covers the myriad ways in which reality, natural and cultural, manifests the divine signature of the Trinity, and concludes with a number of observations about fire, light, and heat. It has three speakers. The opening links outsider to insider through an intermediary, as Bernardus (presumably a novice monk) asks John (presumably Nicolas's secretary) if the Cardinal, who appears to be in a state of reverie, may be approached. "So let us draw near the fire," John assures him. "Here is the Cardinal, seated and ready to accommodate your desires." The Cardinal then speaks: "Come near. The cold, which is more severe than usual, presses us close together and excuses us if we sit together around the fire."[27] The circle of three gathered around the fire is a symbolic *complicatio* of the meanings and emotions of the work. "Stand still," Donne begins his lyric plea for constancy, "A Lecture upon the Shadow," enfolding his poem in a single resonant command.[28]

More generally, Cusan enigmas anticipate the Neoplatonic conceptions of artistic creation so widely disseminated in the Renaissance. There is always trouble between dualities, and the Platonic-Christian dualism of the intelligible (mind) and the sensible (body) left imagination in a tough spot. Usually it was consigned to the body. The popular psychology of the Elizabethan period thought of imagination as a crude craftsman sawing up old memories and fitting them together in ridiculous and deceiving ways.[29] Hobbes refurbished this tradition with the new language of internal physics. But in Plotinus and the Arabian Aristotelians, imagination split into two or more layers, the higher of which served as our entrance into transcendent realms of truth.[30] The higher imagination was rediscovered so often in the Renaissance that it is virtually impossible, and for most purposes unnecessary, to disentangle the precedents. Versions appear in the overlapping neighborhoods of magic, theology, medicine, philosophy, literature, and fine art. The vocabulary for segmented imagination, like that for mental faculties in general, varies considerably. Although their maps were comparable, Renaissance cartographers of the mind never did agree on the place names: *mens* here means *intellectus* there; one man's fancy is another man's fantasy.[31] But the higher imagination by whatever name was said (on the way down, as it were) to incarnate ideas, and (on the way up) to transcend the linear process of ordinary reasoning.

Expand the circle, Nicolas asks. Imagination complies. Yet in obeying the next order, to make the circle infinite, imagination is extinguished, and in this blindness the symbol arrives. The eyes of the portrait track a monk walking to the left. This may be a wonder, but it is not yet, for Nicolas, an enigma. It does not occasion *uisio*, his word for the way we behold the infinite God. When the monk hears that the portrait simultaneously tracks another monk walking to the right, the exercise has produced the unimaginable, and is now a proper enigma. Cusan images, again in contrast to Ficino, lack inherent powers. One would not think of performing magical operations with them: provisional only, they disappear at the birth of the symbol. In relation to subsequent theories of the higher imagination, this one does not claim to be communicating with some repository of superideas. Nothing is contacted. Yet Nicolas may have something to teach us about how this busy elevator between the sensible and intelligible stories of mind was to serve the ends of our self-deification. For it is immediately obvious why imagination, as the maker of what is not, should be like the creator, or in demonic terms, God's competitor. For Nicolas, however, imagination is unmistakably analogous to Christ, union of disproportionate realms. Imagination is the power of mind that lives out in its self-sacrificing creation of theological symbolism the *nulla proportio* between the finite and the infinite.

His enigmas have a rare lucidity. A philosophy equally respectful of mysticism and mathematics has closed with literature, and the offspring are symbols refined to a glassy essence.

Recently an anthropologist has described symbolism's effect as first a jamming, then a redirection, of thought. Symbolic statements are mentally "put in quotes" because they do not make sense either in terms of the ordinary meanings of words or the encyclopedia entries attached to them. They prompt us to "focalize" on "the underlying condition responsible for the initial defect," and thus directed to search our memories for information that would somehow unscramble the initial defectiveness of the statement.[32] Broadly speaking, the focalizations are transcultural. A leopard is being treated as a man, a man as a woman, a wooden cross as God. Symbolism violates categories of classification.

This admittedly rough account of symbolism permits us to appreciate the thoughtful beauty of Nicolas's enigmas. They are symbols of unusual logical purity, in that "the underlying condition responsible for the initial defect" is generated in the open. The circle expands until, passing beyond the imaginable, it is curved and straight. We do not require a guess to move from the defectiveness to the focalization: the two converge in what Nicolas calls *coincidentia oppositorum*. The "is" and "is not" lurking in ordinary metaphor are brought into the open, and displayed in their full logical tension. Cusan enigmas exhibit their symbolicity, which is not the way symbolism ordinarily behaves. Paradox had long been a mark of theological discourse, but the main symbols for God, such as father, king, and shepherd, did not obstruct the pathways of religious emotions with signs of his unthinkableness. Nicolas transforms Christian philosophy into the enfolding creation of, and unfolding discussion of, purified enigmas. The focalizations point to God. This is a strange God, however, seen from extreme angles, and it is not clear what, beyond a sense of wonder, our emotions will be. Nicolas also stirs the thought-mass of religious devotion.

Although he may seem to aim at a philosopher's God appealing only to an elite, Nicolas is surprisingly willing to associate *docta ignorantia* with ignorance of the usual kind. In the three *Idiota* (layman, a person who does not know Latin) dialogues, Nicolas offers an unlettered artisan as his Socrates. A trained philosopher perplexed over immortality has come to Rome for the jubilee of 1450, and, in the company of an orator, they discover the idiot as he sits in his underground quarters carving a wooden spoon that he intends to sell.[33] *Mens,* the idiot with his little Latin somewhat incongruously explains, derives from *mensurare* (to measure). He then adduces his spoon, the manual extension by which we eat and through which the idiot earns his bread, as proof that the human mind does not exemplify preexistent ideas, but creates them, like God. The *Idiota* dialogues belong, however tangentially, to the gradual dignification of manual labor associated with the evolution of science. They were translated into English in 1650, at a time when numerous works expressing the alliance between Puritanism and Baconianism issued from British presses. Appropriately enough, this translation was next published in America under the auspices of a WPA project hoping to encourage the pragmatic ingenuity of the common man.[34]

Perhaps this last fact will dispose our readers to entertain the final, and in some ways most farfetched, of this chapter's prefigurations. Does Nicolas's spoon-making Socrates remind us of an English Renaissance author who methodically, genre by genre, conjured forms from airy nothing and sold them in the marketplace of London theater? Subsequent ages have sought for documentary evidence of his *mens*. Instead, they have found inventories, account books, lawsuits, an itemized will, and other examples of mundane measurement.

The path from Nicolas to Shakespeare has been traversed in a recent book by Ronald Levao. It is a work of some historical interest in Renaissance studies. The author begins with what is more or less Cassirer's Nicolas; he winds up close in spirit to the new-historicist Shakespeare. The Renaissance "dilemma" supplies the bridge between—"an increasing awareness of the mind's power to create fictional worlds that outstrips its ability to justify them."[35] Nicolas tries to justify self-surpassing conjecture within a medieval framework of God and church. By the time we reach Elizabethan England, the justifications themselves have begun to resemble fiction. On this view, the subversive implication of Shakespearean drama is that no one in this world has more than a conjecture. In particular, Levao places in an epochal context the familiar observation that the Vice figures in Shakespeare wield a theatrical energy that exceeds, even overwhelms, the didacticism of the convention.[36] From Richard III to Iago, dark plotters become intriguing emblems of the playwright. It is not implausible to see them as unreckoned offspring of the first major Renaissance philosopher, with his view of man as an inveterate conjecturer.

Whatever this bold, loose stitch joining the edge to the middle of the Renaissance design may allow us to see in Shakespeare, it points up the most arresting lacuna in Nicolas. The dialectical trick of *docta ignorantia* does not greatly improve the situation for human knowledge. "There is no end of symbolisms," he writes, "since no symbolism is so close that there cannot always be a closer one."[37] Yet there can be no "closer" with respect to infinity. Why does man conjecture ceaselessly? Why does speculative reason have anything to do beyond policing its own excess? Why do we not simply stop, lapsing into the nominalist resignation, when convinced that our theories will never be carried through, the edges of our would-be circles never round? God wants to be known, God's image wants to know God and truth: minds, that is, just come that way, conjecturing. As an approximation of God, man does what he is. Nicolas has no other explicit answer to the question of motive.

"For the naturalists state that a certain unpleasant sensation in the opening of the stomach precedes the appetite in order that, having been stimulated in this way, the nature (which endeavors to preserve itself) will replenish itself. By comparison, I consider *wondering* (on whose account there is philosophizing) to precede the desire-for-knowing."[38] This passage from the beginning of *De docta ignorantia* suggests that wonder, before it feeds on the conjectures of infinity, is an involuntary and unpleasant conviction of emptiness inside the self: a desire, a want. Perhaps the motive for his methodical production of God-symbols includes more than thought's devotion to its own defeat. Here we can with profit turn to Kant again, remembering that Cassirer's translation of Nicolas into "Kantian language" rests on genuine structural homologies in their philosophies.

Kant took it for granted that a consciousness of ignorance could lead in two directions. It could be conceived of as necessary, which moves toward skepticism, or as a goad to curiosity. "The consciousness of my ignorance (unless at the same time this ignorance is recognized as being necessary), instead of ending my enquiries, ought rather to be itself the reason for entering upon them."[39] In the thought of his contemporaries, Kant diagnosed pathological extremes of these responses to ignorance that his own philosophy was designed to temper. Certain that the mind could know only its own insides, and was prone to misinterpret even these, the skeptic nourished his doubt; unable to admit limits on knowledge, the fanatical dogmatist insisted on piercing through subjectivity to things as they are. Both the skeptic and the dogmatist sensed the inaccessibility of the *Ding an sich*. Yet neither could make peace with this necessary, though not disabling ignorance, which was Kant's concession to the Renaissance discovery that man cannot know as God knows. (Method is the last subject addressed in the *Critique of Pure Reason;* the book was dedicated to Francis Bacon.)

There is little of the skeptic in Nicolas, though some of his assumptions have lured others down that path. But he does have a touch of Kantian fanaticism—an unwillingness to leave the inaccessible alone. The wonder engendered by his paradoxical games yields a cer-

NICOLAS OF CUSA'S SYMBOLIC RENAISSANCE

tain by-product of psychological, vaguely forbidden satisfaction. In this passage from *De uisione dei*, Nicolas joins the company of his readers, apparently to evoke the marvelous vision of God, who, like an omnivoyant scholar, reads everything:

> When I open a book to read, I see the whole page confusedly, and, if I wish to distinguish separate letters, syllables, and words, I must needs turn my particular attention to each individual thing in succession. I can only read one letter in turn after another, and one word after another, and one passage after another. But Thou, Lord, dost see and read the whole page together, in an instant. If two of us read the same thing, one more quickly, the other more slowly, Thou readest with us both, and dost appear to read in time, since Thou readest with them that read; yet dost Thou see and read it all together, above and beyond time. For with Thee to see is to read. Thou from eternity hast seen and read, together and once and for all, all written books, and those that can be written, regardless of times; and, in addition, Thou dost read those same books one after another with all who read them.[40]

Recalling that the author was a keen collector of incunabula who spent a good deal of money in assembling a library that he himself scarcely had time to enjoy, we may hear a faint undercurrent of envy in this *admiratio*. God reads with us. In the course of the passage we get to read with God. Here and elsewhere, a statement about the difference between man and God gently abolishes that difference by evoking God-consciousness with such precision that we are invited to participate in it, cross the great divide, and figure ourselves, for a wishful moment, as God. How, Nicolas asks, can we imagine that the triune godhead is lover, beloved, and the bond between them? His answer to this medieval question reverberates throughout the Renaissance: "And seeing that I love myself I see myself as loveable, and myself to be the most natural bond between the twain: I am lover, I am loveable, I am bond."[41] This is one of many trinitarian signatures in the work of Cusanus. It is not pondered at length. Yet the complex of beliefs and attitudes which converges in the depths of this idea must bear profoundly on the secret of Nicolas's serenity: the divine self-involvement of self-love heals the ache of privation at the source of wonder.

Nicolas's many attempts to capture the not-other of the deity were not just an acknowledgment of, but a partial compensation for, our embedment in a finite and approximating mentality. "Wonder" is a treacherous word in *Paradise Lost,* the first word of the serpent to Eve (9.532). The Cusan's appetite for wonder, inasmuch as it licenses a desire to be God, contains a hint of the ambitious selfhood later released in Renaissance philosophy and literature.

SIX

The Neoplatonic Individualism
of Marsilio Ficino

Many were the singularities of the Florentine philosopher Marsilio
Ficino (1433–99).

Only a fragment of Plato—*Meno, Phaedo*, sections of *Timaeus* and
Parmenides—was known in the West during the Middle Ages. Under
the patronage of the Medici, Ficino was given a villa outside the city,
his so-called Florentine Academy, and supplied with manuscripts of
the complete works, including some dialogues now considered apoc-
ryphal. A lit candle always illuminated the bust of Plato in his villa:
Renaissance poets would doubtless have seen in that candle the emblem of Ficino's intellectual dedication. He translated the entire corpus
into Latin, attaching brief summaries or *argumenta* and sometimes
lengthy commentaries.

Although Ficino found uses for Aristotle, his outlook was predom-
inantly Neoplatonic. Just as deeds, he wrote in a letter, sway us more
than accounts of deeds, so exemplary lives are better teachers than
moral precepts; and on these grounds "imitation of the Socratic way
of life leads more people more surely to virtue than the moral teaching
of Aristotle."[1] It is clear from his key commentary on *Philebus* that the
Aristotelian and Ciceronian tradition of civic virtue was subordinate
in Ficino's mind to the *summum bonum* of rapturous contemplation. To
this extent, the new Florentine Platonism re-creates in philosophy the
epochal gesture of Renaissance humanism: in the name of a retrieved
classical purity, Aristotle, "the philosopher" of the medieval school-
men, must either be dethroned or absorbed into an "older" language.

As is the case with other Renaissance revivals, this philosophical classicism seems on detailed inspection to be in its main energies decidedly "impure," more Hellenistic and even Byzantine than Athenian. Ficino's first work was a translation of the Orphic *Hymns,* and before tackling the Platonic dialogues he translated another product of late antiquity presumed to have been written many centuries earlier, the *Pimander,* attributed to an Egyptian sage named Hermes Trismegistus.[2] These texts, along with works ascribed to Pythagoras, Zoroaster, and others, constituted for Ficino an "ancient theology," the last in the line of *prisci theologi* being Plato.[3] We now know, as the Renaissance was gradually to learn, that all these supposed precursors of Plato stem from the late classical or early Christian periods. They are laden with the pseudo-mysterious occultism, fragmentary practical magic, and eclectic philosophical *bricolage* characteristic of those times.

Himself the son of a physician, Ficino initiated the tradition of medico-philosophical magic in the Renaissance, based on a vitalistic materialism that, congruent with metaphors already established in late medieval love poetry, went through several major transformations during the next centuries.[4] Because of affinities between the *spiritus* in the human soul and the aether of the celestial spheres, Ficino reasoned, astrologically inspired images could pull down corrective influences from the daimons in the heavens. His work savors of the modern self-help enthusiast. Besides astrological magic, he was interested in the occult effects of music, in experimental diets, amulets, marvels of all kinds. Nicolas produces wonder in his own texts as he hones the enigmas. Ficino often prefers the role of circulating wonders he has come upon.

The attraction to this sort of material must not be set down to mere delusion, as if the attraction would have disappeared had the true origins of the ancient theology been known. Sometimes, indeed, when the truth *was* known, the authority of these texts did *not* diminish. The impression of the Renaissance's devotion to the unmistakably major achievements of antiquity, the classical classics, cannot be retained without severe qualification. There was rather a pronounced taste for the late, dubious, and bizarre. Bogus and mistakenly backdated poets such as "Musaeus" and "Orpheus" crop up again and again on the trails of Renaissance literary imitation. Apuleius's influence is not wholly dwarfed by Ovid's. The panegyrics of Claudian probably inspired Renaissance pens as often as the public poems of Horace did. Other late genres, such as Greek prose romance, flourished anew. The drama is notably more Senecan than Sophoclean. Even in Milton the echoes of Homer and Vergil come to be mingled with many later voices from the epic tradition. In Renaissance philosophy, too, we find this interesting affinity for the belated, somewhat extreme instances of shattered *paideia*. The whole period liked a hodgepodge: the unabashed anomalies of *A Midsummer Night's Dream,* where Elizabethan craftsmen act out a mangled story from Ovid for the nuptials of a legendary Athenian king whom Shakespeare calls a duke, make a fair emblem for Renaissance classicism as a whole.

Something in Ficino, something in his age, responded to the forged authority of later classical culture, in which, out of forgetfulness and misinformation, or maybe out of great fecundity (it seems crucial to this allure that such differences be undecidable), paganism and Christianity appear simultaneously possible. Despite its stated policy of returning to the *fontes* of Western culture, what the Renaissance often did was to resume the classical tradition at the point where it ended.

The *prisci theologi* were the bizarre means by which Renaissance philosophy introduced an idea we associate with the eighteenth century, natural religion. Dismissing the several versions of a "double truth" dividing philosophy or reason from religion or revelation in scholasticism, Ficino taught what might be termed "reiterated truth." The Platonic tradition was, if not in every respect the duplicate of the Bible, then wholly consistent with it: add Christ and the Trinity, which for Ficino did not present serious difficulties, and reason stood complete.[5] Though it stopped short, philosophy was on the way to Christianity, an Old Testament for pagans.

Belief in the ancient theology projects onto the history of classical thought the favorite Neoplatonic structure of diversity emanating from an initial oneness. The achievement of such oneness, reconciling the *prisci theologi* with Plato, and all of that with Christianity, making classical philosophy speak with the same complex unity that the Bible was thought to possess as the singular "Word" of God, demands a peremptory system of hermeneutics. Biblical interpretation had always required normative passages (the Epistles of Paul, the sayings of Jesus), a sense of the overall theme (Fall, bondage, redemption, Apocalypse), and strategies for resolving apparent disunities (typology, for example, or rules such as Augustine's that obscure symbolism must be supposed to mean or semantically duplicate the normative and therefore clear writings of Paul). Ficino equipped Neoplatonism with an interpretative system of this kind; at one point he declared that Plato could be read in a manner analogous to the fourfold meanings of medieval biblical commentary.[6]

The key figure for Ficino in this project of huge syncretism was Plotinus, finest of the Hellenistic minds, the Paul of Platonism—with the difference, typical of the Platonic tradition as a whole, that there should be a yawning break in time and textual transmission between the Gospels and their most influential interpreter. After publishing his Plato translations in 1484, Ficino, perhaps following the suggestion of his famous pupil, Pico della Mirandola, began laboring at the *Enneads,* which appeared, with commentaries, in 1492. It is hard for a modern reader of his work to believe that much prompting was necessary.

We are tempted to make this point as strongly as possible, to say that the reconciliation of Plato and Christianity was more accurately the yoking of Plotinus and Christianity. It is certainly our impression (we have not undertaken a statistical study) that Plotinus is cited over Plato by the seventeenth-century school of Cambridge Platonists at about 2 to 1; important doctrinal statements, such as John Smith's "The True Way or Method of Attaining to Divine Knowledge," are saturated with the writings of the later philosopher.[7] Long before the Renaissance, of course, Plato was usually being read through the filter of Plotinus. As A. O. Lovejoy once remarked, "without going back to Alexandrian Neo-Platonism little in subsequent European metaphysics can be understood in its proper historical setting."[8]

There are many differences between Ficino and Plotinus. Suggesting the centrality of Plotinus is not meant to deny that Ficino is often "Platonic" or acceptably "Christian." Both adjectives apply. However, the backbone of his *theologia platonica* is best described as a Christian reading of a Plotinian reading of Plato.[9]

The doctrine restated throughout the commentaries and treatises of Ficino is the religious meaning of contemplative ascent, and this he drew mostly from the rational mysticism of Plotinus. The soul thirsts for an absent source. In its journey back to this origin, the soul traces in reverse the stages of its genesis: the story of its ascent to the One cannot be told apart from the story of creation, or, to put this another way, the religious destiny of the good soul is fused with cosmology.

There are three levels, or "hypostases," in the Plotinian system. Only the One is infinite, uncreated, unconditioned by any other priority, indeterminate; it is Plato's Idea of the Good invested with a novel transcendence. Every subsequent oneness presupposes the One, yet in its very oneness declares the absence of the One. Derrida, who has taught us to read with special care the notes of other philosophers, tells us in a note that Plotinus is not only the main exception to his critique of "the metaphysics of presence" but also the main precursor of deconstructive philosophy, a beholder of traces rather than self-sufficient entities.[10]

The other hypostases derive from a sequence of emanations. Thus the One spills over into an indistinct alterity or diversification (*strophê*). In the next stage (*epistrophê*), this unruly outpouring turns back to its source, to the One, and in the image of the One recognizes or finalizes its own unity as the Nous or Intelligence, then reflexively closes in upon this unity, self-gathered in the contemplation of itself. In historical terms, Plotinus created the Nous by putting Plato's realm of Ideas inside the vacuous self-contemplation of Aristotle's unmoved mover. The Nous is a form of consciousness which, enjoying the sempiternity of motionless succession, requires no memory.[11]

An emanation from the Nous engenders Soul—the exemplification of Ideas in time. Soul therefore has memory, which for Plotinus operates under the dread of lapsing into the nonpresent. Soul possesses two sides, one of which, the World Soul (*psychê tou pantos,* soul of everything), is in some fashion communal, while the other is individual and embodied. Nature or matter might be designated the fourth hypostasis but, unlike the higher levels, is barren, in the sense that it can only repeat itself within its own material zone. As may be clear from this brief account, our souls are not trapped in the prison of nature. The universe, Plotinus claimed, is an immense sea of mind, into which matter has been thrown like nets.

Plotinus reworked aspects of Plato that Christianity might have found troublesome. For example, the soul in Plotinus is always already in the Nous but, because the Nous endures without memory, lacks awareness of this immanence; the *anamnêsis* of Plato, the recognition through which ideas are recovered, is therefore discarded, and with it a strong metaphysical commitment to the unchristian notion of preexistence. Plotinus also seems to posit that the Nous contains ideas of individuals.[12] Socrates is a genus, one of a kind, and this adjustment eases the way from Neoplatonism's aloof One to the Christian God's loving concern for particular souls. In reascending to the One the Plotinian soul sheds its distinctness, if by that we mean an awareness of personality, but at the pinnacle of contemplative ascent the "I" remains separate. As Émile Bréhier contends, the act of contemplation in Plotinus is arrestingly "formal and empty."[13] The accent falls less on the object contemplated than on the soul's internal transformations during the process of ascent. In its ecstasy the soul is "oned" with the One, as a point can be contiguous with a center without ceasing to be other than the center.

Ficino laid out many versions of this psychic cosmology, varying the vocabulary without changing the essential contours.[14] The One, which Plotinus had identified with Plato's Idea of the Good, Ficino in turn identified with the Christian God, who has the two aspects of self-involvement and self-proliferation characteristic of a Plotinian hypostasis. Thus Ficino distinguished the sublimity of God in his transcendence from the goodness of God in his self-bestowing creation.[15] Sometimes he referred to the highest, Nous-inhabiting part of the soul, able to know all all at once, as *intellectus*. In the *De amore* and elsewhere the Christian Nous becomes *mens angelica* (angelic mind). Plotinus wrote only one treatise on guardian spirits, although the themes of doubling and delegation are fundamental in his cosmos; the word *logos* in Neoplatonism means the "operation of a higher power on a lower plane." Subsequent Neoplatonists, magic-prone, seizing on the notion of spiritual intermediaries able to crisscross the hypostases, populated the Plotinian cosmos with messengers and envoys charged with various tasks of mediation.[16] Ficino embellished this aspect of his tradition.

All of the telling differences between Plotinus and Ficino are not reducible to the opposition between paganism and Christianity, though that is indeed a difference. Ficino, for instance, is notably more florid. Every thinker must be conceded his givens, but this one makes considerable demands on our capacity for suspending disbelief. Unlike Plotinus, who is distinguished among Neoplatonists for the relative sparsity of his metaphysics, and unlike the deists of the seventeenth and eighteenth centuries, who generally tried to keep their religion of reason as lean, abstract, and therefore unobjectionable as possible, Ficino teems with assertion. He articulates the psychic cosmos of Neoplatonism with a thickness of detail comparable to the unprecedented minutiae of the body illustrated in Vesalius. He has a great penchant for lists—the five of these, the seven of those. This recurrent itemization is not simply a stylistic mannerism; Ficino adores numerology. Plotinus, who arranged his treatises (perhaps) in nine groups of nine, was not innocent of number magic. But Ficino relies heavily on the authority of such demonstrations, in part because numbers have always provided seekers of world harmony with exactly what they need most, a ready and easy sanction for analogy. The layers of the universe correspond—which is to say, the structures on any layer have a "one-to-one" reiteration on every other level. So the lists in Ficino tend to double, triple, quadruple—the five of these and the five of those, the seven of these and the seven of those, world harmony without end: listing is the rhetoric of reality. What was a pedagogical technique in scholasticism, or a convenience in referring to particular places in a manuscript, became in Ficino the world's anatomy.

Some of Ficino's liveliest ideas are tucked away in these Neoplatonic inventories. In the *De amore* he considers from several angles the number of worlds enjoyed by a pair of lovers, and in one of these computations declares that their oneness is fourfold, inasmuch as they possess their beloveds, and in the regard of their beloveds repossess themselves.[17] The excellence of a poet such as Donne is to strip this idea of its cosmological formalism, then, like the Heidegger of *Being and Time,* to bring metaphysics down to the earth of our existence. The sudden profusion of the world ("each hath one, and is one") comes as love's prime realization of itself in "The Good-Morrow." How do you know, neophytes have always asked, when you are in love? This is how you know, answers Donne's lyric with the lucidity of dawn: love multiplies the world. Donne awakens into life the slumbering numerological declensions of Ficino.[18] Still, though we prefer Donne on this score, it is only fair to note that his clarity, and that of other good Renaissance lyricists, owes much to the resources of an ambitious and contemporary philosophy of love.

This tendency to proliferation, while it burdens the reader of Ficino with a swelling throng of candidates for belief, serves ultimately to display unity. Unity, in the end, claims priority, and the fate of distinctions in Ficino, as to some extent in all Neoplatonism, is finally not to matter. His vexing treatment of intellect and will provides a good example.

This pair would seem to be one of the mainstays of intellectual history. It allows us to feel confident that we know, in a masterfully abbreviated form, the differences between Aquinas and Duns Scotus. Holding to the same distinction, we think we grasp at least one of the great divides that made Luther and Erasmus into enemies. When we reach Bacon's "Knowledge is power," we sense that all our tracking has not been in vain, and the old shibboleth has at last mutated into an idea recognizably ours. Ahead of us stretches the tradition of will in modern philosophy (Schopenhauer, Kierkegaard, Nietzsche, Heidegger). A new appreciation for the stubbornness of the old philosophical schools is our reward for following this distinction through the ages: Heidegger attacking Husserlian rationalism is now haunted by Scotus (on whom, we learn with a nod to destiny, Heidegger wrote his dissertation) and Aquinas. The distinction is also crucial, or seems to be crucial, to Ficino.

Interpreting the wings of the charioteer in the *Phaedrus* as intellect and will, Ficino appears to introduce into Plato the Augustinian concept of the will. He put the difference this way in his *Platonic Theology* (14.3): "The intellect is united with things by transforming them into itself; the will, on the contrary, by transforming itself into the things. . . . Moreover, the will does not desire the things as they are inherent in the soul, but rather as they exist in themselves." Intellect transforms the external world "into itself," into ideas; will, like Sancho, must have the *Ding an sich*. "To conclude, our soul by means of the intellect and the will as by those twin Platonic wings flies toward God, since by means of them it flies toward all things. By means of the intellect it attaches all things to itself; by means of the will, it attaches itself to all things." [19] Ficino is surely aware of Aquinas's *Summa contra gentiles,* which contains his famous discussions of the priority of knowledge over belief. For Aquinas, we must first know what we desire. Our way to God is, at least in terms of its initial prompting, intellectual, a case in which knowledge first proposes an object for the will to seek. Truth precedes goodness. In his commentary on the *Philebus,* Ficino adopts the Thomistic position on Neoplatonic grounds. (In Plotinus, too, the emotive ascent through enjoyment of beauty found in the *Symposium* ends at the Nous.) But in *De amore* and *De felicitate* Ficino reverses the polarity. Now will or desire are the goads to seeking God, who is known only insofar as he is loved. In a letter commenting on this discrepancy, Ficino notes that certain extraordinary men are guided by their volition to God. [20] Does this equate the pagan way of Eros with Christian grace? And is this Ficino's "mature" opinion?

Historically, this antagonism reaches back to the very project of a Christian philosophy. It is Jerusalem and Athens all over again—the will, Augustine's late addition to Western psychology, pitted against reason, with its impeccable classical credentials. In Ficino, however, will has little of the Augustinian richness. His uncertainty over the victor in the contest is less a sign of deep philosophical ambivalence than an inadvertent confession that nothing much, for him, hangs on the outcome. Truth or goodness? Contemplation or action? The knowledge of God or the blind love of God? In the inebriations of contemplative ascent, these divisions implode: "But what is the good? That which is sufficient, desirable and perfect; or rather, desirable and perfect simplicity; or rather, the sufficient act, the desirable life, the perfect one; or rather, the sufficient life, the perfect unity, the total act; or rather, the one act of the one life in the one." [21] When one achieves a certain height in the Neoplatonic cosmos, distinctions become equivalences. The two wings, beating together, get the soul where it knows to go and longs to go. From the summit, intellect and will look to be no more than alternative descriptions of the same climb. Michael J. B. Allen discerns a "new conception of consciousness" in Ficino's evocation of the "indissoluble unity of the inner world." [22] But this is to mistake the usual disappearance of tension between key differences as Neoplatonic discourse approaches the One for a genuine philosophical result. The Cusan spread-eagles oppositions, fixing at the maximum the tension between impossibility and necessity. Accommodating Ficino either arranges them in analogous hierarchies or ushers them up the stairs to sameness.

To have no sense of the enduring tension between distinctions is akin to having no patience with narrative, which is always embroiled in conflict. Much of the allegorizing of classical myth produced by the Renaissance Neoplatonists is really an expression of their distaste for story. We may consider, in this regard, Giordano Bruno's appeal to Ficino's indistinct distinction between intellect and will in interpreting the Actaeon myth.

The narrative has two climactic events, the hunter's sight of naked Artemis and his destruction by his own hounds. In Ovid's version, the two contiguous events are causally related: because the hunter sees Artemis, she transforms him into a stag. George Sandys, making the tradition of "moralized" Ovid available in seventeenth-century English, requires two contrary lessons for the double climax of the story. The sight of Artemis teaches us not to pry into the secrets of princes—a moral for courtiers and citizens; the turning of the hounds on their master teaches the self-interested man not to be destroyed by his own entourage, like Timon of Athens—a moral for the kingdom of the individual.[23] In neither reading does Actaeon have any idea what is happening to him, that the woman is Artemis and that he has been made into a stag. The Petrarchan love poets were in part attracted to the myth by this absence of awareness: discovering beauty innocently, then suffering a hideously undeserved fate, was the image of their own plight.

In Bruno, however, the sight of the goddess is the consummation openly sought by the hunter-intellect:

> *The great hunter sees:* he has understood as much as he can, and he himself *becomes the prey;* that is to say, the hunter set out for prey and became himself the prey through the operation of his intellect whereby he converted the apprehended objects into himself. . . .
>
> You know very well that the intellect understands things intelligibly, that is, according to its own mode; and the will pursues things naturally, that is, according to the manner in which things exist in themselves. Therefore, Actaeon, who with these thoughts, his dogs, searched for goodness, wisdom, beauty and the wild beast outside himself, attained them in this way. Once he was in their presence, ravished outside of himself by so much beauty, he became the prey of his thoughts and saw him-

self converted into the thing he was pursuing. Then he perceived that he himself had become the coveted prey of his own dogs, his thoughts, because having already tracked down the divinity within himself it was no longer necessary to hunt for it elsewhere.[24]

Seeing the goddess is the triumph of intellect, yet the dogs, apparent representatives of will, are also "thoughts." What makes the difference in the first place is that intellect pursues its own internal perfection, while will aims at gaining external objects. Yet at the moment of visionary fulfillment, difference yields to indifference, and will turns inward to embrace the beautified intellect, or intellect contemplates the entrancing stagnation of itself: will thinks, thinking wills. The narrative segmentation of the myth also suffers a meltdown. In effect, the episode of the dogs simply repeats the sighting of the goddess.

It seems likely that what Bruno was striving for is a positive version of the Narcissus myth.[25] In an important sense, all myths subject to the hermeneutic system of Neoplatonism become the Narcissus story, with its disastrous conclusion refashioned, as in Bruno's reading of Actaeon's slaughter, into a triumphant revolution within the questing soul. Neoplatonism, to carry this a step further, is itself one of the positive versions of the Narcissus myth in Renaissance culture. Without distinctions, the Neoplatonist would have almost nothing to think about or with, no schemes for mapping the design of the universe. What is there left to think in the presence of the One? Oneself. The system at its fulfillment implodes in self-reference—a conclusion virtually conceded in Bruno's transvaluation of Actaeon's end.

The other alternative, of course, is that one could be annihilated in the presence of the One, which would make a better fit with Actaeon. Had its champions chosen to do so, this philosophy could have abolished the individual soul. After all, the parallel hierarchies of the cosmic hypostases and the psychic faculties are to some degree redundant; because there are a World Soul and a Nous, there might as well be, at such stages, one mind. Plotinus, as we have seen, thought that Socrates would no longer be thinking of Socrates when he ascended to the One, though in other ways he sought to preserve the soul's individuality. Ficino and his followers belong to Burckhardt's Renaissance in preserving, indeed strengthening, the individualistic safeguards of Plotinus. They exorcized the monadic tendencies of their system in the time-honored fashion, creating a philosophical scapegoat who, having owned up to their own anxieties, could then be opposed, scorned, and driven from the precincts of sense. This was the Arabian Ibn Rushd, known to the West as Averroës. The topic of the human individual arises for Ficino largely in the context of refuting the abhorrent doctrine of Averroës.

In his commentary on some troublesome passages in book 3 of Aristotle's *De anima,* Averroës contended that the "agent" or "active" intellect is immortal and wholly unmixed with matter.[26] There is only one program running; all thinkers share a single mind. This is by no means a foolish interpretation. Viewed from within the Neoplatonic tradition, it is a somewhat elegant proposal, as we have suggested, and one that puts pressure, like the intellect/will distinction, on the very notion of a Christian philosophy. Christianity as a religion wanted to assert, against the discouragement of the Old Testament, God's eternal concern for the individual soul. But from Greek thought it imbibed a rationalism focused on the what, why, and wherefore of classification—essence and instance, the individual in its species in its genus. What is the genus of reason? Averroës must have seemed to some Christian thinkers a dangerous infidel because his interpretation of Aristotle revealed once again the potentially unchristian directions of pagan philosophy. Idea at its most powerful can consume individuality, leaving impersonal reason to reign supreme.

Averroës externalizes threatening implications within the tradition of Ficino's Neoplatonism. It is not so very far from a realm of Ideas to a transcendent consciousness thinking those Ideas, and not so very far from the Nous of Plotinus to the Agent Intellect of Averroës. Monopsychism of one brand or another reappears constantly in the Neoplatonic tradition, which of course became, in time, Romantic idealism. The *Geist* of Hegel is perhaps the best-known of the late variations on the Averroistic "heresy." Averroës himself did not consider his doctrine inconsistent with personal immortality.[27] The idea of a communal mind can be coupled with the most vigorous enthusiasm for individuality, and indeed often is, as if to compensate for the potential hazards of solitary autonomy. Emerson, for example, in his concept of the Over-Soul: "meantime within man is the soul of the whole; the wise silence; the universal beauty, to which every part and particle is equally related; the eternal O N E."[28] Ficino would surely have attributed to a follower of Averroës the first sentence of the first series of Emerson's *Essays:* "There is one mind common to all individual men."[29]

Ficino wholly refuses to seek such accommodations with monopsychism. For him, "one mind" and "individual men" constitute one of the few dialectical pairs that really are, at every layer of the universe, incompatible, and to defeat the common soul he is willing to sacrifice his usual commitment to unification. When attacking Averroës in book 2 of *Summa contra gentiles,* Aquinas was not disturbed about whatever difficulties a singular agent intellect might pose for personal immortality, as Kristeller has noted.[30] In Ficino's work, however, Averroës becomes the chief opponent of individual immortality—of the belief that his natural religion must secure on rational grounds, the belief that alone, in his view, can make philosophy divine and Platonism a theology. Kristeller has arrived "at the curious and unexpected conclusion that the doctrine of immortality did not play a major role in medieval thought."[31] The interest in immortality as a philosophical doctrine dates from a group of treatises written in the fifteenth century, but Ficino is the first thinker to make this doctrine into the centerpiece of a large body of work. We thus have every reason to suppose, citing Kristeller once again, that the personal immortality which Ficino and other Renaissance philosophers need to secure gets some of its heat from being a metaphysical projection of the Renaissance cults of fame and individualism stressed by Burckhardt.[32]

Ficino devotes the long book 15 of his major philosophical treatise, the *Platonic Theology,* to refuting the menace of monopsychism. Some of the arguments seem tellingly extreme, and some of them could just as well be turned against Ficino's Christian Platonism. The recurring assumption is that there cannot be one intellect, though of course there is one truth, because minds do not agree. The doctrine of the individual in Western philosophy is born, so to speak, of contention: we know that our obvious space-time uniqueness translates into significant metaphysical and religious uniqueness because we have intellectual and temperamental differences. We do not see eye to eye, therefore we are; we are Renaissance Italians, therefore we are. "For at the same time, some affirm and others deny the same thing; some want it, others do not."[33]

Now this is a fine irony. The major proponent of a unitary philosophical heritage, the believer in a natural appetite directing all of us to God, the man who saw unity where European intellectuals for the past one thousand years had been seeing diversity, must have recourse to the notion of hard-and-fast differences in order to guarantee his individual selfhood. In a letter on Averroës, he maintains that the best argument against a unitary agent intellect is that some people doubt it, a pregnant hint that, as Descartes was to show Western philosophy, skeptical doubt will be necessary to certify individual existence. Being oneself is certainty's bedrock: "Whenever we consider the unity of mind, we find it repugnant and turn to plurality if only for the desire to survive."[34] Being oneself means being oneself forever.

The doctrine of immortality in Ficino returns us in a new light to the problem of intellect and will. That we know we are immortal seems arguable; if it were not, Ficino would not need to make it the central feature of a philosophical theology. That we *want* immortality, however, seems in the context of this philosophy radiantly evident, and Ficino's "proof" consists primarily of underscoring this desire.

All things move; motion seeks an end in rest. The supreme motion of the soul lies in contemplative ascent: it seeks God, and therefore seeks to become God.[35] Strikingly enough, the argument for our immortality goes right through the theme of our deiformity, and Ficino pauses there in his *Platonic Theology,* stating the case in an unusually passionate list of the twelve ways in which man is like God. Both are administrators, for example. Both are great makers and inventors; given the resources, man might have made the cosmos. But Ficino really catches fire, dimming the modest flames of Nicolas on deiformity, when he comes to the self-styled greatness that later struck Burckhardt:

We have also said that man strives to rule over himself and all other creatures, men as well as animals; and that he is unable to bear any kind of slavery. Even if he is forced to serve, he hates his lord, since he serves against his nature. In everything he strives with all his strength to overcome others; and he is ashamed to be defeated even in small matters and the most trifling games, as if this were against the natural dignity of man.

As for our desire for victory, we can easily recognize the immeasurable splendor of our soul from the fact that even dominion over this world [*mundi huius imperium*] will not satisfy it, if after having subdued this world, it learns that there is still another which it has not yet subdued. Thus when Alexander heard Anaxarchus the follower of Democritus asserting that there are innumerable worlds, he exclaimed: How miserable am I who have not yet subdued even one world. Thus man wants neither superior, nor equal, and he does not suffer that anything be excluded from his rule. This condition belongs to God only. Hence man desires the condition of God. This can be easily inferred from the fact that many philosophers and princes have sought divine honors for themselves. It did not satisfy them to be considered as good men unless they were considered also as divine. They even wanted to be worshiped like gods. Innumerable men have made the attempt; in particular, among the philosophers Empedocles, among the princes Alexander of Macedonia, are said to have had this desire. But all men have the same desire, and would make the attempt if they could but hope to succeed, as if they could as a natural right claim divinity for themselves.[36]

Ficino seizes on the inverse of a more familiar Alexander anecdote: here he sorrows at having infinite worlds to conquer, not at having one only. There is a breathtaking easiness, a sense of the incontestable, about the way Ficino offers this Alexander as the Renaissance Everyman.[37] We begin to get a feel for how the will might have appeared to Ficino if the subject had not been attenuated by the overall intellectualism of his philosophy. It is not just that desire is insatiable, that the infinity of worlds here becomes a postulate of the will far more than (as it is for Cusanus) an object of the intellect: for men strive, like God, to be recognized as gods. Self-deification has acquired an astonishing aura of piety, perfectly reversing the medieval denunciation of pride. This is a truth that gradually in the course of European history migrated to the periphery of empires, which is where Kurtz must go to discover it in *Heart of Darkness*. But the unrepressed, unembarrassed, trouble-free delivery of Ficino shows him to be utterly at home with the idea. Burckhardt had such moments in mind when he wrote of a revived paganism.

Yet men are also incomplete. Vision is momentary. Reason wanders, "always uncertain, vacillating and distressed."[38] We are the restless ones, the only creatures whose satisfactions do not exist in nature:

> This seems to be that most unfortunate Prometheus. Instructed by the divine wisdom of Pallas, he gained possession of the heavenly fire, that is, reason. Because of this very possession, on the highest peak of the mountain, that is, at the very height of contemplation, he is rightly judged most miserable of all, for he is made wretched by the continual gnawing of the most ravenous of vultures, that is, by the torment of inquiry. This will be the case, until the time comes when he is carried back to that same place from which he received the fire, so that, just as he is now urged on to seek the whole by that one beam of celestial light, he will then be entirely filled with the whole light.[39]

Prometheus, more profoundly than Adam, must be redeemed.

On the other side of Ficino's sanguine account of the transcendent joys awaiting the individual soul lies this evocation of gnawing, ineradicable grief. Ficino suffered from acute bouts of depression, which he attributed to the exaggerated influence of Saturn in his horoscope. The magical images of his *De triplici uita* were intended to correct the imbalance. Maybe they helped. Society, he tells us, was not the cure:

"For we think that we can expel our hidden and continual grief through the meeting of others and through a manifold variety of pleasures. But we are only too deceived. For in the midst of plays of pleasure we sigh at times, and when the plays are over we depart ever more sorrowful."[40] The dominance of the saturnine was not exactly a pathological condition in Ficino's view. It was a symptom of extraordinary intellectual endowment, of a calling for contemplative excellence, a yearning for, as Ficino sometimes called it, "the sublime fatherland" or "celestial fatherland."[41] More than his jovial fellows, the melancholy man grieves for his absent source. In their famous book *Saturn and Melancholy,* Erwin Panofsky, Fritz Saxl, and Raymond Klibansky argue that Ficino created the first psychology of genius in modern thought by transvaluing the pathological *melancholia* of medieval medicine.[42]

At death we will reconnect with God's infinite rest. "This must indeed be true, for the same infinite power which attracted the soul to itself from afar will, when close by, hold it fast within itself with indescribable power."[43] But why must that be so? Because we want it and seek it, we can be assured of attaining it: will instructing intellect is in this instance another name for wish fulfillment, to which this argument obviously reduces. But the word "reduces," however inevitable in a modern commentary, loses the point. For the wish powering this argument is blatant and wholly recognized. It is indeed the very wish that engenders the certainty. The universe has not dared to obstruct the desires of Ficino's individual.

When we assess the worldly ambitions of Renaissance individualism, which were often extreme, we should remember that one of its abiding metaphysical ambitions was to guarantee, out of its own resources, everlastingness, "eternal life and the brightest light of knowledge, rest without change, a positive condition free from privation, tranquil and secure possession of all good, and everywhere perfect joy."[44] Thought had conceived an empire grander than any this earth could ever know. Ficino was an ordained priest of the Catholic church. But his Platonic theology was in obvious ways a religion complete within the individual soul. Proving through philosophy the mind's immortality is no mean end, making reason its own revelation, its own Bible, and its supreme argument its own Christ.

SEVEN

Pico della Mirandola and Renaissance Ambition

As we gather from the way Ficino used Alexander the Great's response to the philosophy of Democritus, the conquest of one world is a mundane ambition by some standards. Ficino had brought rule to the Platonic tradition and made peace with Christianity. Giovanni Pico della Mirandola (1463–94) spent his brief life broadening the exegetical horizons of his friend and teacher. Like Alexander himself a student of Aristotle, Pico dusted off the old philosophers' dream of reconciling Plato and Aristotle, merging, that is, the new empire of Platonism conquered by Ficino with the more familiar territory of the Aristotelian tradition, including the Greek, Arabic, and Latin commentators. Boundaries ancient and modern were now to be transgressed. For Ficino it was either Averroës or Christian Platonism; Pico thought he could prove the unitary agent intellect consistent with personal immortality, though we do not know precisely how the argument would have gone.[1] All the standard disagreements, the occasions for philosophical decision, became cruxes in the journey toward harmonious interpretation.

Even his occultism was, in relation to Ficino, expansionist. Pico added the new world of cabala to Ficino's ancient theology, studying Hebrew in the hope of decoding occult secrets waiting in the letter of the Bible; perhaps he also, like subsequent occultists influenced by his example, dreamed of conjuring angels.[2] The large syncretism of Ficino is limitless in Pico. He several times announced his desire to write a "poetic theology" on the doctrines symbolized in the whole of classical mythology, which were the doctrines beneath the warring sur-

faces of the philosophers, the doctrines revealed in cabala, the doctrines everywhere in place in the universal empire of tradition. He
told, and we shall soon retell, a famous story about the creation of
man, who began life before the panorama of a finished universe. Pico,
his labors sanctioned by this account of Adam, begins philosophy before a panorama of texts.

Those texts all belong to a vast concordant statement. Philosophy's
task is the exegetical exercise of assembling it. The Cusan rhythm of
explicatio and *complicatio* appears in Pico's work as the process of reading texts under the assumption of their ultimate unity, drawing out
meaning only to rediscover it in dense epitomes, which must then be
pressed back out into exposition: "We shall at one time be descending,
tearing apart, like Osiris, the one into the many by a titanic force; and
we shall at another time be ascending and gathering into one the
many, like the members of Osiris, by an Apollonian force" (p. 10).[3]
Intimates of his circle, amplifying his hereditary title to the lordship
of a minor Italian city-state, referred to him as *Princeps Concordiae*
(Prince of Harmony).

We can see already that Pico is a master of Bloomian alchemy. As
he arrives on the scene, philosophy is over, like the creation confronting Adam. The texts are arrayed before him, and their marks do not
change. But he makes gold of rusty iron, novel energy of belatedness,
by posing in a newly radical way the mission of exegesis, setting the
marks into motion, with himself, as magical interpreter, at the center
of this re-creation. Adam made it new by naming the creatures; Pico
will remark the marks. We can also see that the Prince of Harmony, if
he is ambitious in the usual Renaissance way, will have to do something about the problem of sameness. If knowledge is one and the
same, if knowing is the exegetical recovery of the same meaning in
diverse texts, then the Prince's kingdom appears to be finite, complete, exhausted. A major urgency in Pico's thought is somehow to
fuse his love of concordance with openness and infinity, gaining for
his conception of philosophy the great motivating power offered in
the standard view of a philosophical tradition riddled by decisive intellectual differences: rivalry, the wish to know more and better.

In 1486, at the age of twenty-three, he finished nine hundred theses,
or *conclusiones,* and declared himself ready to defend them the following year in public disputation at Rome. Such a challenge, he claimed,
was not unprecedented in his day (p. 21). But this performance would
surely have been one of the great shows of arrogance in the history of
intellectual theater. The event was aborted by Pope Innocent VIII,
who found some of the theses unbearably controversial. We possess

the text of what would have been Pico's introductory lecture, the so-called *Oration on the Dignity of Man*. The work has often been taken to be constitutive of the Renaissance as a period in the history of ideas. We may no longer believe what Pico said about man. Yet we tend to believe that he divulged the self-conceived dignity of Renaissance man.

The format of the proposed disputation allows Pico to act as both the unorthodox loner challenging tradition and the discoverer of a new philosophical supertradition. He decrees a *pax philosophica,* "the friendship whereby all minds do not merely accord in one intellect that is above every intellect but in some inexpressible fashion become absolutely one" (p. 11); he ends prepared to come to grips with opponents of this community: "Let us now, as by a trumpet summons, engage hands in combat" (p. 34). The synthesis of harmony and aspiration recurs throughout. For instance, we are repeatedly exhorted to compete with other members of God's party. In the Christian tradition the name for this sanctioned envy, for desirable same-side rivalry, is emulation. Pico deflects *aemulatio* from saints, holy men, and moral exemplars, its usual objects, to angels.[4] Emulation concerns man as a species. It is our means for ontological self-promotion.

In Pico's revision of the Genesis myth, man is the afterthought of a magnificent God, a God who wants respect. Having completed the universe, "the Artisan desired that there be someone to reckon up the reason of such a big work, to love its beauty, and to wonder at its greatness" (p. 4). God, too, is caught up in the problem of finitude and openness; creation, like philosophy, needs an exegete.[5] But there is no open *quidditas*. There are no empty slots on the chain of being. "Everything was filled up" (p. 4). So, in a passage that reminds modern readers of Heidegger's early proclamation that *Dasein* is the being for whom his being is an issue, God fashions "a work of indeterminate form." Rocks rock. Trees tree. Certain wonderful pieces of creation metaphorically evoke mankind; Shakespeare was fond of clouds in this context. But clouds, strictly speaking, cloud. Above all, angels angel. Other creatures act out of an essence inserted into them from the beginning. Man alone chooses his essence, or acts toward his essence. In place of *quidditas,* we have the power of metamorphosis. In place of an essential self, we have the self *als Kunstwerk.* "Thou," Pico's God told Adam, "art the molder and maker of thyself; thou mayest sculpt thyself into whatever shape thou dost prefer" (p. 5).[6]

Because of his uniquely unchained being, Piconian man is the top gun among emulators. He shares with God the predicate of radical freedom, and this deiformity extends, as in Ficino, to our appetite for recognized greatness: "The state that is allotted to man in the succession of things . . . is capable of arousing envy not only in the brutes but also in the stars and even in minds beyond the world" (p. 3). We are created to register the deity's art. But as we proceed to assimilate the essences of those creatures fixed in the hierarchy of being, especially the angels, the art of our own self-sculpture becomes the supreme object of admiration in the universe. "Let a certain holy ambition invade the mind":

> Let us fly beyond the chambers of the world to the chamber nearest the most lofty divinity. There, as the sacred mysteries reveal, the seraphim, cherubim, and thrones occupy the first places. Ignorant of how to yield to them and unable to endure the second places, let us compete with the angels in dignity and glory. When we have willed it, we shall be not at all below them. (P. 7)

There follows a remarkable passage urging us to surpass the angels order by order, excellence by excellence, until "we come to rest in the bosom of the Father, who is at the top of the ladder, and are consumed by a theological happiness" (p. 10). We find in Pico exactly the new Genesis one would predict for Renaissance thought on the basis of Burckhardt's thesis. Aristotle asserted that philosophy begins in wonder. In Pico, the task of wonder folds back on us, and philosophy also begins in the gratification of being wondered at. When Vives revises Pico's creation myth, man becomes the actor rather than the sculptor, applauded by the gods he is driven to imitate.

Harry Berger, Jr., has observed that the rhetoric characteristic of Pico's emulations is a movement from the demarcation of a distinct entity, such as an order of angels, to incorporating metaphor—from the world to the self, "remote exemplar to indwelling attribute."[7] The creation myth of the *Oration* lifts any restraint, whether by moral precept or ingrained spiritual modesty, from an appetite for appropriation, which now occupies the place of our humanity: man is Pac-Man, existing only in the act of devouring the essential excellences of others. Berger notes the same hunger in Ficino: "One has the rather odd feeling, in reading Ficino and Pico, that while they imagine themselves to be climbing up the ladder to God, God is actually lowering the ladder while they climb in place."[8] Emulation diminishes otherness.

There are things to be said on the other side of this question.[9] It would be possible to accept Berger's description, but remove the onus. Emulation diminishes *unapproachable* otherness. If we feel that it lessens the degree of majesty in the universe, we must be talking about the sort of majesty that depends on concealment and taboo. No doubt the size of the immodesty released in Pico, if not in Ficino, will astonish many contemporary intellectuals, who rather feed their vanity on paraded negativity, and send them scurrying back to a language of moral prudence evolved by their forefathers to check all sorts of things that they themselves have learned to indulge. Condemnation of Pico will probably reflect our own ambivalence, for he is the first Western intellectual to confront us unmistakably with the self-centered motives for thought. God lures the will and intellect in Ficino. The high road beckons. But in Pico the languages of will and intellect mutate into "holy ambition." The soul is ascending, following the same old upward path. The goal is still named reason. But beneath all the familiar trappings, Neoplatonism has retrieved something close to the Greek *thymos*, the competitive high-spiritedness of the Homeric warrior that became, in Plato, the second, or passionate, layer of the soul. Through embarrassment or calculation, that part of the soul is usually kept hidden. Pico displays it in the center.

"Who does not wonder at this chameleon we are?" (p. 5). Like his ontological animal, Pico takes on the emotional colors of his subjects, and in this very instance poses a question that, by wondering at the chameleon we are, chameleonlike answers itself. Where Ficino is declarative, Pico is performative. His habitual reflexivity is perhaps our best clue to his unthreatened dismissal of Ficino's fears of personal extinction in an Averroistic Nous. This reflexivity derives from the double tracks of emulation, the simultaneous angel-rivalry and self-rivalry that fuel his version of contemplative ascent. It would seem that the catastrophe of diffusion would be more terrifying if it could be thought to steal upon one; the contemplator might be looking ahead, so to speak, at the beloved and beautiful truth, and suddenly he might be gone, leaving only the truth. In Pico, however, the sculpting of self-definition is the express means of ascent; the inward eye moves constantly from the view ahead to the self; the admiration of the bypassed angels coincides with a self-applauding interior audience. This sheath of performative ambition deflects the invasion of impersonality feared by Ficino. There is no pressing need to certify ahead of time, with clinching arguments, the enduring existence of the self, for the competition of the self with the self never relaxes in the rapture of absorption.

It might be objected that our text is an introductory lecture, and that introducing is always a self-conscious procedure. But Pico's work in its entirety has the character of an introduction. It is a project so vast that it can only be foretold. In this sense, the *Oration* stands out all the more boldly as Pico's definitive testament, and its traditional place in Renaissance studies seems all the more appropriate when we reflect that the age produced not only immense and fragmentarily realized projects known to us primarily through their introductions, such as Ralegh's *History of the World* or Bacon's *Magna Instauratio,* but also developed along with the dissemination of print numerous genres of introduction—proems, prefaces, engravings, keys, analytic diagrams, envoys, epigraphs, dedicatory epistles, honorific poems, and the like. The printed book was an ambitiously self-aware commodity. Indeed, one great culmination of Renaissance thought is Descartes's *Meditations,* which is also an introduction, a statement that must precede a larger statement, and in a profounder sense a philosophy *of* the introduction, arguing that the key to metaphysical success lies in determining "first philosophy." At the heart of this philosophy of the introduction stands self-consciousness.

Pico was known in England almost immediately after his nephew published the *Opera omnia* in 1496, two years after his death, though his works were probably less influential than Gianfrancesco Pico's *Life,* which Thomas More translated.[10] Yet Pico is, like Nicolas of Cusa, an uncanny figure whose rightness for the period far outweighs the empirical question of his direct influence. In particular, Pico's retelling of man's creation supplies a historical model, a founding instance, for one of the recurrent gestures of Renaissance culture. Let us call it the Piconian moment: we are given a list of items, all of which, save one, are said to be finite; praise, choice, or imaginative excitement is then vested in the sole case of indeterminacy.

We of course find several examples in the *Oration.* Pico repeats the structure of his creation myth when he inventories the great philosophers, giving each of them a defining epithet. Thus Duns Scotus possesses "certain vigor and breadth," Albertus Magnus "spaciousness and grandeur," and so on (pp. 22–23). In Plotinus, however, "there is no one thing in particular for you to wonder at, for he offers himself to our wonder in every part" (p. 23). What man is to creation, Plotinus, wonder of wonders, is to Platonists.

In the Middle Ages God customarily occupied the infinite slot in this rhetorical structure. Often he continued to fill this position for the Renaissance. But this period experimented with new candidates for the infinite exception: first and foremost, man himself. The relocation in man of the traditional predicates for God, which we found implicit in Cusanus and explicit in Ficino, is now flagrant in Pico; Genesis has been rewritten to accommodate our new parity with God.

Neoplatonism, of course, supplied only one of the visions of man explored in the Renaissance. Yet it is a point of continuity that the others often demanded the Piconian moment.

Montaigne's rapturous self-regard might be described as an inverted Neoplatonism, a descent into the earthly self from the false world of rational ambitions. It is madness to detach soul from body: "Instead of changing into angels, they change into beasts; instead of raising themselves, they lower themselves. These transcendental humors frighten me, like lofty and inaccessible places; and nothing is so hard for me to stomach in the life of Socrates as his ecstasies and possessions by his daemon, nothing is so human in Plato as the qualities for which they say he is called divine" ("Of Experience," p. 856).[11] This paragraph goes on to discuss other doomed attempts to transcend our mortal limits, such as immortality, fame, self-deification—a train of association sensitive to the unfolding of Neoplatonism in Italy. For Montaigne, on the contrary, "greatness of soul is not so much pressing upward and forward as knowing how to set oneself in order and circumscribe oneself" (p. 852). Rejecting the expansive cosmic vanity of the Neoplatonists, Montaigne created a narcissism of the particular over the idea, the habit over the quest, mundane experience over contemplative flight. When being expressly polemical, he circumscribed man with finite terms. But there was an ambitious streak in Montaigne that wanted to reverse the distribution of such terms: the desire to escape human limitation invariably exposed it; infinity lay in his own circumscribed, mundane selfhood. He required the Piconian moment of his opponents to distinguish his "I study myself" (p. 821) from other studied subjects. Those were false in their pretense of success. "I, who make no other profession, find in me such infinite depth and variety, that what I have learned bears no other fruit than to make me realize how much I still have to learn" (p. 823).

Even as he abandons the metaphysical ambitions of the philosophical tradition, Montaigne builds into the new and unique subject of himself the promise of infinity, of moreness and inexhaustibility, that those ambitions also sought to secure. Like Piconian man, he is without *quidditas*—a creature of habits, perhaps, and even ruling patterns, but not of a particular, invariant essence. Discerning this truth was Montaigne's claim to originality. He was the infinite example in the array of authors: "Authors communicate with the people by some special extrinsic mark; I am the first to do so by my entire being, as Michel de Montaigne, not as a grammarian or a poet or a jurist" ("Of Repentance," p. 611).

As in every time, perhaps, but floridly in the climate of the Renaissance, praise was the index of ambition. The objects of admiration were desires rendered external—the objective confirmation, as it were, of subjective commitments. Thus Sidney on the theme of *solus poeta*, which we quote in full, despite its familiarity, as a particularly clear instance of the Piconian moment:

> There is no art delivered to mankind that hath not the works of nature for his principal object, without which they could not subsist, and on which they so depend, as they become actors and players, as it were, of what nature will have set forth. So doth the astronomer look upon the stars, and by that he setteth down what order nature hath taken therein. So do the geometrician and arithmetician in their diverse sorts of quantities. So doth the musician in times tell you which by nature agree, which not. The natural philosopher thereon hath his name, and the moral philosopher standeth upon the natural virtues, vices, and passions of man; and "follow nature" (saith he) "therein, and thou shalt not err." The lawyer saith what men have determined. The historian what men have done. The grammarian speaketh only of the rules of speech; and the rhetorician and logician, considering what in nature will soonest prove and persuade, thereon give artificial rules, which still are compassed within the circle of a question, according to the proposed matter. The physician weigheth the nature of a man's body, and the nature of things helpful or hurtful unto it. And the metaphysic, though it be in the second and abstract notions, and therefore be counted supernatural, yet doth he indeed build upon the depth of nature. Only the poet, disdaining to be tied to any such subjection, lifted up with the vigor of his own invention, doth grow in effect another nature, in making things either better than nature bringeth forth, or, quite anew, forms such as never were in nature . . . ; so as he goeth hand in hand with nature, not enclosed within the narrow warrant of her gifts, but freely ranging only within the zodiac of his own wit.[12]

Other discourses are "determined," "compassed," and "enclosed," bound to nature as nature itself is bound to essence in Pico. Poetry in its ontological freedom is the only use of language answerable to the full range of human wit. The implication of the Piconian moment here is that poetry deserves our praise because its nature-besting nature is singularly ambitious and stands out in competition with the nature-bound natures of other discourses. The thing itself is a winner. Winners compel recognition.

Thus far we have considered only versions of intellectual vocation or selfhood as Renaissance substitutes for God in the Piconian moment. In these cases individuals already possess the infinite item. We have Pico's unchained being, Montaigne's worldly self, Sidney's cosmic wit; and the Piconian moment exhorts us to cultivate our own gardens. But the enjoyment of certain Renaissance infinites binds others to finitude. Politically, of course, the nations we associate with Renaissance culture all exemplify or yearn for the infinite instance among forms of nationhood: empire.

The capacity for perpetual increase is the excellence of empire's body politic, Bacon argues in his essay "Of the True Greatness of Kingdoms and Estates": "To conclude: no man can *by care taking* (as the Scripture saith) *add a cubit to his stature,* in this little model of a man's body; but in the great frame of kingdoms and commonwealths, it is in the power of princes or estates to add amplitude and greatness to their kingdoms; for by introducing such ordinances, constitutions, and customs, as we have now touched, they may sow greatness to their posterity and succession." [13] Here the politics of imperial aggrandizement merge in the classical manner with Renaissance dynasticism. In theory, at least, the infinite extending of empire means that things will always be getting better for everyone's posterity.

This growth, however, is to be won at the cost of warfare, and the bulk of Bacon's essay offers counsel on the virtues of a well-structured, and well-exercised, military establishment ready to push back by force the boundaries of the empire. Toward the end of our period, distaste for such expansionism will take the form of an equation between political virtue and the sufficient goodness of the homeland. This viewpoint will also deplore the financial complement to imperial growth, the infinitizing of capital. In chapter 2 we discussed the moral anxiety in the Renaissance over the loss of intrinsic value, an uneasiness that orbits about the subject of money. Money, too, occasions the Piconian moment. Here Tasso imparts a Renaissance spin to the medieval condemnation of usury: "Money-changing is not natural because, like usury, it can multiply profits infinitely and therefore can be said to have no fixed end, but nature always has a fixed end, and all the arts that imitate nature aim at fixed ends too. . . . the money involved in money-changing is not thought to be applied to anything except the process of making money itself." When money is exchanged for something else, it obeys nature. But when money breeds with money, as in usury, the result is an accumulation of potentially infinite (and therefore unnatural) profits. [14]

The rhetorical structure of the Piconian moment becomes a scenario for villainy when the infinite must be won from other men; then the infinite instance constitutes not the singularity of mankind or imperial foreign policy, but rather the conspicuous power of a single man over others. Presented sometimes against the backdrop of foreign war, the race for power within the state, the war of the individual against his competitors, receives particular emphasis in tragedy. Marlowe's drama thrives on the villainous excitements of the Piconian moment. Thus Tamburlaine, surveying the goods accessible to our "aspiring minds," finds the appropriate object of human strife in "That perfect bliss and sole felicity, / The sweet fruition of an earthly crown" (*1 Tamburlaine* 2.7.18–19)—absolute and infinite power of command. There is perhaps the still higher felicity of commanding kings, and Faustus, in his famous opening speech, moves one by one through the varieties of human knowledge to light upon the discipline offering just this pay-off:

> These metaphysics of magicians
> And necromantic books are heavenly.
> Lines, circles, signs, letters, and characters—
> Ay, these are those that Faustus most desires.
> O, what a world of profit and delight,
> Of power, of honor, of omnipotence
> Is promised to the studious artisan!
> All things that move between the quiet poles
> Shall be at my command. Emperors and kings
> Are but obeyed in their several provinces,
> Nor can they raise the wind or rend the clouds,
> But his dominion that exceeds in this
> Stretcheth as far as does the mind of man.
> A sound magician is a demi-god.
> Here try thy brains to get a deity!
> (*Doctor Faustus* 1.1.50–63)

Every other art has an "end" (1.1.10); divinity teaches death, the grimmest end of all. Only magic, holding out the possibility of "omnipotence," is truly "divine." The speech is virtually a demonic revision of Pico. The power sought by Faustus precisely equals the power allowed to Satan, for which another name is damnation. Inevitably, or so it seems to us in retrospect, the Renaissance indulgence of the theme of man's deiformity produced its dark satanic counterpart.

Given the adaptability of the key rhetorical structure of Neoplatonic piety to extravagant evil, it is not surprising that the Piconian moment came under attack by Renaissance moralists. What *is* surprising, perhaps, is that this attack was not more widespread. For often piety simply restated the old medieval version of the infinite item: whereas the things of this world are limited and death-bound, crowns and all, God alone is limitless and eternal, the truly omnipotent sovereign, the perfect lover, the supreme poet. This is temperate advice, but it preserves the source of the disease. The greatest moralists of the Renaissance evinced a more intimate understanding of the self-aggrandizements at the root of the new individualism.

One such figure has already been discussed in chapter 2. After we have expressed our dismay over his appalling defense of tyranny, the moral clarity of Hobbes remains impressive. More powerfully than anyone else, he saw the terrible, restless egotism that beset both sides in the Puritan revolution; he becomes the praiseworthy exception in our own Piconian moment because he realized what the unique historical mixture of Renaissance and Reformation cultures had produced on his island. Generally, part 1 of *Leviathan* ("Of Man") indicts the absolutist ambitions imported from Renaissance Italy. Ambition's Renaissance hallmark, the principle of moreness or inexhaustibility, lives in the anxious soul of power; a fixed degree of power always threatens to be felt as insecurity, and the powerful therefore seek more power in an unending spiral of self-surpassing domination. It is not magnificence that drives them, but dread. Hobbes also comprehends the deep alliance between aspiration and recognition: "For the nature of power is in this point like to Fame, increasing as it proceeds; or like the motion of heavy bodies, which the further they go, make still the more haste" (chap. 10). He would have learned nothing from Burckhardt's astute remarks about the vanity that lurks in honor: "For honor consisteth only in the opinion of power" (chap. 10). Milton, in imagining the psychology of Heaven's arch-rebel, was no more insightful than this: "To have received from one, to whom we think our selves equal, greater benefits than there is hope to requite, disposeth to counterfeit love, but really secret hatred. . . . For benefits oblige; and obligation is thraldom; and unrequitable obligation, perpetual thraldom" (chap. 11). Part 3 of the book ("Of a Christian Commonwealth") turns the same hard light on the Protestant version of absolutist individualism—the self-appointed prophets and petty Jesuses who claim by divine election the authority to invent and rule their own spiritual communities.[15]

Our attunement to infinite expansion becomes in Hobbes a description of our cursed unsociability. Pico retrieved Greek *thymos,* but neutralized its destructive competitiveness by aiming us, as a species, toward the angels. Hobbes sees Piconian man destroying himself in the state of nature, as every instance of mankind tries to gain dominion over every other instance: holiness is not our ambition; we are a race of would-be kings. Man, then, must repeat creation and reinstitute the Piconian moment. There can be one sovereign only, one infinite will, one unlimited power, one victor, one exception: what man is to the other creatures in Pico, the Hobbesian sovereign is to his subjects. As Hobbes put it, invoking Genesis, "the pacts and covenants by which the parts of this body politic were at first made, set together, and united, resemble that *Fiat,* or the *Let us make man,* pronounced by God in the Creation" (introduction). Man makes a godlike man in his own image to redeem the tragedy of his creation. Reinterpreted under the pressures of English history, Pico's revised Genesis has acquired a sequel—the social contract, sovereignty *als Kunstwerk.*

Another clear head, if also extravagant and irregular, belonged to Sir Thomas Browne. He is sometimes said to lack a subject, which must be another case of the hiddenness of the obvious. He is thought to be passing on, pointlessly, the bromides of conventional wisdom. To understand Browne, to grasp the aptness of his concerns, we must view him against the large backdrop of his cultural epoch. The object of Browne's address is the Renaissance selfhood born in Italy and exported to Europe: the self absolute in its ambitions, certain, defiant, superior, rivalrous, uncharitable, intolerant, fame-crazed. He schools this individual by example when defining himself. His neglected masterpiece, *Christian Morals,* is a sustained dialogue with this individual.

The idea that death proves the folly of huge ambition is indeed conventional, but, in the context of the Renaissance, this proverbial truth could be charged with energy as the obvious counterargument to the premises of the new selfhood, with its keen desire for immortality of all kinds. Pico converted his belatedness into contentious originality. Browne revels in belatedness: "'Tis too late to be ambitious" (p. 120).[16] The conviction that the end is at hand usually inspired fear or vengeful spite, and during the revolutionary years it underwrote ambitious programs of political and social reform. Browne, typically, becomes sleepy, like an audience that has already seen the main action of the play, and writes with weary elegance of futility and oblivion. Ambition, though, is constantly on his mind, and constantly being disciplined by the counterthemes of ignorance, charity, tolerance, and death. Why should we contort ourselves, he wonders, in the desperate search for metaphysical certainty about the mysteries of this world? The knowledge we prize so highly, "death gives every fool gratis" (p. 66). Browne scatters the poppy of oblivion on the hearse of Renaissance individualism. The inverse of Pico, he strives to convert contentious originality into opulent belatedness.

He sometimes reminds us of Montaigne in his skepticism toward the varieties of human pretension. Yet he is not afflicted by the somewhat pushy vanity of his precursor. Browne has not enjoyed the greatest of all friendships; he has not refuted all knowledge; he does not imagine his published volumes being fingered in the boudoir. To be sure, he heartily indulges in the vanity he attacks, as for example in his fancy prose style: man is a pompous animal, and pompous on the page. He makes room in himself for almost every one of the pursuits of Renaissance selfhood, but in a moderate form, allowing none of them to claim him utterly. Unlike Hobbes, who kept the spiritual aspirations of Renaissance philosophy at a distance with his defiant materialism, Browne has incorporated the enemy in a reduced version. Contentment with middling achievement is a recurrent note; he would be happy to "bring up the rear in heaven" (p. 53). The "oh altitudo" (p. 9) he often enjoys when conning over the subtle designs of the Creator is almost domestic in comparison to the full-blown contemplative migrations of serious Neoplatonism. His little transports of enthusiasm are linked to the observation of the world, do not presume special benefices of grace, and contain no hints of an authoritativeness that would press them forth as crucial evidence in political or metaphysical debate. He keeps to himself. He has seen the more public displays of homemade neighborhood religious enthusiasm which have drawn praise from left-wing scholars: Miltons and Winstanleys were few and far between. Zeal, the Puritan form of *thymos,* is a sectarian warrior. "Particular churches and sects usurp the gates of heaven, and turn the key against each other, and thus we go to heaven against each other's wills, conceits and opinions, and with as much uncharity as ignorance" (p. 53).

Extremes are not virtuous. Browne can play the tune of everyday Stoicism in recommending that one be "Caesar within thy self" (p. 204), but the drastic versions of self-control that could march behind the banners of such maxims are abhorrent to him.[17] He defends laughter against the champions of weeping Heracleitus and the supposedly humorless Christ of the Gospels (*Pseudodoxia Epidemica* 7.16). Virtue is like the dispersal of the plants in our world: no place has it all. As for the Piconian emulation of angels, Browne recognizes the satanic potential:

Since we delight not to imitate inferiors, we aggrandize and magnify those we imitate; since also we are most apt to imitate those we love, we testify our affection in our imitation of the inimitable. To affect to be like may be no imitation. To act, and not to be what we pretend to imitate, is but a mimical conformation, and carries no virtue in it. Lucifer imitated not God, when he said he would be like the highest, and he imitated not Jupiter, who counterfeited thunder. Where imitation can go no farther, let admiration step in, whereof there is no end in the wisest form of men. Even angels and spirits have enough to admire in their sublimer natures, admiration being the act of the creature and not of God, who doth not admire himself. (P. 229)

Unchecked imitation, he acutely notes, proceeds from an inward addiction to self-admiration. Neoplatonism, like other Renaissance philosophies, depends for its initial appeal on an act of worshipful veneration. We should not owe so much to an author: "He that chiefly owes himself unto himself is the substantial man" (p. 220). *Christian Morals* presupposes throughout our capacity for self-fashioning. Yet we human actors are warned away from histrionic parts on the stage of life. "Though the world be histrionical, and most men live ironically, yet be thou what thou singly art, and personate only thy self. Swim smoothly in the stream of thy nature, and live but one man" (p. 240). In brief, a modest individualism, repeating the gestures of Renaissance magnificence minus their characteristic agitations, is the wisdom purveyed in his companionable books. What Hobbes would cure with tyranny, Browne, a good physician indeed, treats with doses of humane circumspection.

In the *Christian Morals,* falling into his Baconian mood and playing imaginatively with Bacon's vision of history, Browne considers the idea of the Renaissance:

The world, which took but six days to make, is like to take six thousand years to make out: meanwhile old truths voted down begin to resume their places, and new ones arise upon us; wherein there is no comfort in the happiness of Tully's Elisium, or any satisfaction from the ghosts of the ancients who knew so little of what is now well known. Men disparage not antiquity who prudently exalt new inquiries, and make not them the judges of truth, who were but fellow inquirers of it. Who can but magnify the endeavors of Aristotle and the noble start which learning had under him, or less than pity the slender progression made upon such advantages, while many centuries were lost in repetitions and transcriptions sealing up the Book of Knowledge? And therefore rather than to swell the leaves of learning by fruitless repetitions, to sing the same song in all ages, nor adventure at essays beyond the attempt of others, many would be content

that some would write like Helmont or Paracelsus, and be willing to endure the monstrosity of some opinions, for diverse singular notions re-
quiting such aberrations. (P. 221)

Browne's notorious whimsy is not, as some have maintained, incidental to his statement. His darting, vagrant attention demonstrates
right before us that nothing need be thought in such a way that our
other curiosities are suppressed. T. S. Eliot was on the right track in
defining such wit as "a recognition, implicit in the expression of every
experience, of other kinds of experience which are possible," and right
to find one of its enemies in Puritan zeal.[18] He was wrong, though, to
reduce this style of consciousness to experience and sensibility, as if it
were a preexistent given of mental life that could be tuned down to
monochromatic flatness in particular individuals or periods. Browne's
taut nonchalance is a polemical creation, made in response to the fiery
partiality of Renaissance culture: to the search, be it through sovereignty, wealth, magic, contemplative ascent, or religious enthusiasm,
for what Tamburlaine calls a "sole felicity." So Browne re-creates the
Renaissance in himself, but with his usual leisureliness. A mind can,
and should, do more than quest for certainty; whimsy is conviction
suffused with other sorts of pleasure.

The Renaissance has improved on the Middle Ages, with its "repetitions and transcriptions." But the Renaissance is itself a repetition,
as "old truths voted down begin to resume their places": Neoplatonism, Neostoicism, Neoepicureanism, Neoimperialism, and all the
rest. The Renaissance in its scientific edition has devalued veneration.
"In sum," Bacon wrote of the humanist revolt against medieval learning, "the whole inclination and bent of those times was rather towards
copy [copia, repetitious amplitude gained from varying an original
model] than weight [substance]."[19] Living at the end of a golden age,
Cicero could ease his fear of mortality by anticipating his conversa-
tions with the great minds in limbo. But Renaissance men who im-
prudently "exalt new inquiries" and do therefore "disparage antiquity"
have no great forefathers to rejoin in the hereafter. "Ah yes, Aristotle,
you old duffer, you'll have to excuse me. Well, my God, Paracelsus!"
Yet veneration is stubborn, and Renaissance ambition remains unable
to surpass the classical exemplars and "adventure at essays [weighings,
determinations] beyond the attempt of others." The result in his own
profession is a vogue for authors such as Jean-Baptiste Van Helmont
and Paracelsus, full of seething polemics against the classical tradition
in medicine, but offering in its place only "diverse singular notions."

The late days of the world are rife with fitful ambition, marked by a taste for "monstrosities" and "aberrations." Browne's thick monosyllabic prose, heavy with doublets and other devices of repetition, captures the energy of the Renaissance and subjects it to relaxing inertia.

The underlying weariness here is expressed yet more powerfully in George Herbert, who stands somewhere between the "holy ambition" of Pico and the skeptical moralism of Browne. It is predictable that Piconian emulation might become, in devotional verse, a griefstricken competition with the sorrows of Christ, and this is what Herbert stages in the two poems following "The Sacrifice" in *The Temple*. Herbert would perform for Christ the role that Christ performed for Christians, taking upon himself the sorrows of his God. This imitation must fail, however, because Christ's supreme grief, the departure of God the Father, can never again happen to a Christian. Making oneself admirable through rivalrous emulation is thus the first of many failed strategies in *The Temple* for becoming worthy of salvation. This intimate attunement to frustrated ambition informs his highly evocative lyric, "The Pulley," where we find the new creation myth of Pico and Vives told in another tone:

> When God at first made man,
> Having a glass of blessings standing by;
> Let us (said he) pour on him all we can:
> Let the world's riches, which dispersed lie,
> > Contract into a span.
>
> So strength first made a way;
> Then beauty flowed, then wisdom, honor, pleasure:
> When almost all was out, God made a stay,
> Perceiving that alone of all his treasure
> > Rest in the bottom lay.
>
> For if I should (said he)
> Bestow this jewel also on my creature,
> He would adore my gifts instead of me,
> And rest in Nature, not the God of Nature:
> > So both should losers be.
>
> Yet let him keep the rest,
> But keep them with repining restlessness:
> Let him be rich and weary, that at least,
> If goodness lead him not, yet weariness
> > May toss him to my breast.

"So strength first made a way": what could be more Burckhardtian, more of the Renaissance than this? Strength is the first gift of God to man, prior to beauty and (surprisingly) to wisdom, which lags behind in third place. Man is not given "rest," which is to say, a fixity or essential identity, a being in which to rest. Thus it is by the end of the poem that our first gift has been consumed. As restlessness goes up, strength goes down; such are the pulleys of the Lord. To have no nature, to be forever making oneself because one is nothing definite, to be given over ontologically to the toils of ambition: Pico's indeterminacy becomes in Herbert a mixed blessing. The God of the *Oration* wanted man to climb beyond the stars to his supercelestial lair. Herbert's God foresees that the unchained ego will become deeply fatigued in its own infinite freedom and will have reason to seek out, fallen exhausted to its knees, the peaceful breast of its creator.

EIGHT

Descartes's Beginning

A scientist prefacing his results with unembarrassed metaphysics, a self-clarified ego methodically determining its clear and distinct ideas: the promised end of this story of the Renaissance inspired by Burckhardt and Cassirer is the most seductive alliance of subjectivity and objectivity in modern intellectual history. In six days God created the world. In six days René Descartes (1596–1650) rethought the world, and we have been rethinking it ever since, pondering his pages to find the world unrethought, or ourselves unrethought, or, if we cannot find them, to visit the mental landscape where they got lost. *Meditations on First Philosophy* enthralls us, and no Canon Aspirin has been able to dispel the headaches of our addiction.

We write in full awareness of the swelling numbers of detractors. This Renaissance author fulfills a unique function in the mythology of contemporary intellectuals. The ordinary rules of fair demonstration do not apply. Cartesianism is like television: everything may be blamed on it. We use Descartes to measure our ambition. Year after year, at the podiums of Western universities, lecturers take it as their pride to have gone beyond, around, or beneath "Cartesian dualism," thought's root of all evil. A newer and related target is "essentialism," or "humanist essentialism," or, with the flip of a chiasmus, "essentialist humanism." We would not normally ask if the polemicist knows what an essence is; University Boulevard needs its language of abuse as much as any other street. But if one pressed, Descartes would almost certainly be adduced as an example (an instance of the essence) of essentialism, though perhaps not of humanism.[1] The living mythology of the Renaissance includes the widespread belief that it ended in self-deception, and passed on the vice, until we ourselves became responsible enough to root it out. We have made over Descartes in the image of his own evil genius. To mention his ideas is instantly to generate doubt.

Preparing rejoinders to this author is a venerable genre. Descartes himself invited objections, and he replied to seven sets of them. Contemporaries became especially meticulous about his revival of Anselm's argument for the existence of God. Today we mostly exercise our scruples on *cogito, sum*.

The pivotal chapters of Richard Popkin's superb *History of Skepticism* are entitled "Descartes: Conqueror of Skepticism" and "Descartes: Sceptique Malgre Lui."[2] A divided press is probably the fate of any mind that closes with skepticism. Doubt is the Antaeus of philosophical protagonists, and whatever stops the onslaught of corrosive doubt will become in turn an object of doubt. Nor is doubt the only force released by doubt. The coexistence in the *Meditations* of skeptic doubt and apodictic bliss fairly invites a hostile audience.

Skepticism has a revealing two-sidedness. Our own seems to us intriguing and dramatic, while the skepticism exhibited by others usually comes across as intellectual snobbery. The skeptic is forever announcing that *his* standards are just too high to accept this or that candidate for belief. This assumed superiority seems to manifest its concealed aggression when the faultfinding skeptic trains his doubt on the existence of other minds. Again, our own efforts to discover how we know, if we know, that passersby are not robots may seem honest, even heroic, as if we were bearing the doubts that other men are not strong enough to tolerate. But when we read Descartes, Husserl, or Stanley Cavell on this theme, we know from the very fact we are reading them that the argument is on some level an indulgence, that we are not being granted an existence as complete as the one they have granted themselves, that the attention we are bestowing on them is being greeted with an indifference that has the audacity to try to justify itself philosophically—and the aggression we sense breeds our own aggression, which then works in concert with doubt.

Skepticism begets skepticism. But Descartes would be the conqueror of skepticism, taking the old question about how, if the skeptic knows nothing, he can *know* he knows nothing, and thinking it through: skepticism is certain, doubt is certain, and therefore I, as doubter and skeptic, exist. We take aim at this moment in the *Meditations* partly because the faultfinder has at last shown us his idea of a perfect candidate, and we would dearly love to give him a dose of his own pathogenic medicine.

Yet it is also true, though seldom remarked, that attacks on the *cogito* tend to imitate the weighty brevity of its formula. The sentence beguiles. The temptation to fit our own truth, whatever it may be, into Descartes's container probably has something to do with its immense compression. No other sentence ever formulated has to such a degree the Cusan quality of *complicatio*. *Cogito ergo sum* purports to be the thought implicit in every thought, the summation of consciousness.

Descartes himself delighted in varying it. *Cogito ergo sum* has become the canonical form, though in the *Meditations* he actually wrote *cogito, sum;* because, at the moment of its discovery, the thinking is doubting, the original version must be, as Descartes noted in *The Search for Truth, "I doubt therefore I am;* or, what comes to the same, *I think therefore I am."*[3]

In English the tradition of retracing or reformulating the famous certainty goes back at least as far as Dryden's reworking of Milton.[4] The Adam of *Paradise Lost* bounds to his feet in health and happiness, looks "about me round" at the landscape and its other inhabitants, inspects his body, exercises in "lively vigor," and then, aware that he does not know "who I was, or where, or from what cause," discovers speech in naming and finally addressing his surroundings, questing for the maker who put him there (8.257–82). Rhyming Milton's blank verse in *The State of Innocence,* Dryden also regularized his thought. The first human idea in *Paradise Lost* wants for logic. Immersed in the novelty of how things are, the Miltonic Adam leaves out a step. Dryden's Adam will not be permitted to elide this truth more certain than the sun, the hills, the rivers, the animals, the body, curiosity, or speech. He awakens a professional philosopher:

> What am I? or from whence? For that I am,
> I know, because I think.[5]

Perhaps Wallace Stevens was writing better than he knew when he declared in "Notes toward a Supreme Fiction" that "The first idea was not our own. Adam / In Eden was the father of Descartes."[6] Whenever we delve down to first things, the classic formula appears to become almost irresistible. Canon Aspirin, the solitary sage at the end of "Notes" who would scrub the world clean of rigidified fictions, asks "What am I to believe?" and supplies an answer fathered by Descartes and Jehovah: "I have not but I am and as I am, I am." Romantic individualism lives in the Cartesian clearing it strives to vacate. "Man is . . . no longer upright," Emerson wrote in "Self-Reliance," "he dares not say 'I think,' 'I am,' but quotes some saint or sage."[7] The prescription for originality here is certain to self-destruct, for even if a man *were* upright enough to say "I think," "I am," he would be quoting a seventeenth-century sage.

Heidegger, reviving ontology in *Being and Time,* indicted the artificial and derived character of Cartesian thinking. But he, too, could not resist rewriting the formula:

> If the *"cogito sum"* is to serve as the point of departure for the existential analytic of Dasein, then it needs to be turned around, and furthermore its content needs new ontologico-phenomenal confirmation. The *"sum"* is then asserted first, and indeed in the sense that "I am in a world." As such an entity, "I am" is the possibility of Being towards various ways of comporting myself—namely, *cogitationes*—as ways of Being alongside entities within-the-world. Descartes, on the contrary, says that *cogitationes* are present-at-hand, and that in these an *ego* is present-at-hand too as a worldless *res cogitans.*[8]

In other words, I am therefore I think, and not like Descartes.

Paul Ricoeur opened his *Freud and Philosophy* with the suggestion that Freud's discovery of the unconscious can be understood historically as a trauma for Cartesian consciousness.[9] This notion certainly illuminates Jacques Lacan, whose magisterially unclear reading of Freud begins to make sense as a prolonged treatment of the illnesses of a Cartesian ego. Merging Freud's "where id was, ego shall be" with the famous self-delineation of his countryman, Lacan produced a *cogito* of tortuous qualifications:

> That is to say, what is needed is more than the words with which, for a brief moment, I disconcerted my audience: I think where I am not, therefore I am where I do not think. Words that render sensible to an ear properly attuned with what elusive ambiguity the ring of meaning flees from our grasp along the verbal thread.
>
> What one ought to say is: I am not wherever I am the plaything of my thought; I think of what I am where I do not think to think.[10]

In this case, the fascinated retention of the formula of the *cogito,* along with other mannerisms of rationalist clarity (graphs, algebraic formulae, geometrical schematisms) rendered impenetrable and surreal in Lacan's writings, betrays a stubborn countertransference to the philosophy on his couch.

Nobody will be alone, these days, in professing to despise Descartes. Contempt for the *cogito* runs high in the Wittgenstein tradition as well. To our knowledge, Wittgenstein never attempted a revision, perhaps because his own thinking was so intimate with skeptical doubt that he recognized the self-defeat in trying to provide a philosophical bulwark against it. The famous argument against private languages for interior states rejects the presumption that we know ourselves as atomic individuals with a certainty unavailable in our other dealings with the world; in that direction, Descartes's direction, lay unbridled doubt. Wittgenstein developed an array of counterphilosophical concepts, primarily "the ordinary," to circumvent the Antaeus of skepticism: best not to grapple with him at all. Yet the Wittgenstein tradition is haunted by Cartesian subjects such as dreams and pain. When the question of the *cogito* becomes explicit, the taut sensibleness of analytic prose sometimes gets ruffled. Thus A. J. Ayer, his irritation showing: "It is, therefore, a peculiar statement; and not only peculiar but degenerate. It is degenerate in the way that the statements which are expressed by such sentences as 'this exists' or 'this is occurring now' are degenerate." [11] Degenerate in relation to what norms, whose norms? Much of the commentary on Descartes in English has been touched by this distaste. The *cogito* is confused; the "am" is presupposed in the "think," or both in the "I"; it is circular; in the name of history or community or language, it is wrong, or, if true, trivially so. These are the judgments of philosophers convinced that they have a better antidote to skepticism. If we reflect that Descartes is in a sense philosophy's supreme egotist, these Monday morning quarterbacks begin to resemble punitive superegos belittling the evidence of their own ambition.

The unflinching champion of the *cogito* in twentieth-century thought was Edmund Husserl. In the *Cartesian Meditations,* he declared (as Heidegger did) that Descartes misinterpreted the difference between the ego and mundane objects. Nonetheless, the opening gesture of the *Meditations* remains, for Husserl, definitive:

First, anyone who seriously intends to become a philosopher must "once in his life" withdraw into himself and attempt, within himself, to overthrow and build anew all the sciences that, up to then, he has been accepting. Philosophy—wisdom—is the philosopher's quite personal affair. It must arise as *his* wisdom, as his self-acquired knowledge tending toward universality, a knowledge for which he can answer from the beginning, and at each step, by virtue of his own absolute insights. If I have decided to live with this as my aim—the decision that alone can start me on the course of a philosophical development—I have thereby chosen to begin in absolute poverty, with an absolute lack of knowledge. Beginning thus, obviously one of the first things I ought to do is reflect on how I might find a method for going on, a method that promises to lead to genuine knowing. Accordingly the Cartesian *Meditations* are not intended to be a merely private concern of the philosopher Descartes, to say nothing of their being merely an impressive literary form in which to present the foundations of his philosophy. Rather they draw the prototype of any beginning philosopher's necessary meditations, the meditations out of which alone a philosophy can grow originally.[12]

Philosophy is the discourse of the individual, indeed the only genuine discourse of the individual. Descartes discovered authentic intellectual privacy, from which all philosophers must now set forth. His beginning is like staged rebirth, "in absolute poverty, with an absolute lack of knowledge," that makes possible the originality ("*his* wisdom . . . his self-acquired knowledge") of a self-fashioned mind.

Husserl took Descartes pretty much at his own estimate. Radical doubt was intended to clear the slate of mere tradition. Man needs skepticism, he wrote in *The Search for Truth,* because he "comes into the world in ignorance, and as the knowledge of his earliest years rests only on the weakness of the senses and the authority of masters, he can scarcely avoid his imagination being filled with an infinite number of false ideas."[13] Bestowed from within, the *cogito* was not contaminated by authority, which is to say, by the past. When Pierre Gassendi remarked that the presentation of the *cogito* suppressed a syllogism ("Whatever thinks, is"), Descartes replied that someone thinking this idea "is not syllogistically deducing his existence from a thought, but recognizing it as something self-evident, as in a simple mental intuition," and in his letter to the Marquis of Newcastle insisted that his nugget of truth was not "something taught you by your masters; your mind sees it, feels it, handles it."[14] Always, no matter what, my existence is mine. The Renaissance had long desired to make a beginning, but so far had largely disguised this ambition as the revival of a past beginning. A great number of novelties were produced in its various programs of veneration. Descartes was in a sense just setting the score straight when he decided to get along without a glorious sense of the classical and, having shed that origin, move on to the supreme instance of origin and veneration, God. Science tended to advance the humanist scorn for, and doubt of, medieval learning all the way back to antiquity. In Descartes, we find the logical end product of a mistrustful disillusionment with history in its entirety.

The *cogito* can be described in epochal terms as the urge for an ambitious new beginning purged of the pretense of a classical model. In place of the tripartite periodization in the humanist idea of the Renaissance, Descartes in the heart of his metaphysics offers one age only, the moving "now" of the *cogito*, modernity ever-new and history ever-doubtful, the tradition of originality passed on from individual philosopher to individual philosopher. In its first instance of certainty, Descartes's truth-seeking ego has moved out of the monasteries of the Middle Ages, out of the church, the state, the schools, every "general category" save its own individual existence: the secular intellectual has declared himself. He will believe only what he can believe.

From this new position of outsideness, the ego can no longer lay claim, at least overtly, to the motivations that ignited the period initially. Reviving a great past is a deliberate attempt to generate fame; traditions, as the humanists understood them, were instructions for the correct dispensation of fame—a knowledge of who was great, and why. Because an intellectual of this kind was a producer of fame, he felt wholly justified in seeking this public amplification, during his life and during aftertimes. Descartes understood that the mainspring of tradition was this calculus of veneration. Fame was the spur—to error: the familiar intellectual "likes better to interrogate others, to weigh what the ancients have written, than to consult himself on the judgment which he should form; and as from his childhood he has taken as reason what rested only on the authority of preceptors, now he gives his authority as a reason and desires that others should pay to him the tribute which he formerly paid them." [15] So Descartes had to forge a new psychology of authorship independent of the satisfactions that tradition alone could supply.

Claiming in *Discourse on Method* to "dislike" glory, he gave several reasons for publishing his work. Because some reputation was inevitable, his might as well have a chance to be accurate; also, he needed help with key experiments (1:149). More interestingly, however, writing was an aid to self-scrutiny, especially if the author proceeded as if he were going to publish: "For this will give me all the more reason to examine them [my writings] closely, as undoubtedly we always look more carefully at something we think is to be seen by others than at something we do only for ourselves; and often what seemed true to me when I first conceived it has looked false when I tried to put it on paper" (1:145). Publication was the thinker's entirely private affair. Fame might follow, but the justification for preparing one's text for the press was wholly internal. It promoted certainty. The thinking of the ego was written thinking, thought in anticipation of being published thinking.

Descartes must have realized that his own fame was a unique contrivance. He had destroyed the foundations of the old idea of positive historical community. Any clear and distinct idea subsequent to the *cogito* would have to fall to the future's doubt, insofar as his method got handed down. All that could be sure to last of his work, then, was the negative gesture of doubt and the bare outline of individuality— the existence of the thinking capable of doubt and certainty. Husserl received him in precisely this manner.

So, with some variation, has Derrida, who began his career as a close student of Husserl. Michel Foucault maintained in *Madness and Civilization* that Descartes's *cogito* was, like any other rationalist origin, a violent act of exclusion, setting up norms for distinguishing reason from madness. Derrida replies to this "naïve" reading with his own version of Descartes's beguiling sentence: "Whether I am mad or not, *cogito, sum.*" [16] Then, repeating Husserl repeating Descartes, he defines the prototypical beginning for the kind of thought he wants to encourage:

> I am not proposing the separation of the wheat from the tares in the name of some *philosophia perennis*. Indeed, it is exactly the contrary that I am proposing. In question is a way of accounting for the very historicity of philosophy. I believe that historicity in general would be impossible without a history of philosophy, and I believe that the latter would be impossible if we possessed only hyperbole, on the one hand, or, on the other, only determined historical structures, finite *Weltanschauungen*. The historicity proper to philosophy is located and constituted in the transition, the dialogue between hyperbole and the finite structure, between that which exceeds the totality and the closed totality, in the difference between history and historicity; that is, in the place where, or rather at the moment when, the Cogito and all that it symbolizes (madness, derangement, hyperbole, etc.) pronounce and reassure themselves then to fall, necessarily forgetting themselves until their reactivation, their reawakening in another statement of the excess which also later will become another decline and another crisis. [17]

The negations here must be read with considerable elasticity, almost in the spirit of Freud's "On Negation." Derrida is *not* proposing that the *cogito* without the other ideas unpacked from the Cartesian ego represents a *philosophia perennis* because he abhors "philosophy" as a settled, once-and-for-all totality, or the quest for such a totality. Yet by "exactly the contrary" Derrida *does* mean that he is separating the wheat from the tares in a perennial antiphilosophy named "hyperbole." If a hyperbole carries the day, it will no longer be a transgression and, as another "normal philosophy," will generate a new hyperbole. Inasmuch as the history of philosophy is the resurgence of "the Cogito and all that it symbolizes" against closed totalities, *cogito ergo sum* does in fact constitute the prototype for healthy philosophical crisis—*deconstructio perennis,* as it were. After Derrida has said everything he has to say against Husserl, which is a very great deal indeed, he still defends the Cartesian beginning as a reawakening handed down from age to age.

We do not wish to make too much of Derrida's reading of the *Meditations,* which is to be understood in the context of a disagreement with Foucault. We do not feel that it is a matter of dire necessity to correct his view. Yet he does provide us with a useful point of reference. It might be a considerable relief if there were one sentence in the history of philosophy that could be taken at face value. We cannot, however, allow Descartes originality at his own estimate. The *cogito* belongs to a tradition of Renaissance aspiration that can be sensed throughout Descartes's rationalism. Moreover, by dismissing the ideas that follow the *cogito* as timid retreats from its open indeterminacy, which is by no means an uncommon reading, Derrida overlooks the strong continuity between the first certainty of Descartes's ego and the "echoes" of this stability in the ontological argument and the theory of judgment.

The *Meditations* is a story about an ego that makes a lot of trouble for itself, and the trouble turns out to be the condition of its success. "All is best," Milton began the final speech of *Samson Agonistes,* "though we oft doubt" (1745). In Descartes's Christian tragedy, Milton's "though" becomes "because." Doubt alienates the ego from everything, until there is only the ego, whence the peripeteia of *dubito ergo sum.* Doubt identifies, isolates. As a strategy of identification, it seems the polar opposite of Renaissance vainglory. For that mentality, fame or the crown or some self-forwarding act identifies, isolates. Beneath this opposition, we hope to show, lies a pronounced kinship.

In the usual formulation of the "All the world's a stage" topos, men act parts. As we have suggested in our parable about Machiavelli and Shakespeare, some of the literary and political dynamics of the new Renaissance individual spring from his actorly self-consciousness. But the playhouse affords another position about which human identity might be structured. Descartes remarked in the *Discourse* that he spent nine years roaming about the world, "trying to be a spectator rather than an actor in all the comedies that are played out there" (1:125). Both formulations appear in a notebook entry: "Actors, taught not to let any embarrassment show on their faces, put on a mask. I will do the same. So far, I have been a spectator in this theatre which is the world, but I am now about to mount the stage, and I come forward masked" (1:2). Is this about assuming a pseudonym? The mask, in any case, permits the actor to remain an unseen spectator. This odd dissociation would be a fairly accurate metaphor for the condition of Descartes's soul surrounded by *res extensa*. The body itself is a theatrical mask, which, like the brutes, only seems to be alive.

Both Heidegger and Dewey emphasized the "spectatorial" ego in Descartes; the fundamental metaphors that sustain his metaphysics, such as "clear and distinct" ideas or "natural light," derive from looking.[18] We think the doubting does, too. A spectator at the theater, as he becomes conscious of his spectatorship, generally loses the reality of the show. He steps out of the deception. If he keeps thinking about his own position, he may entertain the idea that the show would not exist without his presence, that the entire spectacle of the world is but a performance intended to deceive him (Descartes's fiction of the evil genius), or that the spectacle of the world is a self-produced dream (the first doubt devised in the *Meditations*). Suddenly, having indulged a train of thought, a spectator is all alone on the stage of the world.

Many of the ringing declarations of selfhood in Renaissance drama are brought forth by real or threatened dissociation. Under the pressure of external events or internal ambitions, personality has become fragmented and elusive, as in Richard III's midnight meditation. Descartes brought rule to this sort of mental state; he showed how it made sense. For example, we mentioned in chapter 1 the illeism ("Othello's occupation's gone") featured in the rhetoric of pressured selfhood on the Renaissance stage. Self-reference in the third person may indicate that the self is aware of its own magnificence, belongs to its own audience, recognizes itself. It may also signal the loss of this perspective, a desire to be reunited with an earlier and irretrievable dignity. The *cogito* does not quite qualify as illeism, but it is surrounded on every side by an impersonality that transforms the self into its own spectator; Descartes gives a third-person distance to terms such as "ego" and *"res cogitans."* The ego in Descartes lives a first-person existence, every thought prefaced by "I think." The body and the emotional life, however, have been subjected to a systematic illeism, pushed across the line of Descartes's notorious dualism into the zone of third-person neuter.

The Passions of the Soul is a Renaissance love treatise written in the new language of mechanism, Descartes's *Symposium* and *De amore*. Wonder, the cherished emotion of the Neoplatonists, appears as the first of the six root passions (1:373); there is even a discussion of Aristophanes' myth about sexual attraction (1:360). Ficino's magical pneumatology has been drained of life. Passions result from the clockwork circulation of spirits through the interior of the body. Here, for instance, is the new look in revenge:

> The desire to ward off harmful things and to avenge oneself is the most compelling of all desires. It is desire, joined to self-love, which makes anger involve as much agitation of the blood as courage and boldness can bring about; and hatred causes this agitation to affect primarily the bilious blood. . . . This blood enters into the heart and . . . produces a heat more extreme and more intense than any that may be produced by love or joy.
>   . . . Those who restrain themselves and resolve to take a greater vengeance become sad at the thought that the action which makes them angry obliges them to take such vengeance; and sometimes they also have anxiety about the evils which may ensue upon the resolution they have taken. This makes them first turn pale and cold, and start trembling. (1:399)

"And thus the native hue of resolution / Is sicklied o'er with the pale cast of thought" (*Hamlet* 3.1.83–84). The body of thought projected in Shakespeare is no longer metaphorical or in any sense the expression of thought. What we call "expression" becomes in Descartes an inert designation, like the tumblers on a slot machine. Such a description of emotional states had long been available in the medical tradition. Descartes transferred the dispassion of the doctor/patient relationship to the whole of emotional introspection. The articulate *thymos* of Renaissance drama and philosophy is now a machine.

From Descartes's general evocation of mental dissociation, indeed of thinking *as* mental dissociation, we turn to the radical doubt of the *Meditations*. Commentators have wondered how it is possible for Descartes to doubt what Kant would later term analytic truths. My perception can readily fall prey to doubt; the invention of an evil genius dedicated to my deception will render most of my beliefs doubtful. But how can I doubt arithmetical operations or geometrical axioms? Descartes himself hinted at some special dubiety at work in these cases:

> Yet when I turn to the things themselves which I think I perceive very clearly, I am so convinced by them that I spontaneously declare: let

whoever can do so deceive me, he will never bring it about that I am nothing, so long as I continue to think I am something; or make it true at some future time that I have never existed, since it is now true that I exist; or bring it about that two and three added together are more or less than five, or anything of this kind in which I see a manifest contradiction. And since I have no cause to think that there is a deceiving God, and I do not yet even know for sure whether there is a God at all, any reason for doubt which depends simply on this supposition is a very slight and, so to speak, metaphysical one. (2:25)

Here the doubt seems to arise from the uncertainty of memory; apparent certainties are secure when they are thought, but not when remembered as having been thought. But Émile Bréhier, arguing from letters, traced this "metaphysical" doubt to a rare and drastic voluntarism in Descartes's theology.[19]

Memory is not the only problem. God, Descartes believed, could at any minute change the rules; 2 + 3 equaled 5 the last time you reckoned it, but in principle God might install another system, making the new answer 4. Essences were willed, as in scholastic nominalism; Descartes, however, abolished the restriction that God could not will a contradiction. Hence, in the theological part of the *Meditations,* Descartes maintained that existence requires two acts of God, who must sustain whatever he creates. God must be proven, that is, not just to be, but to be constant. For he might in principle create anew, and the result would be hopeless disarray in the concept of tradition: nothing at all could be securely handed down.

Descartes thought that the knowledge of *dubito ergo sum* was "better, more certain, and more useful than that derived from this great principle which we usually establish as the basis or center to which all other principles are referred and from which they start forth, viz. *it is impossible that one and the same thing should both be and not be.*"[20] Perhaps this was so because, although the simultaneity of A and not-A makes nonsense of most propositions, it is experienced in the state of doubt; Nicolas's coincidence of opposites, pulled down from the transcendent, has become Descartes's willed uncertainty. In order to destroy the strongest fortresses of reason, Descartes must appeal to a God like himself, a schizoid God, vulnerable to doubts. Four? Five? Is it to be this? Is it to be that?

The apparent implication of Bréhier's enlightening appeal to voluntarism is that scientific mechanism, the world view toward which the *Meditations* are headed, expels the fearful specter of mad discontinuity. Ultimately Descartes's God, like Descartes's ego, will sail into the safe harbor of a reliably regulated world; constancy restrains the transmutations of the piece of wax. No doubt Descartes was tolerably at ease in the world he ultimately achieved, all laid out on graph paper and ready for the attention of scientists. But is it so certain that he feared discontinuity? Perhaps the solipsism of the *cogito* was not the innocent product of systematic doubt, what just happened to prove indubitable, but deliberately sought from the beginning. Certainty was not so very different. The mind of Eudoxus, his mouthpiece in *The Search for Truth,* has outgrown the disturbing suspicion that other minds bask in the certainty of larger truths than his own. "For it [my mind] enjoys the same repose that the king of an isolated country would have were he so separated from all others as to imagine that beyond his frontiers there was nothing but unfertile deserts and uninhabitable mountains."[21] In our view, Descartes's inconstant God was, as God often was in the Renaissance, the creature of his ambition. The ego of the *cogito* has obliterated objectivity. Its turbulent uncertainty about the not-self cannot be, in this line of thought, the simple opposite of mechanism, what must be overcome to achieve the mechanism: these are rather two ways of conquering the external world, one by abolishing it and one by regulating it. On its way to science, the Renaissance ego tarried with the possibility that its ambition to become "the king of an isolated country" did not require anything beyond metaphysics.

I think therefore I am, my ego performatively confers birth and being upon itself. Here we again encounter the epoch's yearning for a positive version of the Narcissus myth. The main revision necessary was that the image in the pond not be a doubtable deception: it must really be Narcissus, the existing ego clear unto itself. The most famous sentence in philosophy secured this revision.

The experiment in perfect solipsism failed, however. As Hegel was to observe, a conquest too complete leaves nothing of sufficient dignity to register the greatness of the conqueror. Scientific objectivity would be needed after all. It was important to be certain, therefore, that God is not an evil genius.

The idea of God curbs the narcissism of the *cogito,* in that the ontological argument requires Descartes to concede his own imperfection. If he had created himself, he would *be* God: "Yet if I derived my existence from myself, then I should neither doubt nor want, nor lack anything at all; for I should have given myself all the perfections of which I have any idea, and thus I should myself be God" (2:33). Part of the odd poignance of the ontological argument lies in the open confession that, given the chance, Descartes would have been the infinite God; this aspiration constitutes his idea of God: "That is, when I turn my mind's eye upon myself, I understand that I am a thing which is incomplete and dependent on another and which aspires without limit to ever greater and better things; but I also understand at the same time that he on whom I depend has within him all those greater things, not just indefinitely and potentially but actually and infinitely, and hence that he is God" (2:35). Thus God would appear to be inseparable from vanity, or rather from the privation of vanity—all that we aspire to be and are not. This strangely egotistic deference is "the mark of the craftsman stamped on his work" (2:35).

With the ontological argument Descartes does, in a certain sense, make common cause with the Middle Ages. But when Anselm proved God's existence from our idea of God, this was not *his* idea in the way that Descartes's is; it was not an idea lodged in the ego of the *cogito*. Descartes has assimilated the Renaissance ambition to prove the soul immortal on the basis of its own existence. The subtitle of Ficino's *Platonic Theology* is *De immortalitate animarum;* likewise, the first edition of the *Meditationes* (1641) promises its readers a book *in quibus Dei existentia et animae immortalitas demonstrantur,* reminding us that the original point of Cartesian dualism was to demonstrate the independence of soul from body, which is to say, the soul's immortality.[22] In Ficino, the wish is father to the fact; man is immortal because he wants immortality. We are almost two centuries further along now, and the author of our present text was the most effective scientific polemicist of his day. Wish no longer carries weight, though it carries through the argument, just as in Ficino. It has been forced into the privacy of a disguise, Anselm's disguise, and behind this rational mask fashions the idea of God into the certain existence of God.

Because I must think God is, God is. The ontological argument shares with the *cogito* the shift from thinking to existing, the first purporting to prove the second. In a sense, the thesis that we have been urging repeatedly, that God in his infinity became the model for human ambitions in the Renaissance, comes to its epitome in this argument. For the existence of God is made to depend on our idea of God, which is our idea of what we ourselves would be: the creature shapes his creator. A God secured in this manner, as an item of rational certainty, does not seem to us very well fortified against the secularizing currents of the following centuries. The key secular turn has already been made, transferring God from a communal way of life to an intellectual proposal by "the king of an isolated country." Just as Heidegger could dismantle the Cartesian or Kantian "I think" by opening questions such as "What is called thinking?" so the ontological argu-

ment betrays God to forthright denial. Because I do not have the idea
that God exists, God does not exist.

For Descartes, the idea of God is wholly entwined with the theory
of judgment. After the achievement of the *cogito,* the remaining meditations can be viewed as a prolonged philosophical theodicy.[23] Milton
explored in mythological narrative the problem of how God can be
good when evil thrives. The rationalist version of evil is error, and
Descartes must justify the ways of God to *res cogitans* by showing that
God, "who is supremely perfect, . . . cannot be a deceiver" (2:43).
Rationalist man is responsible for his own errors. Mounting this argument, Descartes allowed both of those traditional teammates, intellect and will, a role in the act of judgment.

The Cartesian ego surveys its faculties, and, in the rhetoric of the
Piconian moment, discerns the infinite instance:

> Indeed, I think it is very noteworthy that there is nothing else in me which
> is so perfect and so great that the possibility of a further increase in its
> perfection or greatness is beyond my understanding. If, for example, I
> consider the faculty of understanding, I immediately recognize that in my
> case it is extremely slight and very finite, and I at once form the idea of an
> understanding which is much greater—indeed supremely great and infi-
> nite. . . . Similarly, if I examine the faculties of memory or imagination,
> or any others, I discover that in my case each one of these faculties is weak
> and limited, while in the case of God it is immeasurable. It is only the will
> or freedom of choice, which I experience within me to be so great that the
> idea of any greater faculty is beyond my grasp; so much so that it is above
> all in virtue of the will that I understand myself to bear in some way the
> image and likeness of God. (2:39–40)

Will, then, must bear the idea of God; God, as we have seen, is
what the ego would will to be. But in the act of judgment, will and
intellect have different aims. Reason recognizes clear and distinct
ideas. Paucity, the amount of truth, is not a consideration. But the
infinite faculty has an innate propensity to believe. Will's consent to
truth runs ahead of reason's recognition of truth, thus producing error, a privation of the will:

> So what then is the source of mistakes? It must be simply this: the scope
> of the will is wider than that of the intellect; but instead of restricting
> it within the same limits, I extend its use to matters which I do not un-
> derstand. Since the will is indifferent in such cases, it easily turns aside

from what is true and good, and this is the source of my error and sin. (2:40–41)

In judgment, something must be added to understanding—an assent stamped on a rational proposal. We mark the truth with the mark God left on us. But will often supplies this assent without the rational endorsement, which is a mistake. Presumably, the two powers are ideally coordinated in the performative *cogito*. As we do it (will it), we understand it; as we understand it, we do it.

The two-phase theory of judgment has seemed clumsy to some modern commentators. Anthony Kenny appeals to J. L. Austin's notion of the "onus of match." [24] The onus is on the house to match the architect's blueprint, but on the guidebook drawing to match the house. Similarly, when we think "*X* is true," *X* must match a state of affairs, but when we think "I consent to the truth of *X*," we must match, or remain faithful to, the truth of *X*. We take this argument to be claiming that will is extrinsic to judgment, that "*X* is true" is all that understanding ordinarily involves. Descartes has lumbered the determination of truth with his characteristic self-consciousness, inserting a relationship to our ideas where there are, most of the time, only our ideas.

The activity reserved for the will in Cartesian judgment answers to what we ordinarily call "conviction" or "commitment." A great deal of Renaissance thought has been subliminally remembered in this account of belief's force. The *thymos* of the dramatists and Neoplatonists was not submerged altogether in mechanism. A representative of it— the desire for infinite knowledge, the deiformity in the human—attends the truth. Or we might say, to come into line with contemporary discussions of truth, that Cartesian understanding is attuned to truth as correspondence, and all the accompanying virtues of rationalism—accuracy, experiment, logical entailment. Will is attuned to truth as coherence; something "seems right," it sorts well with a large ensemble of beliefs, and we believe it. Descartes, of course, thought the will was mistaken in such cases. But his prescient theory of judgment supplies us with a prototype of the insight that we use today to deflate the pretenses of rationalism.

The will was Descartes's version of the principle of inexhaustibility that formed the core of Renaissance ambition. Descartes tried to discipline the holy ambition that invaded the mind of a Pico, putting pride back in its place. He wanted us to prefer "the knowledge of some few truths to the vanity of appearing ignorant of nothing" (1:147). This was a timely warning, though of course his ego, as we

have tried to show, enjoyed in disguised form a number of vainglo-
rious triumphs. For the price paid for the infinitization of human ambition was higher than zealous wars, the atrocities of sovereigns, or
the racial arrogance of colonialism. A pragmatic critique must be
added to the moral and political ones; unlimited strife was not finally
self-interested. "Let him be rich and weary," said Herbert's God. The
new *thymos* made its major literary impression in the genre of tragedy.
Freud's essay on Shakespeare's knowing victim of "vaulting ambition"
is entitled "Those Wrecked by Success." If ambition must be infinite,
it will also be insatiate. "More!" Tantalus cries in hell.

The aspirations treated in our last three chapters have a sublimity
that still touches us, maybe inspires us, for these are still our ambitions, visible despite our curtailing settlements with necessity, as they
are visible in the subterfuges of Descartes. It will not do to feel so
superior to superiority that we fail to understand our own. The high
grand style of Renaissance ambition was, in psychological terms, a
true revelation.

Where has it gone? The full extent of human vanity was clear to
Hobbes, but he wound up signing our names to a contract for tyranny; it is excluded from Rousseau's state of nature, which may be
one reason why he can recommend democracy hopefully. Ever since,
the hyperboles of pride have been somewhat hidden in the theory of
democracy, though encountered daily in practical politics. Today our
Western democracies combine Hobbes's state of nature with Rousseau's politics. We are permitted a straitened version of unlimited
competitive acquisition in the capitalist marketplace, while a common
ceiling is put on our worth politically, through egalitarian rights, tol-
erant public debate, the ideal of public education, and the like. Every
generation learns that the two systems, projecting different visions of
the individual, are difficult to keep apart.

Now and then an idea helps. It is important for individuals to feel
that their spiritual resources are deep and rich, that they need not pun-
ish themselves with drivenness to fulfill their highest ambitions. Romanticism was a great boon in this regard. The structure of the Piconian moment, for example, reappeared in Kant's mathematical sublime:
an apprehension of the majesty of the illimitable, the sublime was
distinct from the beautiful in producing a restless aspiration similar to
that of Pico's Adam.[25] Felicities akin to the raw ambitions of the Renaissance were now available, potentially, to everyone on the common
ground of nature and art. Emerson found Renaissance selfhood in the
leisure to exist alongside nature: "How does Nature deify us with a
few and cheap elements! Give me health and a day, and I will make

the pomp of emperors ridiculous. The dawn is my Assyria; the sun-set and moon-rise my Paphos, and unimaginable realms of faerie; broad noon shall be my England of the senses and the understanding; the night shall be my Germany of mystic philosophy and dreams." [26] One might be rich as Alexander, but not weary. With Freud, at last, we gained a powerful, clear-sighted body of thought aimed at teaching us to shrink our narcissism, and to discern the baby in "His Majesty the Ego." The pomp of emperors had never been mocked so well.

FREUD'S EXCELLENCE, Richard Rorty has observed, was to have broken down the alienating barrier between the Cartesian self and the world machine in a way that made sense for personality:

> This Baconian attitude was the culmination of the mechanizing movement that had begun in the seventeenth century. That movement had replaced the attempt to contemplate the essences of natural kinds with the attempt to tinker with the machines that compose the world. But not until Freud did we get a usable way of thinking of *ourselves* as machines to be tinkered with, a self-image that enabled us to weave terms describing psychic mechanisms into our strategies of character-formation. [27]

Extending the tradition of *The Passions of the Soul,* Freud presents a straightforwardly mechanistic account of sexual excitement in his *Three Essays on Sexuality.* We see, and are moved to touch; we touch, and are moved to embrace; we embrace, and are moved to intercourse. It is all familiar to us: the same old story. But Freud notes that the pleasure in this drama of two is importantly unlike the pleasure principle, where tension is followed by renewed equilibrium. By contrast, the pleasure in sexual foreplay serves to increase tension, just as in business the offer of an incentive bonus will increase the amount of work. We realize a certain degree of satisfaction. Yet at every stage short of orgasm, which reasserts the calculus of the pleasure principle, we must achieve more pleasure, lest the pleasure we then enjoy be transformed into unpleasure or, in ordinary language, frustration. [28] Freud refers to this distinctive mechanism as the forepleasure principle.

It strikes us that the main pursuits of Renaissance ambition obey the incremental structure of the forepleasure principle. Power: capture a certain amount of power, as Hobbes maintained, and you must capture more power; otherwise the power you have will be felt as powerlessness or insecurity. Fame: achieve a certain amount of fame, and you must then achieve more fame; otherwise the fame you have will be felt as limited or insufficient recognition. Knowledge: gain a certain amount of knowledge, and you must somehow have the hope of gaining more knowledge; otherwise the knowledge you have will be felt as a frustrating ignorance. Many were the ideas and practices meant to open to infinity these and related pursuits in the Renaissance. Nicolas's learned ignorance, the ascent toward God of the Neoplatonists, the humanist economy of praise, the rhetoric of the Piconian moment, the idea of progress, absolutist monarchies extending their power into the New World through voyages of discovery and colonization, credit financing: all of these were schemes for guarding ambition against the possibility of frustrating limits.

Freud found this Renaissance structure in sexual desire. He also located it in the delaying tactics of jokes, which hold back the punch line until, customarily, the third narrative repetition; and he found it in art, of course: "The writer softens the character of his egoistic daydreams by altering and disguising it, and he bribes us by the purely formal—that is, aesthetic—yield of pleasure which he offers us in the presentation of his fantasies. We give the name of an *incentive bonus,* or a *fore-pleasure,* to a yield of pleasure such as this, which is offered to us so as to make possible the release of still greater pleasure arising from deep psychical sources."[29] Perhaps the discovery of ambition's mechanism in the examples of sexuality and aesthetics will lend an initial plausibility to the discussion of love poetry in the final part of this book. Petrarchism is, in a number of ways, the distinctive lyric genre of the Renaissance. It must have been, at least in part, the shared structure of the forepleasure principle that enabled these expressions of frustrated love seeking "to make possible the release of still greater pleasure arising from deep psychical sources," these highly self-conscious works of art that contain internally the dynamic Freud found in art's consumption, to encode in their "conceits" the full array of Renaissance ambitions.

THREE

Love

NINE

Petrarch Refracted: The Evolution of the English Love Lyric

"The most striking distinction between the erotic life of antiquity and our own," Freud ventures in a late footnote to his *Three Essays on Sexuality*, "no doubt lies in the fact that the ancients laid the stress on the instinct itself, whereas we emphasize its object. The ancients glorified the instinct and were prepared on its account to honor even an inferior object, while we despise the instinctual activity in itself, and find excuses for it only in the merits of the object" (*SE*, 7:149). The immediate context here is the question of unconventional object choices, homosexual and other, but we think the generalization will bear more weight than Freud asks it to carry. There is nothing in classical literature comparable to the exaltation of woman that arises with the troubadours of the Pays d'Oc in the twelfth century and is transmitted from them to the rest of Europe: to northern France and the *trouvères*, to Germany and the *Minnesänger*, to Italy and the *stilnovisti*. These poets sing, time and again, of the woman who is the decisive event in a man's life, whose arrival divides that life in two ("Incipit uita noua"), who makes all other concerns trivial in comparison. Among the classical poets, Catullus adumbrates such an enthrallment, but he has other things, and other kinds of love, to write about. Freud is right to see the elevation of the feminine object into the alpha and omega of existence as in some ways the special mark of postclassical Western culture.

The significant figure in this consequential innovation is Francesco Petrarca, known in English as Petrarch (1304–74), the inheritor of Provençal and stilnovist lyric who gives it the shape in which it becomes the accepted form for serious love poetry during the next three centuries. His ephebes are legion. In the general European Renaissance, it is Petrarchan imitation that trains the lyric poets of the developing vernaculars: imitation Petrarchan in form—the sonnet, which owes its preeminence among the wide repertoire of Italian verse forms to Petrarch's example—but also, and more surprisingly, Petrarchan in content. Italian, French, Spanish, English, German poets, and others, recount, as though on their own experience, a love that in its general outlines and often in its specific details mimics that presented in Petrarch's own *Canzoniere,* the sequence of lyrics about his love for the blond woman with black eyes whom he calls Laura. He saw her first during services at the Church of Saint Claire in Avignon, 6 April 1327, and she took over his life:

> I' vidi Amor che' begli occhi volgea
> soave sì ch' ogni altra vista oscura
> da indi in qua m'incominciò apparere.

> I saw Love moving her lovely eyes so gently that every other sight from then on began to seem dark to me. (*Canzoniere* 144.9–11)[1]

His devotion remained constant and all-consuming; even her death from the plague twenty-one years later—at exactly the same hour and day of the year at which he first saw her—did not loosen her hold on him.

Petrarch's inability to think of anything else ramifies through the Renaissance and beyond. We note immediately that this is the love lyric in its epochal guise: a lover and a beloved, a subject and his object, the main questions being his knowledge of the beloved, the ambitiousness of his desire for her, the anticipation of her conquest, the urge to manifest the ever-deepening consequences of her refusal, and become, if not her lover, then her monument. Petrarchism was in fairly precise ways the distinctive genre of the English Renaissance, its literary life bracketing the era. We find it first in the lyrics of Sir Thomas Wyatt and the Earl of Surrey, written during the reign of Henry VIII; the Italian export had arrived, and these poems are among its earliest unmistakable symptoms. In no subsequent period of English literary history will love be the dominant preoccupation of lyric poetry, or would-be poets feel compelled, as a public demonstration of their ambition, to animate the reigning conventions of literary love. However, few Renaissance careers were without some episode of Petrarchism. It flourished under Elizabeth I and can still be observed in the sexier, superficially anti-Petrarchan lyrics of the following century. The long arc of the tradition, from the sequences of frustrated or ideal love to the Ovidian variations of the seventeenth century, comes down on Milton, and with particular force on the epic that fuses in literature the two great historical forces brought to the island under Henry VIII, Renaissance and Reformation.

So the historical record almost compels us to discuss Petrarchism in terms of the period concept. Coming to the subject from Burckhardt and Cassirer, we easily perceive the family resemblance: Renaissance individualism chooses to fall in love in this style. Yet literary history has some explaining to do about why Petrarch's lyrics should have become so central.

For his is a peculiar story, and peculiarly told. Virtually nothing happens. The preceding paraphrase includes all the clearly recoverable events, and some of those can be specified only from information available outside the poems. Most of the poems do not essay direct presentation of Laura at all. She shows up obliquely, sometimes as a fetishized object such as a veil or a glove.[2] Most famously, she appears in abstracted symbols for parts of her body which become the conventional décor by which later Petrarchan verse is most quickly recognized: "La testa or fino, et calda neve il volto, / ebeno i cigli, et gli occhi eran due stelle" (Her head was fine gold, her face warm snow, ebony her eyebrows, and her eyes two stars) (157.9–10). Often such details appear in the merest shorthand, and take on an odd life of their own which can make the poetry seem surreal and baffling at first encounter; an ongoing topos in discussions of Petrarchan poetry has been to wonder if the ladies in question were, you know, real.[3] The situation Petrarch writes about is largely a static one, and at least ostensibly for a simple but definitive reason: Laura responds with implacable indifference, if not active hostility, to her lover's attention; the very point of the sequence's main event—Laura's death, announced in poem 267—is that it changes almost nothing. In the face of this, Petrarch can muster few resources. Mostly he rehearses his despair.

The *fin amor* celebrated by Petrarch's precursors was itself unconsummated a good bit of the time, though never at his pitch: "The concept of true love was not framed to include success."[4] Petrarch's extraordinary elongation of that frustration is echoed in almost all of the *Canzoniere*'s Renaissance descendants, a run of masculine bad luck so insistent that it becomes almost a joke, a sign of Petrarchism's monotonous conventionality. But jokes have their reasons. Why should Europe's lyric celebration of the feminine object of desire begin with several centuries fixated on the unavailability of that object?

The major kinds of lyric poetry have their own emotional zones—
the grief of elegy, the admiration of panegyric, the grouchiness of
epigram, the exaltation of victory ode. Though each of them may
create visions of the fullness of life, the visions can be traced back to
the core of characteristic states of mind. Inside Petrarchan verse the
mood is the frustration of unrequited sexual love. Action hits a wall,
and the rebound goes inward, into the resources of the poetic self.
Petrarchism as it unfolds in the Renaissance dilates the individual in a
condition of unwanted isolation. It is another in the line of dissociated
mental states that fascinated the period. It, too, will strive to produce
stable versions of the Narcissus myth.

Frustration is only half its core passion, for the rule of the genre
demands that the lover's isolation inspire a prolonged imaginative aggrandizement in the name of two overlapping motives: to display the
worthiness of the love, to demonstrate the essential injustice of its
refusal. Imagination, however, has its own self-bestowed rewards, and
the Petrarchan ego often comes to rest in an exaltation of its initially
unwanted autonomy. Some of the most convincing and substantial
passages of relief in the *Canzoniere* arise not from the brief moments
when Laura's favorable response is (probably) hallucinated, but rather
from a deeper plunge into alienation. The poet of incurable love is
also the poet of delighted solitude. Away from all human interference,
desire can exercise itself with a new freedom and ease, projecting an
image of the beloved onto the passive landscape. Petrarch is at his
most rapturous in just this mode:

> I' l'ò più volte (or chi fia che mi 'l creda?)
> ne l'acqua chiara et sopra l'erba verde
> veduto viva, et nel troncon d'un faggio
> e 'n bianca nube, sì fatta che Leda
> avria ben detto che sua figlia perde
> come stella che 'l sol copre col raggio;
>   et quanto in più selvaggio
> loco mi trovo e 'n più deserto lido,
> tanto più bella il mio pensier l'adombra.

I have many times (now who will believe me?) seen her alive in the clear
water and on the green grass and in the trunk of a beech tree and in a white
cloud, so beautiful that Leda would have said that her daughter faded like
a star covered by the sun's ray; and in whatever wildest place and most
deserted shore I find myself, so much the more beautiful does my thought
shadow her forth. (129.40–48)

The woman's very distance enables a heady sense of power on the lover's part, of the capacity of his own mind to transform or displace external reality. At its most cogently celebratory, Petrarchan love poetry exalts the poet's own imagination. No doubt this is one reason why most of the Renaissance poets spent some portion of their youth in Petrarch's school.

It also helps to explain the historical alliance with Neoplatonism. According to Castiglione's Bembo, erotic enlightenment begins when the absence of the presumed object of desire prompts the lover to replace it with a more secure one of his own making: "To escape the torment of this absence and to enjoy beauty without suffering, the Courtier, aided by reason, must turn his desire entirely away from the body and to beauty alone . . . and in his imagination give it a shape distinct from all matter; and thus make it loving and dear to his soul, and there enjoy it; and let him keep it with him day and night, in every time and place, without fear of ever losing it."[5] On both practical and ontological grounds, loving the woman's image is better than loving the woman herself. Petrarchism intersects Neoplatonism because this philosophy can guarantee that a withdrawal from external reality gives access to the true ground of reality. The One, we have learned, consumes everything. But for precisely that reason, this happy frustration will not give us the anguish in the core passion of the *Canzoniere*.

Petrarch himself suggests, through the Narcissus myth (*Canzoniere* 45), that one problem with Laura is pride.[6] The stone has been lobbed from a glass house. In the great pun that spreads throughout his lyrics, Laura, the object of his all-consuming desire, can be indistinguishable from *lauro*, the laurel of poetic achievement. The play on Laura's name is perhaps the strongest connection available between the dazed obsessiveness of the *Canzoniere* and normal human business. Her pride mirrors and incites Petrarch's own. Somehow, frustrated desire and professional success belong together. In one way or another, Petrarch wants the laurel of her refusal. Laureation is a thread we shall follow through the English love lyric in these two chapters, for it is woven of the themes of our book: revived antiquity, infinite ambition, man's self-deification, and the cult of fame, to which must now be added public courtship in verse.

Pride is clever with disguises. Petrarch broods in his philosophical writings on its ability to pass itself off as virtue.[7] Such wariness derives primarily from the work of Augustine, who identified pride as the primal sin of the fall: "'Pride is the start of every kind of sin' [Ecclus. 10:15]. And what is pride except a longing for a perverse kind of exaltation? For it is a perverse kind of exaltation to abandon the basis on which the mind should be firmly fixed, and to become, as it were, based on oneself, and so remain. This happens when a man is too pleased with himself" (*City of God* 14.13).[8] Augustine's polemic was aimed at the heroic values of classical culture, which was not so severe on self-regard and had no trouble praising *autarceia* as a positive goal. But the Empire had provided ample evidence of the dangers of such values. A vice seeming to be a virtue was the plot of man's Fall; it was also the plot of Christianity's supreme apologist. Augustine spoke for a new ethical dispensation from which classical narcissism was to be uprooted: "The earthly city was created by self-love reaching the point of contempt for God, the Heavenly City by the love of God carried as far as contempt of self" (14.28). Humility now became the crucial standard. The self's comfort depended on something beyond its borders. During the Middle Ages, the contrast between self-love and the love of others, Eros and Agapê, acquired a moral energy unknown in antiquity.

In his most directly personal work, the scathingly introspective dialogue *De secreto conflictu curarum mearum,* Petrarch invokes the very spirit of Augustine to interrogate and accuse him about "the causes that inflate your mind with pride." A lengthy denunciation of his lust for Laura yields to a climactic assault on his other desire, which is *superbia* in its Renaissance form, *honos et gloria* reborn: "Ambition still has too much hold on you. You seek too eagerly the praise of men, and to leave behind you an undying name. . . . I greatly fear lest this pursuit of a false immortality of fame may shut for you the way that leads to the true immortality of life." "I freely confess it," Petrarch replies, though the admission gains no purchase on the passion itself: "But I have not strength to resist that old bent for study altogether." With a parting shot from Augustine ("what you call lack of strength is in fact your own doing"), there the dialogue ends. We have already seen in chapter 1 how complex Petrarch's negotiations with fame could become. Under the pressure of his ambivalence, fame splits in two: there is good fame, won from posterity, and suspect fame, won from one's contemporaries. In the divided mind of *De secreto,* that second possibility offers no relief. The desire for fame testifies in itself to a mortal sin, an insidiously complacent selfishness that is the greatest impediment to Petrarch's salvation: "The story of Narcissus has no warning for you."[9]

It would be too simple to identify Laura with fame. The interpretation tempts us because we are prone to feel that a woman has been lessened and manipulated in the *Canzoniere,* absorbed into the self-interested calculations of a male ego, and in the face of this psychic crime we need, like Petrarch's own Augustine, to point a finger at male egotism. No one has ever denied the egotism. But Laura is more profoundly its cost than its privilege.

A writer, sitting alone, facing a blank sheet of paper, puts on that paper words that are the words of speech but are not being spoken, and translates into this silent medium the gestures of speaking to someone who in all but the most peculiar circumstances is not there, but whose presence the writer nevertheless tries in some form to imagine. Similarly, when that writing is read, the writer ostensibly speaking is, in all but very special circumstances, not there, although we tend to say, of course, that writers succeed to the extent that they can make us feel their presence. Cutting in two the face-to-face encounter that speech, one assumes, originally developed to serve, the skill of writing traffics at both ends in absent presences. A simulacrum of speech, it diverts language from literal to fictive others whose existence depends on the operations of a solitary's fantasy.

Most of the important human connections in Petrarch's life seem to have been mediated by writing. He produced an immense epistolary corpus, carefully organized and revised. The letters make no firm distinction between actual and imagined recipients. In addition to the autobiographical letter to Posterity, there are Herzog-like letters to Cicero, Seneca, Homer, and the like. Petrarch noted a strange self-sufficiency in the urge to write, indifferent to ulterior motives: "Incredible as it may seem, I desire to write but I know not about what or to whom to write."[10] The indecisiveness of the De secreto persisted to the end. In one of the last letters, he responded in this way to Boccaccio's plea that he ease up on his studies: "I do hope that death may find me reading or writing, or, if it should so please Christ, in tearful prayer."[11] Thomas M. Greene reads Petrarch's story as a "lifelong wait" for a repeatedly deferred Augustinian conversion, colored by "his growing fear, his growing realization that the miracle of will and grace was not to be vouchsafed him."[12] Reading and writing, all that reading and writing meant, were Petrarch's fate. The myth of Apollo and Daphne intersected the myth of Narcissus and Echo. It is here that we may begin to seek the most cogent reasons why the Renaissance should have rewritten so many times the story of a tongue-tied lover devoted to a distant woman to whom he can barely bring himself to speak, and who scarcely deigns to answer him when he does. The generative core of this story is speech failing systematically in its ostensible external goal, then doubling back on its originator, as writing. Like the thinking of the Cartesian ego, the troubled ruminations of the Petrarchan ego are, in no incidental way, written.

These themes are dramatized in Petrarch's longest, most compelling, and most difficult poem, *Canzoniere* 23. It is also the poem that contains the fullest narrative unfolding of the Laura-laurel pun, in a personalized retelling of several of Ovid's myths of metamorphosis, beginning with Daphne and Apollo:

> . . . sentendo il crudel di ch' io ragiono
> infin allor percossa di suo strale
> non essermi passato oltra la gonna,
> prese in sua scorta una possente Donna
> ver cui poco giamai mi valse o vale
> ingegno o forza o dimandar perdono;
> ei duo mi trasformaro in quel ch' i' sono,
> facendomi d'uom vivo un lauro verde
> che per fredda stagion foglia non perde.

> That cruel one of whom I speak [Love], seeing that as yet no blow of his arrows had gone beyond my garment, took as his patroness a powerful Lady, against whom wit or force or asking pardon has helped or helps me little: those two transformed me into what I am, making me of a living man a green laurel that loses no leaf for all the cold season. (Ll. 32–40)

The lover himself becomes the laurel. Yet Laura does not, as we might expect she would, occupy the position of Apollo. Petrarch is both pursuer and pursued:

> Qual mi fec' io quando primier m'accorsi
> de la trasfigurata mia persona,
> e i capei vidi far di quella fronde
> di che sperato avea già lor corona.

> What I became, when I first grew aware of my person being transformed and saw my hairs turning into those leaves which I had formerly hoped would be my crown. (Ll. 41–44)

Subsequent myths figure the growth of the lover's poetic vocation. The repeated failure of his presumption loosens his tongue, gives him his voice. True to its origins, this is a special kind of voice:

> Così lungo l'amate rive andai,
> che volendo parlar, cantava sempre,

mercé chiamando con estrania voce;
né mai in sì dolci o in sì soavi tempre
risonar seppi gli amorosi guai
che 'l cor s'umiliasse aspro et feroce.

Thus I went along the beloved shores, and, wishing to speak, I sang always, calling for mercy with a strange voice; nor was I ever able to make my amorous woes resound in so sweet or soft a temper that her harsh and ferocious heart was humbled. (Ll. 61–66)[13]

Speech, which aims to persuade its addressee, is diverted into song, a use of language that may ravish with its beauty but makes nothing happen.

The woman's own most direct act is to deny speech its usual purpose:

Questa che col mirar gli animi fura
m'aperse il petto el' cor prese con mano,
dicendo a me: "Di ciò non far parola."
Poi la rividi in altro abito sola,
tal ch' i' non la conobbi, o senso umano!
anzi le dissi 'l ver pien di paura;
ed ella ne l'usata sua figura
tosto tornando fecemi, oimè lasso!
d'un quasi vivo et sbigottito sasso.

She, who with her glance steals souls, opened my breast and took my heart with her hand, saying to me: "Make no word of this." Later I saw her alone in another garment such that I did not know her, oh human sense! rather I told her the truth, full of fear, and she to her accustomed form quickly returning made me, alas, an almost living and terrified stone. (Ll. 72–80)

Following the logic of this suppression, the lover's career becomes literary:

le vive voci m'erano interditte,
ond' io gridai con carta et con incostro:
"Non son mio, no; s'io moro il danno è vostro."

Words spoken aloud were forbidden me; so I cried out with paper and ink: "I am not my own, no; if I die, yours is the loss." (Ll. 98–100)

The word *interditte* (forbidden) takes its rhyme, after a long postponement, from line 92, *scritte* (written).

To speak in paper and ink is to speak *con estrania voce,* with an estranged voice that the speaker almost does not recognize as his own.
The process of estrangement moves toward the complete split of
speech from speaker:

> . . . ancor poi ripregando i nervi et l'ossa
> mi volse in dura selce, et così scossa
> voce rimasi de l'antiche some,
> chiamando Morte et lei sola per nome.

> When I prayed again, she turned my sinews and bones into hard flint, and
> thus I remained a voice shaken from my former burden, calling Death and
> only her by name. (Ll. 137–40)

Forbidden *vive voce,* a petrified Petrarch hears his voice calling on
Death, not love. Again there is an Ovidian text in the background,
perhaps the most Petrarchan of Ovid's stories: "tamen haeret amor
crescitque dolore repulsae" (though rejected, her love sticks and grows
with her grief; *Metamorphoses* 3.395). The character in question, who
is about to separate into petrified body and abstracted voice, is Echo.[14]

Remembering Narcissus and Echo helps us to track the movement
from the opening event of the poem to its violent end:

> I' segui' tanto avanti il mio desire
> ch' un dì, cacciando sì com' io solea,
> mi mossi, e quella fera bella et cruda
> in una fonte ignuda
> si stava, quando 'l sol più forte ardea.
> Io perché d'altra vista non m'appago
> stetti a mirarla, ond' ella ebbe vergogna
> et per farne vendetta o per celarse
> l'acqua nel viso co le man mi sparse.
> Vera dirò; forse e' parrà menzogna:
> ch' i' senti' trarmi de la propria imago
> et in un cervo solitario et vago
> di selva in selva ratto mi trasformo,
> et ancor de' miei can fuggo lo stormo.

> I followed so far my desire that one day, hunting as I was wont, I went
> forth, and that lovely cruel wild creature was in a spring naked when the

sun burned most strongly. I, who am not appeased by any other sight, stood to gaze on her, whence she felt shame and, to take revenge or to hide herself, sprinkled water in my face with her hand. I shall speak the truth, perhaps it will appear a lie, for I felt myself drawn from my own image and into a solitary wandering stag from wood to wood quickly I am transformed and still I flee the belling of my hounds. (Ll. 147–60)

This, of course, is the story of Actaeon. In the context of Petrarch's poem, Bruno's Neoplatonic version of the myth seems considerably less perverse.[15] In Petrarch's hands, the Actaeon myth parallels the altered Apollo/Daphne myth: at the end of the poem as at the beginning, the lover suddenly, catastrophically, becomes the object of his own pursuit. A wave of implication that has been building throughout the poem breaks on the sounds of the lover's pursuers. The belling of the hounds, we suggest, is the plaintive song whose development the *canzone* has narrated, returning to its now speechless creator.[16] The terror on the other side of narcissistic beguilement is the experience of one's own self as an outsider. Petrarch's lover flees from the sound of his own poetic voice, echoing murderously in the bell jar.

The poem is almost, but not quite, over. A final and deeply characteristic turn remains:

né per nova figura il primo alloro
seppi lassar, ché pur la sua dolce ombra
ogni men bel piacer del cor mi sgombra.

Nor for any new shape could I leave the first laurel, for still its sweet shade turns away from my heart any less beautiful pleasure. (Ll. 167–69)

The allure of the deadly object is suavely reaffirmed. The lover appears to have learned nothing at all; we might almost wonder if Petrarch is tacking on a *commiato* written for another, less ferocious poem. Yet there is at least a continuity of action in the way the present tense sustains itself, as if insisting on the tenacity of the state to which the lover has come. No mere terror is going to change things. We recall that the inquisitorial Augustine of *De secreto* had no trouble achieving self-indictment, but equally no hope of achieving reform. Montaigne was not the first writer of the age to discover the senselessness of repentance.

Under the shadow of Petrarch, Renaissance poets worked to bring his story to some other conclusion. We do not find anything approaching this despairing yet stubborn loyalty to a morally and psychologically dubious poetic vocation in the early Petrarchism of England. Christianity is not aligned against love in the poetry of Wyatt. He does not suffer the rigors of nonconsummation. Overtly at least, fame is not an issue; secrecy, indeed, may well have been the poet's wish. The conflict that generates his best poems arises within love itself. Translating *Canzoniere* 140, Wyatt adds an un-Petrarchan emphasis on faithfulness, the rules that govern reciprocities between master and servant. Love has been allowed to show in his face and, when rebuked by the woman for this forwardness, retreats to the "heart's forest":

> What may I do when my master feareth,
> But in the field with him to live and die?
> For good is the life ending faithfully.
> (Rebholz 10)[17]

Throughout his lyrics Wyatt, who served his inconstant monarch as a diplomat, makes pacts of fidelity with certain key abstractions, such as "truth" and "steadfastness." The plain, proverbial style that appears alongside Petrarchan ornamentation represents a commitment to fairness, which surfaces at the end of his most famous poem, "They flee from me" (Rebholz 80): "But since that I so kindly am served / I would fain know what she hath deserved." Merely raising the question of just and symmetrical treatment consoles, just as fidelity to a master gives dignity to the rebuked lover in his Petrarch translation. If "field" means "face" rather than "heart" (which seems likely, because the heart is a foresty retreat, whereas the field is where love shows himself, to win or lose), then good faith with love has given him the boldness to express love again.

At its most powerful, this devotion to fairness must reassess itself in the face of deception, not only in the woman but also in himself:

> It was my choice, it was no chance
> That brought my heart in other's hold,
> Whereby it hath had sufferance
> Longer, perdie, than reason would.
> Since I it bound where it was free,
> Methinks, iwis, of right it should
>   Accepted be.
>
> Accepted be without refuse
> Unless that Fortune hath the power

All right of love for to abuse;
For, as they say, one happy hour
May more prevail than right or might.
If Fortune then list for to lour
   What vaileth right?
(Rebholz 93)

It is at just about this point that Petrarch and many of his followers would either end the poem or veer off into complaint. Wyatt, though, forced to persist by his formal commitment to linked stanzas, consigns love to a realm of fortune and chance in which complaint is pointless, because "choice," "reason," and "right," the triad of abstractions that stage his injustice in the first stanza, have no court to back them up:

What vaileth right if this be true?
Then trust to chance and go by guess.
Then who so loveth may well go sue
Uncertain hope for his redress.
Yet some would say assuredly
Thou mayst appeal for thy release
   To fantasy.

To fantasy pertains to choose.
All this I know for fantasy
First into love did me induce.
But yet I know as steadfastly
That if love have no faster knot
So nice a choice slips suddenly.
   It lasteth not.

It lasteth not that stands by change.
Fancy doth change, Fortune is frail.
Both these to please, the way is strange.
Therefore, methinks, best to prevail,
There is no way that is so just
As truth to lead though t'other fail,
   And thereto trust.

The middle stanzas flirt with a new set of guiding abstractions, "chance," "guess," "uncertain hope," and "fantasy." If love does not work out in one quarter, try another: justice, the belief that a gift given should be answered by a gift received, is not the law in love. But

Wyatt, knowing full well the baselessness of his choice, prefers truth, constancy, trust. Without them, "the way is strange." The word "just" in the final stanza has already failed, and trust along with it, in the previous stanzas. At the end of the poem "just" cannot mean much more than a guideline, a familiar way of proceeding, a trait of character rather than an absolute principle of moral determination. Making poetry of sexual noncompliance, Renaissance lyricists confronted gulfs of irrationality. If Wyatt must concede the severance of reason from fantasy in love, he can reintegrate them in poetry, where he reasserts the continuity of his character against the temptation to lapse into newfangledness. Loyalty to his own knowledge provides the turn in this lyric: "But yet I know as steadfastly. . . ." Whatever happens in love, one can be, as even the proverb-haunted Polonius saw, symmetrical with oneself, choosing one's own choice again. Alternatively, one can decide not to love ("Farewell, Love, and all thy laws forever"; Rebholz 31).

A more authentically Petrarchan Petrarchism does not appear until Sidney's *Astrophil and Stella,* which drives euphuism from the inkwells of fellow poets and inspires the grand decade of oxymoronic sonnet sequences in the 1590s by re-creating, for the first time in English, the elongated frustration of Petrarch.

The poems in the *Canzoniere* exhibit at every turn the resourcefulness of obsession. Fantasy is not only their element but often their subject—the image of Laura, the memory of Laura, the replaying of ambiguous gestures in the process of interpreting Laura. As we have seen, this cultivated obsession is petrifying, toxic, shameful, counter to worldly, moral, and religious self-interest. But—and this becomes one of the defining gestures of the Petrarchan tradition—the love is nonetheless to be affirmed as an ideal. The interpretations of Laura must in the end imply the good sense of her devotee: being herself ideal, she will eventually reward his service to this ideal; somehow or other, hope keeps springing up from apparently absolute despair. Thus, to look ahead, the much-maligned idealizing couplets in the bulk of Shakespeare's sonnets (57: "So true a fool is love that in your will, / Though you do anything, he thinks no ill") should be taken as assertions of genre, submissions to the fundamental rule of idealization.

Sidney's lover has exactly this resourcefulness. His adoration survives hurtle after hurtle in the reproach of friends, the accusations of morality, the disapproval of reason, and above all the repeated humiliation of his failure. Stella's capacity for resistance is geared to Astrophil's capacity for idealization. It is an almost mathematical or mechanistic drama, a battle between her implacable limit and his implacable excess. The "Fourth song" enfolds the sequence in microcosm, as Astrophil renews his suit in each stanza, only to find waiting for him, at the end, her inevitable, unbudging "No, no, no, my dear, let be." When the lover foretells his death in the final stanza, the refrain takes on a soothing meaning. Indeed, within the line itself a hint of ambivalence lives in "my dear," and that turns out to be Sidney's main innovation. Sonnet 69 ("For Stella hath with words whose faith doth shine, / Of her high heart given me the monarchy") makes it fairly clear that Stella is, after all, an Astrophile, and returns his love. Before long they are kissing. In the "Eighth song" she speaks her heart at last, and we hear the entirety of feeling encapsulated in the word "dear":

> If to secret of my heart
> I do any wish impart
> Where thou art not foremost placed,
> Be both wish and I defaced.
>
> If more may be said, I say;
> All my bliss in thee I lay;
> If thou love, my love content thee,
> For all love, all faith is meant thee.
>
> Trust me while I thee deny,
> In my self the smart I try,
> Tyrant honor doth thus use thee;
> Stella's self might not refuse thee.
>
> Therefore, dear, this no more move,
> Lest, though I have not thy love,
> Which too deep in me is framed,
> I should blush when thou art named.

The spirit of Laura informs Petrarch himself in the *Trionfi* that she not only knew of his love but also fully returned it, keeping quiet for the good of both their souls.[18] Sidney's sequence harbors, in its innermost recess, Stella's heart, the mutuality that was Petrarch's wish—a love that, broken out from the enclosure of Petrarchism, will be celebrated in poems like Donne's "The Canonization." The dramatic effect of this is a sudden unblinkered revision of Stella. His act of self-control has been as nothing compared with hers. She is all the things he is in love and faith. They differ in one particular only: she has not been able to withstand the conventional reproaches to desire, particularly the threat of dishonor. "Tyrant honor doth thus use thee; / Stella's self might not refuse thee": love is not the supreme master of her heart. The "blush when thou art named" reminds us of the peculiarly feminine version of honor, which is sexual. In dealing with women, male honor must submit to the limits of its sister virtue. As Sidney dramatizes Petrarchan courtship, the honor of the woman is the sticking point preventing honorable male poetry from recovering an Ovidian excess for Renaissance literature.

Mutual love has come to the same end as male obsession and female indifference. ". . . My song is broken," this poem closes. There is no longer any point in seduction. Forbidden to move his suit again, Astrophil has apparently been banished from her company, the "rigorous exile" of sonnet 104. As in Petrarch, poetic language is now severed from its imaginative connection to the speech situation, and the sequence limps to its end, ruing "honor's cruel might" (sonnet 91) and doing business-as-usual with the one theme that remains to him, absent presence.

Business-as-usual is, of course, poetry, and the sonneteers stirred by Sidney's example dwell at intriguing length on the consolation implicit in this fact. One thing the Petrarchan poet has, in compensation for his anguish, is poems. In the *Canzoniere,* literary immortality serves only obliquely, if at all, to reward the lover's suffering, though in *De secreto* Laura and poetic fame are as close as the twin sins of lust and pride. Fame surfaces unforgettably in the early sonnets of *Astrophil and Stella:* "But if (both for your love and skill) your name / You seek to nurse at fullest breasts of Fame, / Stella behold, and then begin to indite" (sonnet 15). Yet the theme is muted by the end of the sequence, and in sonnet 90 Astrophil proclaims that he wants the woman, not the glory. During the sonnet boom, though, we find at last the sort of calculation that Petrarch himself would probably have reached had he not been so invested in the *Africa.*

Some of the most grandiose claims for the vivifying power of literature in all the Renaissance, the great age of this claim, occur in Elizabethan love lyrics. Literary immortality emerges at last from its medieval oblivion. These poets count fame-making among their prime worthinesses, their capital enlarged by the posthumous fate of Petrarch's own reputation. Undying celebrity can be straightforwardly seductive (I alone among my rivals can make you immortal) or threateningly seductive (Be kind, or I will betray your cruelty to aftertimes). When artistic immortality rebounds from the lady to the poet himself, it can be simply compensatory, as in Michael Drayton:

> Proudly thou scorn'st my world-out-wearing rhymes,
> And murder'st virtue with thy coy disdain:
> And though in youth, my youth untimely perish,
> To keep thee from oblivion and the grave,
> Ensuing ages yet my rhymes shall cherish,
> Where I intombed, my better part shall save;
>   And though this earthly body fade and die,
>   My name shall mount upon eternity.
>
> *(Idea* 44)[19]

Fame is also a major preoccupation in Shakespeare's sonnets, where the ability to render the young man's image immortal in verse substitutes for the procreation urged at the beginning.

The pressure in the 1590s is nevertheless toward some merging of those satisfactions. One can, after all, imagine that Petrarchan love might meet with no impediments, and the poems declaring its self-importance would then be exercises in a stylish seduction ritual. A love such as Sidney's, being, like that of most Petrarchan poets, adulterous, could hardly have taken that course with full respectability. By removing the obstacles of adultery and (thus) honor, Spenser brings the Petrarchan story to an unprecedented happy ending. But in the *Amoretti,* as in *Astrophil and Stella,* the meaning of the woman's resistance gives rise to the most vital poetry. Imaginatively, we are still on the frustration side of the barrier.

Spenser reverts to the theme of Augustinian pride, though focused now fully on the woman, not the poet. Feminine honor might also be the solitary hell of feminine pride:

> Ne none so rich or wise, so strong or fair,
> But faileth trusting on his own assurance;
> And he that standeth on the highest stair
> Falls lowest: for on earth nought hath endurance.
> Why then do ye, proud fair, misdeem so far,
> That to your self ye most assured are?
>
> (58.9–12)

In the offing is not a mere humbling of the woman. As embodied in Spenser, this moral stand comes with an acknowledgment of narcissism's indelibility. The sonnet just quoted is immediately followed by a twin that praises something very close to what the first poem attacks:

> Thrice happy she, that is so well assured
> Unto her self, and settled so in heart,
> That neither will for better be allured,
> Ne feared with worse to any chance to start.
>
> (59.1–4)

Spenser's sequence is moving toward a happy ending in marriage that allows us to say just what the telos of Petrarchan love might be given two hardy people and routine good luck. Petrarch briefly adumbrates this new ending in offering himself as the replacement for Laura's mirror (*Canzoniere* 45). Spenser expands the hint:

> Leave, lady, in your glass of crystal clean
> Your goodly self for evermore to view,
> And in my self, my inward self I mean,
> Most lively like behold your semblant true.
> Within my heart, though hardly it can shew
> Thing so divine to view of earthly eye,
> The fair idea of your celestial hue
> And every part remains immortally;
> And were it not that through your cruelty
> With sorrow dimmèd and deformed it were,
> The goodly image of your visnomy
> Clearer then crystal would therein appear.
> But if your self in me ye plain will see,
> Remove the cause by which your fair beams darkened be.
>
> (45)

The traditional disapproval is there, yet the alternative being imagined is not a fundamental alteration of the woman's *superbia,* but rather its enlistment in a cooperative endeavor. The lover's bid to replace the mirror in a lady's affections involves a promise to perform the function that his old adversary performs: she can continue to admire herself in the mirror of his admiration (for the poet as Narcissus, see *Amoretti* 35 and 83).[20] This possibility is no more than the fundamental congruence of their situation; the chance for happiness lies in her capacity to acknowledge it (as she does, "with her own will beguiled," in *Amoretti* 68) and to trust her lover to live up to his role in it. That trust can reconcile pride and dependence, supplying a basis for communion within which her self-absorption has nevertheless a privileged place. Milton's Eve, as shall be seen in the next chapter, follows a similar path. The Petrarchan drama of apparently selfless devotion has begun to test the possible arrangements between narcissistic selfhood and the world around it.

However, the event in literary history that impends here is often seen as a major change of masters, a decisive break with Petrarch altogether. Seventeenth-century love poetry has conventionally been described as a more or less libertine, Ovidian refutation of the brief fling with serious Petrarchism in the 1590s. So far as it goes, this is incontrovertible. Christopher Marlowe, Ovid's translator, does indeed cross a threshold when the lovers at the end of *Hero and Leander* manage to get out of their weird Petrarchan outfits and into real sexual consummation. Initially overcome with shame, Hero resists "Like chaste Diana when Actaeon spied her" (*Hero and Leander* 2.261). But this chased Diana learns new ways, and learns them, in a magnificent play upon the same and the different, when practicing the old. Push having come to shove, she tries to repel the ungoverned Leander. But in the very rhythm of this resistance—his onslaught prompting her repulsion, her repulsion prompting his onslaught; the mechanism of the Petrarchan sonnet sequence become incarnate—Hero discovers nature's way. She slips into something more comfortable:

> She trembling strove; this strife of hers (like that
> Which made the world) another world begat
> Of unknown joy.
>
> (2.291–93)

Resistance has broken through to the other side of the barrier.[21] From the perspective of literary history, one of the worlds of unknown joy begotten here is that of consummated English love poetry—the verse of, among others, Donne, Carew, Suckling, Randolph, Lovelace, Marvell, and Milton.

The men of no other century have chosen in such numbers to write down in verse their sexual experience or the products of their sexual imaginations. They declared their lust for young women and old, black and blond, ladies with moles and milkmaids from the country. Maybe their happiest epitome is the physician poet John Collop.[22] Thomas Browne, his fellow doctor, said there were no grotesques in nature; Collop worked out the sexual consequences. He wrote poems praising the beauty and desirability of one-eyed ("Thus Love and you at bo-peep play"), plump, and hunchbacked mistresses, yellow, black, and green mistresses, with a variety of dental irregularities, a whole zoo or wonder cabinet of rare mistresses. Collop must not be mistaken for a tasteless joke. The poems have a serious side and are often lovely. Every woman, we come away feeling, has a potential champion in the male libido, which like infinity knows no bounds. Herrick addresses the theme directly in "Love Dislikes Nothing." Petrarchism has become, with the help of Ovid, democratic: every woman can inspire it.

Perhaps the ache of frustration was just too sharp for the available compensations:

> Show me no more those snowy breasts,
>   With azure riverets branched,
> Where whilst mine eye with plenty feasts,
>   Yet is my thirst not stanched.
> O Tantalus, thy pains ne'er tell,
>   By me thou art prevented;
> 'Tis nothing to be plagued in Hell,
>   But thus in Heaven tormented.
>   (Drayton, "To His Coy Love," ll. 9–16)[23]

Certainly Donne, as he crosses the threshold, entwines the emotions of imperial conquest with those of religious salvation. The sexual imperatives of elegy 19 leave us with a naked pair in bed, bringing writing to the uttermost brink of doing. Donne abandons the unconsummated Petrarchan verse of the sixteenth century, which yearned for a first time but made do with lesser favors, and gestures toward the Ovidian experiments of the seventeenth century, which characteristically presuppose consummation; Carew's "A Rapture" begins with allusions to elegy 19, then devotes its main energies to a description of (by our count) the second and third times. The object Donne assaults in his notorious elegy is less a woman than a tradition of male desire, and he seeks an answerable female desire largely in order to overcome this foe. Value, the target of desire, resides for Donne in the unclothed or "dis-covered" woman: "Full nakedness, all joys are due to thee."

All joys are therefore mutual. The sundering of the speech situation in Petrarch has been undone: lovers in *The Songs and Sonnets* are characteristically face-to-face, eye-to-eye. The peculiarity of Donne's love poetry stems in part from the absence of three related themes, each of them familiar in English Petrarchism; he does not encrust the physical image of the woman with elaborate tropes, he does not register distress over the impending decay of the woman's beauty, and he is not especially interested in the usual Petrarchan way of preserving her beauty, poetic immortality. The main exception to that last remark is a telling one: in the central stanza of "The Canonization," immortality ("We die and rise the same, and prove / Mysterious by this love") is claimed for precisely the fulfillment that the Petrarchan lover, unable to enjoy, *cannot* immortalize.

In "The Canonization," as in other well-known lyrics, Donne fuses Petrarch and Ovid by presenting an exclusive devotion enjoying full sexual consummation. It is on the libertine side of his verse that we find a poet dead set, programmatically, against Petrarchism—"whining poetry," as he sneers. Donne's imagination has a Renaissance expansiveness; he thinks in terms of worlds. The libertine Donne promotes a world in which honor is but a hymen, and exclusive, jealous adoration is impossible. The indifferent can love her and her, and you and you, which sounds like Ovid exulting in his omnivorous libidinal tastes. But he adds to his model a new reservation. "I can love any, so she be not true"—so she be, in other words, as indifferent as he. The poem wishfully projects a world without exclusive enamorment, within which the unrequited love at the center of Petrarchism simply could not arise. Save for the few heretics doomed to be true to faithless lovers, the situation that generates Petrarchism will pass from the earth, and all will be rebels and atheists.[24] This is precisely the "strange" way that Wyatt did not choose.

When Shakespeare crosses the threshold, the atmosphere has a moral charge missing in Marlowe and Donne. The Petrarchan ideal is first of all, and oddly, a young gentleman. At the introduction of the dark lady, the convention takes on its customary guise, with the qualification that this woman walks on the ground, meaning in part that the poet's love for her is consummated. Simultaneously, or almost so, the idealization of the female comes into conflict with the idealization of the male: both of them cannot be as Shakespeare has figured them. Finally, the work of the couplets can no longer be sustained. His apprehension of the woman's foul untruth brings him to a self-indictment for ever having sworn her otherwise; in effect, the form of his lies, the literary impetus for his repeated experiments in self-deception, is Petrarchism. Accusation seizes the couplet: "For I have sworn thee fair: more perjured eye, / To swear against the truth so foul a lie" (152). If we cut away the two trivial cupid sonnets, Shakespeare's sequence ends with the explosion of its genre. We stand at another vantage from which literary historians may view the future becoming possible. The novel element of sexual consummation has, in its consequences, destroyed Petrarchism. The ominous note for the future is that conventions of idealization do not easily coexist with erotic satisfaction.

Petrarchan conventions, despite such attempts as Spenser's to adapt them to fulfilled and mutual love, are still most at home with unconsummated and unrequited love. It is the denying mistress who burns like ice, like fire. It is the denied lover, charged with forgetfulness, who seeks to occlude his hopelessness. When the lady consents, other conventions become appropriate—the epithalamic or the libertine— and these are prominent in the seventeenth century. But several aspects of this last phase of the love tradition retain strong continuity with the Petrarchan wellsprings. In particular, there is a new clarity about the deep logic of Petrarchism, as if the later poets, inhabiting a brave new world of sexual success, could understand the peculiar alliances among love, fame, and poetry that their predecessors negotiated, somewhat blindly, in the grip of frustration.

Shakespeare, Daniel, and Drayton, whose art came to maturity in the golden period of English love poetry, leave the impression that their varied deployment of fame arose in the midst of serious disappointment. When Sidney shows rival poets the brimming breasts of fame, and declares like a challenge in a tournament the name of Stella, he is converting sorrow into triumph. Not getting Stella is at least a winner in the competition for honors in frustration; misery loves company so that he can have a contest and be deemed the most exquisitely miserable. In seventeenth-century verse the moves in the game seem known in advance. "What shall I do to be forever known, / And make the age to come my own?" Cowley writes in "The Motto," putting us in mind of Christ's denunciation of fame in *Paradise Regained* (3.100–104), which closes with the observation that things done for the sake of fame and glory become, for that very reason, unpraised. Elsewhere Cowley presents himself as "Love's last and greatest prophet":

> Teach *me* to Love? Go teach thyself more wit;
>   I chief professor am of it.
>   Teach craft to Scots, and thrift to Jews,
>   Teach boldness to the stews;
> In tyrants' courts teach supple flattery,
> Teach Jesuits that have traveled far to lie;
>   Teach fire to burn, and winds to blow,
>   Teach restless fountains how to flow,
>   Teach the dull earth, fixed, to abide,

Teach womankind inconstancy and pride.
See if your diligence here will useful prove;
But, prithee, teach not me to love.
("The Prophet")

Cowley declares with the petulance of Donne that he has nothing to learn: seventeenth-century love poets have seen it all. The rhetoric Donne used in "Go, and catch a falling star" to evoke the alienating cynicism to which life might drive an honest man, Cowley uses to exhibit his smugness.

The moods are crasser, the rivalries less constrained by the etiquette of martial honor. Marvell, looking back to a "candid age" prior to the Civil War, noted that the ability to make fame had become self-important among his contemporaries:

That candid age no other way could tell
To be ingenious but by speaking well.
Who best could praise had then the greatest praise;
'Twas more esteemed to give then wear the bays:
Modest ambition studied only then
To honor not her self, but worthy men.
("To His Noble Friend Mr. Richard Lovelace,
upon His Poems")[25]

But the erosion had started earlier than the Civil War. In "Ingrateful Beauty Threatened," Carew tells a Petrarchan mistress that there is something in the situation she has failed to think through; she's refusing, it must be remembered, a *poet*. Like Jack Warner dressing down Bette Davis, Carew reminds his Celia that mistresses, all the Celiae and Deliae of the Renaissance lyric, are creatures of the media: I made you, I can break you. (In Cowley's "The Given Love" a straightforward deal is proposed: fame for favors.) Toward the end of Marvell's "candid age" of "modest ambition," Edmund Waller writes his astonishingly lucid "Story of Phoebus and Daphne, Applied." The complaints of a grieving youth have failed to win Saccharissa, that artificial sweetener. No cause for lamentation, for the instrumentality of love poetry, despite appearances, is no longer aimed at the stubborn beloved:

Yet what he sung in his immortal strain,
Though unsuccessful, was not sung in vain;
All, but the nymph that should redress his wrong,

179

Attend his passion, and approve his song.
Like Phoebus thus, acquiring unsought praise,
He catched at love, and filled his arms with bays.[26]

"Apollo," in other words, "hunted Daphne so, / Only that she might laurel grow." Had Waller written this couplet, it would mean that approving readers can stand in for an immune nymph. Embracing an armful of bays, the poet can do without the woman. The solitary egotism of Waller's love poet moves Petrarchism toward the hyperbolic solitude of "The Garden," whose speaker takes the divestment a step further by sacrificing not only the woman but also the ambition to wear the laurel, finding his compensation in the radically internal, Neoplatonic crown of "a green thought in a green shade."

Even at the point of sublimest mutuality in the sexiest poem of the century we find the logic by which Waller applies the key Petrarchan myth to cold ambition. Thomas Carew's "A Rapture" announces its extremity with a picture of the Petrarchan lover—indeed, it is Petrarch himself—bringing his courtship to its hitherto impossible end:

> Laura lies
> In Petrarch's learned arms, drying those eyes
> That did in such sweet smooth-paced numbers flow,
> As made the world enamored of his woe.
>
> (Ll. 139–42)

In Carew's paradise, even Petrarch finally gets some, even Laura finally puts out. Yet the fantasy addresses its own past still more searchingly. An even older frustration is undone in the preceding lines:

> Daphne hath broke her bark, and that swift foot,
> Which th'angry gods had fastened with a root
> To the fixed earth, doth now unfettered run,
> To meet th'embraces of the youthful Sun;
> She hangs upon him, like his Delphic lyre,
> Her kisses blow the old, and breath new fire:
> Full of her god, she sings inspired lays,
> Sweet odes of love, such as deserve the bays
> Which she her self was.
>
> (Ll. 131–39)

The loveliness of the conceit is the implication that the pleasure had been worth the wait and even enabled by it. Whereas Petrarch, in *Can-*

zoniere 23, elides Daphne to become the laurel himself, Carew restores
a Daphne who undergoes Petrarch's experience and becomes herself a
poet. She leaves paralysis not simply to bring pleasure to her lover,
but to confront him as a new equal, interested in mutual pleasure;
sexual gratification, at least at this level, comes in the engagement
with an other of something like one's own talents and instincts. Narcissus finds himself reflected in a person rather than a mirror. But
another motor in the fantasy is the equivalence of libido and poetic
inspiration: imagining Daphne with the one inevitably brings on the
other; she sings because she allegorically figures "the bays / Which she
her self was." Donne wrote of "concupiscence of wit," Herrick imagined himself rising in old age to cry "No lust there's like to poetry!" [27]
But when the equation becomes exact, the two can be interchanged,
as in Waller, and gratified ambition take the place of gratified sexuality.

In one of Thomas Stanley's lyrics a mistress is criticized for having
consented to sexual union, which is tantamount to being persuaded
by the poems she has inspired, and thus bestowing the laurel herself—
or indeed, upon herself:

> Was't not enough thou freely didst bestow
> The Muse, but thou wouldst give the laurel too?
> And twice my aims by thy assistance raise,
> Conferring first the merit, then the praise?
> . . . .
> Thy Muse, seeming to lend, calls home her fame,
> And her due wreath doth in renouncing claim. [28]

Ambition is the thing. At the moment of cooperation, when desires
can at last be yoked, this poet sees icy narcissism, Waller's Thyrsis in
the mistress's yielding. The crass but perceptive wit of Stanley yearns
for the old Petrarchan situation because it was, for poets, a better deal.

Poems like Waller's and Stanley's signal the end of a tradition. The
covert pacts and substitutions that gave the tradition its work, that
attracted writers able to make original statements within a prescribed
set of possibilities, that made the tradition a tradition, will usually
suffer unsubtle and unflattering exposure at the close. The end is the
beginning seen nakedly.

Petrarch found rapture in taking the image of Laura to the country-
side. Castiglione attested to the friendliness of the image. During the
late sixteenth century, the psychic transaction by which the image becomes preferable to the woman herself emerges into the open. The
poem we have in mind is "Absence, hear thou my protestation," gen-

erally ascribed to John Hoskyns, though more plausibly attributed to Donne:

> By absence this good means I gain,
>   That I can catch her
>   Where none can watch her,
> In some close corner of my brain;
>   There I embrace and kiss her,
>   And so I both enjoy and miss her.[29]

The mind's a fine and private place, and some, we think, do there embrace. The logic of this consolation reaches a typically seventeenth-century finality in a poem by the writer Marvell was defending when he railed against the vicious egotism of postwar poets, Richard Lovelace's "Love Made in the First Age: To Chloris." Here the speaker, relishing a chance to play the role of the cruel mistress, rejects the invitation of a woman who once scorned him, and vengefully prefers the joy of ravishing her image: "Crownèd with mine own soft beams, / Enjoying of myself I lie."[30] In the solitary enjoyment of his own crowning sunbeams, this Apollo has no interest in external Lauras or laurels. Petrarchism can end in what used to be called self-abuse.

By way of this pronounced tendency to replace the woman with her image, the high-minded sufferings of the earlier Petrarchan verse made a bizarre marriage with the new libertine strands of the seventeenth century.

At first glance the antipathy could not be stronger. Along with attacks on the varieties of female refusal (honor, discretion, coyness), in the libertine tradition there are self-help poems such as Carew's "Boldness in Love" and Suckling's "Why so pale and wan." Petrarchism, Carew counsels, is counterproductive; the strategy does not work. In Suckling, the speaker's arch assumption that the pale silence of the Petrarchan loser *must* be a stratagem, and as such sure to fail, neatly reinstalls self-interest as the true ideal; and the lyric ends by detaching the lover from his unobtainable object: "Nothing can make her, / The devil take her."[31] Closure, as is often the case in seventeenth-century lyrics, involves an act of imaginative violence against the tradition of Petrarch.

This plank in the libertine platform received extensive support from an unlikely quarter—Robert Burton's blistering pages on "Remedies of Love": "she is lovely, fair, well-favored, well qualified, courteous and kind: But if she be not so to me, what care I how kind she be? I say with Philostratus, beautiful to others, she is a tyrant to me, and so let her go."[32] Burton proposes numerous techniques for cooling passion's heat, among them the deliberate manipulation of the beloved's image so as to produce revulsion. These currents in the libertine tradition, with their pious antecedents in patristic literature, left a mark on *Paradise Lost*. Milton's brief evocation of the "serenade, which the starved lover sings / To his proud fair, best quitted with disdain" (4.769–70) is virtually an epitome of Suckling's "Why so pale and wan." Burton's renewed concern with the self-interested use of repulsive images can be discerned in Raphael's suggestion that Adam cure his uxoriousness by realizing that the rites he values are no more than those enjoyed by copulating animals (8.579–85). Not only male sexuality but also male vengeance gets better served in the seventeenth century.

Petrarchism may well be, remembering a Miltonic phrase in Donne's "The Ecstasy," a defect of loneliness. But it is remarkable that so many seventeenth-century love poets encountered defects of union. A hangover of postcoital depression awaited them in the new subject matter of sexual success. Ovid as literary master was not the mere inverse of Petrarch; the closer we look, the more we realize that the century did not so much shut Petrarch out as refract him. In libertine poetry, the old moral and theological critique of sexual love reappears at the level of nature: there is a curse or privation in the very design of it.

Three great poets at the beginning of the century testify to this defect. Shakespeare writes his furious, relentless sonnet on "The expense of spirit in a waste of shame" (129), which discovers the "hell" of conventional Petrarchan suffering on the other side of consummation. The mechanism of disillusionment in lustful sexuality eventually drives out the opposing mechanism of Petrarchan idealization. In his rueful "Farewell to Love," Donne records the truth that intercourse is short, depleting, dulling; one reason why the evocation of Christ's resurrection at the center of "The Canonization" should not be written off as schoolboy irreverence is Donne's likely assumption that the act *needs* redemption. Finally, Jonson lends his authority to the low estimate of sexual intercourse through his translation of *Foeda est in coitu et breuis uoluptas,* believed in the Renaissance to be the work of Petronius: "Doing a filthy pleasure is, and short, / And done, we straight repent us of the sport" (*Underwood* 88). From this perspective, all enjoyments are imperfect enjoyments.

Our species dislikes an unsolvable problem, and today we have whole industries and professions, products and gurus, devoted to the rectification of these and related design flaws. Seventeenth-century poetry also teems with pragmatic advice on this matter. Petronius, in Jonson's translation, offered this pregnant suggestion:

> Let us together closely lie, and kiss,
> There is no labor, nor no shame in this;
> This hath pleased, doth please, and long will please; never
> Can this decay, but is beginning ever.

Shameless, endlessly renewable, the kiss is the most innocent of all sexual acts, and it avoids almost entirely that weight of decay and death felt, linguistically and emotionally, in typical Renaissance descriptions of intercourse. "This hath pleased, doth please, and long will please": here is the same before/during/after structure with which Shakespeare analyzes intercourse in sonnet 129, but kissing is a pleasure in all three zones of the time frame.

Poets followed the suggestion, creating a sizeable body of kiss lyrics. It was probably from heeding Jonson's advice, backed up by several notably delicious kisses elsewhere in his songs and lyrics, that Robert Herrick became the monarch of osculation in seventeenth-century verse. The kisses even come in epochal form. Catullus numbered 3,300 of them in *Viuamus, mea Lesbia*. Kisses in seventeenth-century imitations, naturally, skyrocket to infinity:

> Blush you at this, pretty one stay,
> And I will take that kiss away.
> Thus with a second, and that too
> A third wipes off; so will we go
> To numbers that the stars out run,
> And all the atoms in the sun.
> (Thomas Randolph,
> "A Pastoral Courtship")[33]

Antifruition became a libertine topos. Some of these *paradossi,* such as Cowley's "Against Fruition," appear to be exercises on a set theme. Others bespeak an actual discipline, a program for chastening the sexual drive by confining it to fantasy. Bishop King, famous for his elegy on his wife, delivers the usual complaints with an obvious sincerity. Coition degrades love to lust and causes the lover to devalue his partner; guilt is its inevitable sequel:

Ev'n in the marriage bed, where soft delights
Are customary and authoriz'd rites,
What are those tributes to the wanton sense
But toleration of incontinence?
Nor makes it only our opinion less
Of what we liked before, and now possess,
But robs the fuel, and corrupts the spice
Which sweetens and inflames love's sacrifice.[34]

The alternative is "expectation and delay":

Give me long dreams and visions of content,
Rather than pleasures in a minute spent.
And since I know before, the shedding rose
In that same instant doth her sweetness lose,
Upon the virgin-stock still let her dwell
For me to feast my longings with her smell.

This resolve to leave the rosebuds ungathered, to live with unful-fillable images of fulfillment, supplies a regimen for the flesh comparable to the deliberate schemes of image manipulation recommended by Catholics and Protestants alike for the devotional life of the soul. Again we are reminded of Herrick. Like Ovid and Martial, Herrick tells us that "Jocund his Muse was, but his life was chaste," yet the many instances of interrupted or blocked fruition in his lyrics give us better reason to believe the Renaissance poet. Sir Thomas Browne was not the only seventeenth-century male who "could be content that we might procreate like trees, without conjunction, or that there were any way to perpetuate the world without this trivial and vulgar way of coition."[35] But, wrote the aristocratic Suckling, disposing of Browne's implication that we must, after all, perform this ridiculous act in order to procreate, "since there are enough / Born to the drudgery, what need we plough?" The restriction of sexuality to fantasy produced its own issue: brainchildren, poems of indulged erotic imagination. *Hesperides* may be the fullest record we possess of the actual practice of poetic sexual fantasy as programmatic chastity.[36]

Suckling wrote two poems entitled "Against Fruition," and the better of them, "Stay here fond youth and ask no more, be wise" (quoted above), was taken seriously enough to inspire at least two answers, by Edmund Waller and aptly named Henry Bold.[37] One might be inclined to dismiss Suckling's recommendation as wholly "playful" until, reading his neglected plays, one discovers the centrality of the nonconsummation motif.[38] In the two lyrics orgasmic disappointment is inexorable—the incarnation of our fallen condition, our severance from heaven. Beneath the jauntiness of the poems lies a conviction that the mind may be, tragically, the best bower we have in this world. "'Tis expectation makes a blessing dear: / It were not heaven, if we knew it were."[39] Having is finite, summed, just what it is: a score. Anticipation, however, is untold, incalculable, forever beckoning, and above all preserves the love object from debasement. The answers by Waller and Bold respond to the self-defeating silliness of the worm-seed advice that Suckling pours on the tail of his fond youth. If sex is not, as Browne declared, "the foolishest act a wise man commits," it is certainly the subject about which wise men are given to speak most foolishly.[40] So, Bold replies, "Go on, bold boy! and put her to't, be wise!"

The poems deserve a more reflective reply. In Suckling's hands this topos loses its oddity and reveals its stalwart allegiance to Petrarchism: at stake in the antifruition poems is the preservation of an ideal; they are obedient, in a libertine setting, to the fundamental rule of the Petrarchan tradition. The second of the lyrics, "Fie upon hearts that burn with mutual fire," inverts *carpe diem* by urging the mistress to be coy and unforthcoming, and systematically unmakes the world Donne projected in "The Indifferent" by demanding that the sexual passions of men and women never be in sync. The poems, with all their self-conscious perversity, have a nostalgia for an earlier state of the love tradition. "He that enjoys her hath no more to say" ("Against Fruition [II]"): perhaps Ovid was not such a good idea. Writing after decades of poetic assaults on Petrarchan love, Suckling here reinvents from libertine premises the Petrarchan mistress, and for the sake of ideal sexual pleasure teaches to seventeenth-century beloveds the old virtue of coyness.

Rochester, no less, was alive to the fleshly compensations of this proposal. His lyric "The Platonic Lady" shows us an antifruitional mistress laying down her rules, improving upon the usual advice of the topos by substituting infinite foreplay for infinite fantasy:

> I hate the thing is called enjoyment:
> Besides it is a dull employment,
> It cuts off all that's life and fire
> From that which may be termed desire;
> . . . .
> I love a youth will give me leave
> His body in my arms to wreathe;

To press him gently, and to kiss;
To sigh, and look with eyes that wish

. . . .

I'd give him liberty to toy
And play with me, and count it joy.
Our freedom should be full complete,
And nothing wanting but the feat.[41]

To this day, such advice has its practitioners. In the context of Renaissance love poetry, however, this mistress is training a new generation of Petrarchists with the classic gestures ("To sigh, and look with eyes that wish").

The profoundest answer to Suckling, or at least to the questions he raises for lovers, was given by Andrew Marvell. "To His Coy Mistress" opens with an infinite courtship, which is then rejected by a frantic doing in which the very shortness or hurriedness of the sexual act, the complaint of so many poet-lovers of the century, becomes its excellence in our fallen race with time.

The need to master the faults and privations at the heart of sexuality is everywhere at issue in libertine poetry. These poets want to ensure the renewability, the unending fascination, of sexual love. A bedrock fear of "aphanisis"—the term Ernest Jones coined for the disappearance of sexual desire—drives the verse.[42] Nothing is forbidden in the erotic Elisium of Carew's "A Rapture" except disinterest: "We only sin when Love's rites are not done." The exhilarating first times of *Hero and Leander* or elegy 19 are a generation away; the problem now (as Donne foresaw) is how to "die and rise *the same*," without deflating desire or its object, ready to die and rise again.[43] Carew's lyrics often end with comebacks and renewals, and he left us, appropriately, "A Second Rapture." Here, swept along a vector of debasement, he calls for "a wench about thirteen" able to "re-invite / Old decayed appetite." Restoration, provision, prevenient secular grace, a warrantee against decaying desire: all the libertine poets crave futurity, and this is the wish that, in a Suckling or a Rochester, revives for a moment repressed Petrarchism in a libertine world. The antifruition poems reposition desire on the before side of consummation. With this shift, frustration emerges once again as the ideal: frustration, be thou my pleasure! The topos we have been discussing imaginatively reclaims the innocence that the first wave of English Renaissance Petrarchism was written largely in the hope of losing.

These are the things we see as the *Canzoniere* is refracted at the end of the glory days of Renaissance lyric. The enthrallment of the poet to

his mistress—apparently absolute in Petrarch—is loosened in ways
adumbrated by Petrarch. Love poetry gets written because its authors
love, but also because they seek fame, or the power of bestowing *aes-
timatiua*. Artistic and sexual ambitions are interchangeable; they can
be substituted for each other in the course of reaching countless bar-
gains. A solitude stocked with images may be preferable to having an
amorous partner. The value of postponement, hedonistic as well as
moral, is considerable. In a very small corner of the record we see the
playful but serious concession that orgasm, though it fulfills, is solitary, poor, nasty, brutish, and short—indeed, is all of that precisely
because it *is* a limit, and therefore fulfills; a major element in the complaints of these male poets about the imperfections of sexual intercourse is an intolerance for the satiety that does indeed follow upon
it. Some of the poets say, and others imply: we prefer forepleasure to
endpleasure precisely because the former has the structure of knowledge, fame, wealth, and power, and permits infinite aggrandizement.
The age had its style.

Before turning to Milton, we might stop, as many of our predecessors have, simply to acknowledge the sheer peculiarity of human
sexuality. The reinvention of Petrarchan frustration from Ovidian
premises may be an absurd folly, correctly diagnosed by the Bolds of
this world, but the antifruition topos also concedes, like Petrarchism
in its entirety, an authentic waywardness in male sexual passion. In his
essay "The Most Prevalent Form of Degradation in Erotic Life"—one
especially pertinent to the aspects of Renaissance lyric examined
here—Freud opposes the idea that satisfaction engenders degradation
in all the spheres of our desire. Sexual passion and its objects are
uniquely fragile:

> But is it also true that with the satisfaction of an instinct its psychical value
> always falls just as sharply? Consider, for example, the relation of a drinker
> to wine. Is it not true that wine always provides the drinker with the same
> toxic satisfaction, which in poetry has so often been compared to erotic
> satisfaction—a comparison acceptable from the scientific point of view as
> well? Has one ever heard of the drinker being obliged constantly to change
> his drink because he soon grows tired of the same one? On the contrary,
> habit constantly tightens the bond between a man and the kind of wine he
> drinks. Does one ever hear of a drinker who needs to go to a country
> where wine is dearer or drinking is prohibited, so that by introducing
> obstacles he can reinforce the dwindling satisfaction that he obtains? Not
> at all. If we listen to what our great alcoholics, such as Böcklin, say about
> their relation to wine, it sounds like the most perfect harmony, a model of

a happy marriage. Why is the relation of the lover to his sexual object so very different?

It is my belief that, however strange it may sound, we must reckon with the possibility that something in the nature of the sexual instinct itself is unfavorable to the realization of complete satisfaction. (*SE* 11:188–89)[44]

This wise and humorous passage, which should interest future annotators of Herrick's sack poems, might even serve as a preface to the Renaissance love lyric itself. Freud asks us to reckon with the possibility that complete and unequivocal satisfaction of sexual desire is an impossible attainment, that (in the terms of our discussion) sexuality *does* have the Renaissance character of our other ambitions. Thus we congenital foreplayers protect desire and its object against mutual disillusionment by constructing obstacles between them. Fantasy, poetry itself, may be among these obstacles. We love the not-yet-overcome. There is something Petrarchan in our souls. The barriers we erect to what Milton calls in *Paradise Lost* "Casual fruition" (4.767) are in Freud's view a topos of the unconscious, whose beloveds are images, not realities, and whose ideal is mere desire, not its end in satisfaction.

Despite the many objects of desire celebrated in Renaissance poetry, we end this chapter as we began it, impressed by the protean force of the instinct.

TEN

Lust Captured:
Paradise Lost and
Renaissance Love Poetry

What do poets want? As a Cambridge undergraduate, Milton had already assimilated the Renaissance answer. The happiness of learning in general comes from expanding lifetime to the limits of all history:

> This, my hearers, is to live in every period of the world's history, and to be as it were coeval with time itself. And indeed, while we look to the future for the glory of our name, this will be to extend and stretch our lives backward before our birth, and to wrest from grudging Fate a kind of retrospective immortality. I pass over a pleasure with which none can compare—to be the oracle of many nations, to find one's home regarded as a kind of temple, to be a man whom kings and states invite to come to them, whom men from near and far flock to visit, while to others it is a matter for pride if they have but set eyes on him once. These are the rewards of study, these are the prizes which learning can and often does bestow upon her votaries in private life. (Prolusion 7, *Prose Works,* 1:297)

The blend of influences in this young man was nothing short of uncanny, as if he had already cultivated the ability to see his age from the perspective of the future. This passage is embedded in an argument congruent with Pico's *Oration;* man thirsts to know, and God will not tantalize him, lest the creator "seem to have endowed us to no purpose, or even to our distress, with this soul which is capable and indeed insatiably desirous of the highest wisdom" (1:291). The "universal learning" we seek includes Baconian science. That will not, however, be power enough. Man brooks no confinement:

So at length, my hearers, when universal learning has once completed its cycle, the spirit of man, no longer confined within this dark prison-house, will reach out far and wide, till it fills the whole world and the space far beyond with the expansion of its divine greatness. Then at last most of the chances and changes of the world will be so quickly perceived that to him who holds this stronghold of wisdom hardly anything can happen in his life which is unforeseen or fortuitous. He will indeed seem to be one whose rule and dominion the stars obey, to whose command earth and sea hearken, and whom winds and tempests serve; to whom, lastly, Mother Nature herself has surrendered, as if indeed some god had abdicated the throne of the world and entrusted its rights, laws, and administration to him as governor. (1:296)[1]

Here, almost two centuries later, is the deified creature of Ficino and Pico. God has given him his own attributes, a "divine greatness," then gotten out of his way. The preeminence that belongs to the species can be enjoyed by those timely-happy individuals who win undying fame, "the pleasure with which none can compare." One trusts the professor was pleased. The breeding program had finally paid off: humanism's ideal student.

Humanism had also dreamed of training great princes and states-men. If the regard of kings and commonwealths figures in the "re-wards" of celebrity, would it not be better to succeed in that league? Is not the language of Milton's passage on fame metaphorical, trans-ferred to learning's "private life" from its roots in worldly power? Milton does not deny this, though he insists, ambivalently, that the metaphor excels the fact:

What, then, of public life? It is true that few have been raised to the height of majesty through a reputation for learning, and not many more through a reputation for uprightness. Such men certainly enjoy a kingdom in them-selves far more glorious than any earthly dominion; and who can lay claim to a twofold sovereignty without incurring the charge of ambition? I will, however, add this one thing more: that there have hitherto been but two men who have ruled the whole world, as by divine right, and shared an empire over all kings and princes equal to that of the gods themselves; namely Alexander the Great and Augustus, both of whom were students of philosophy. It is as though Providence had specially singled them out as examples to humanity, to show to what sort of man the helms or reins of government should be entrusted. (1:297)

We are quoting from an academic exercise on a set theme, where one expects to find polemical extravagance, but, even by Renaissance standards, this is a remarkable endorsement of humanist imperialism. A man cannot expect to wear two crowns without suffering the charge of ambition. The desire to wear one crown, apparently, does not count as ambition. The inner kingdom of knowledge is certainly the more magnificent one. Then again, our worldly rulers ought to be chosen from learned men, which is why God gave us the examples of Alexander and Augustus. A great deal happened to this student before he wrote the poem that occupies us in this chapter. We shall not hear again of man as a Piconian magus, or the "divine right" of imperialism. But it is suggestive of some continuity that Milton should have published this undergraduate effusion in the final year of his life.

This poet got what he wanted. Today a sizable body of intellectuals call themselves Miltonists, and they boast it an honorable distinction merely to have had a single glimpse of what he meant by a two-handed engine. In the course of his career, Milton was allowed to strive for both of the crowns. But the centerpiece of his fame is, of course, the Protestant epic *Paradise Lost*, which is "coeval with time itself," stretched between the limits of creation and apocalypse: and beyond, *plus ultra* yet once more. It simply seizes, by the huge self-confessed force of its scope and ambition, the laurels pursued with such dedication by the poets of its age. Milton is to that crown "As is the aspray to the fish, who takes it / By sovereignty of nature" (*Coriolanus* 4.7.34–35). Petrarch's posthumous fame was largely inadvertent; he wanted to be remembered, not as the love-struck victim of the *Canzoniere*, but as the author of an epic as great as Homer's and Vergil's. Few readers, now or then, have thought the *Africa* close. From the beginning, a major frustration in the cultural designs of Renaissance humanism was its inability to field worthy competition for classical literature in epic, obviously the major genre.[2] But Milton, as he himself put it, was one "who would not be frustrate of his hope to write well hereafter in laudable things" (*Prose Works*, 1:890). By filling that gap, and filling it at the end of the somewhat belated Renaissance in England, Milton eventually earned his fame. He concludes the period, and not just chronologically.

Because of Milton, the story works out. Periods tend to begin with fiery manifestoes and model artistic triumphs. They generally end, however, in pastische and formalism, or in the sort of literature discussed at the conclusion of the previous chapter: striking moves that clarify a tradition, but in their apparent finality do not immediately regenerate it. Without *Paradise Lost*, the usual rule would hold true more than we like to admit, and many professors would spend the last weeks of the Renaissance survey course talking about how the vital achievements of Sidney, Spenser, Shakespeare, Donne, and Jonson wind up precious and prettified in the mannerisms of Carew, Herrick, Cowley, Davenant, Cleveland, Vaughan, Crashaw, and Marvell. Instead, the humanism and Protestantism mingling in England at last produced someone as learned, ambitious, and fame-conscious as Petrarch.[3] He comes at the end, not the beginning, and he made the age itself into the kind of story he liked to tell: a story with new energy at the end. It is the plot framing "Lycidas," but dilated from small to great. The epic stands complete. Tomorrow to fresh woods and pastures new.

Like all works of art, *Paradise Lost* is infinitely organizable and can be described with profit from any number of viewpoints. Milton's canniness about tradition, the survival of his youthful devotion to inexhaustible knowledge, invites us to be more painstaking about our descriptions than usual, for most of our viewpoints are in some fashion represented within the poem; epics, and Milton's in particular, tend to find a place for everything. Critics have recognized that Milton uses the narrative positions opened to him during the course of his "great Argument" to evoke varieties of poetic love, making literary conventions into moral revelations. Thus the famous lyric hailing "wedded love" at the close of book 4 offers the epithalamion as the speech act appropriate to the first instance of human love, and this "elect" genre is often contrasted with the "Cavalier" seductions of the devil's early speeches to Eve in book 9, which isolate for praise her singularity while denigrating her "wedded" relationship.[4] But we want to argue that Milton's *agôn* with love poetry is considerably richer and more extensive than these familiar observations suggest.

The task of determining how the poem looks from the viewpoint of Renaissance Petrarchism receives some initial encouragement because its excellence, when compared to prior epics of the period, arises in a substantial way from its solution to the problem of what to do with the love story. Through the main line of Renaissance epic experimentation—*Orlando Furioso, Gerusaleme Liberata, The Faerie Queene*—Petrarch's avatars had sidled toward a fusion of love and heroism in the appropriate Renaissance form of dynastic ambition.[5] But the end reveals the incompleteness of their solutions. *Paradise Lost* is the first and last epic since the *Odyssey* to render its love story both genuine enough to move us and heroic enough to instruct us. The explorations of cosmic space and time in the poem invariably return to the proving ground of a marriage; the themes of a lofty poem all come down to, exert pressure on, this marriage; in the end its wisdom has been compressed into the clasped hands of Adam and Eve, again together on the guided quest for a new bower. Milton's epic stands as a consummate expression of the love tradition, at once a tribute to its wisdom and a commentary on its treacheries.

Love in the 1645 *Poems* is in certain obvious ways subordinate to the subject of male friendship. Yet, as Milton tells us when recounting the contribution of literature to his sexual virtue in *An Apology*, he above all "preferred the two famous renowners of Beatrice and Laura who never write but honor of them to whom they devote their verse, displaying sublime and pure thoughts, without transgression" (*Prose Works*, 1:890). "Famous renowners": a complex phrase, knowingly attuned to the deep structure of Petrarchan verse, into which Dante has been subsumed; the appeal to "honor," and its association with unconsummated love, is similarly deft. This sentence alone informs us that Petrarchism has reached into the man's imagination, not to mention his conduct. And indeed, the volume of 1645 does contain a brief sonnet sequence written in Italian, including a fifteen-line "Canzone," in which we find, sure enough, a laurel crown. Young people of both sexes ask the love-struck poet why he is writing in Italian; on another and English river, they assure him, "the immortal guerdon, the crown of unfading leaves, is already sprouting for your head."[6] Even laymen realize that the crown, *L'immortal guiderdon d'eterne frondi,* is the thing love poets would pluck.

The nexus of love, fame, and crown reappears in the first movement of "Lycidas":

> Were it not better done as others use,
> To sport with Amaryllis in the shade,
> Or with the tangles of Neaera's hair?
> Fame is the spur that the clear spirit doth raise
> (That last infirmity of noble mind)
> To scorn delights, and live laborious days;
> But the fair guerdon when we hope to find,
> And think to burst out into sudden blaze,
> Comes the blind Fury with th'abhorred shears,
> And slits the thin-spun life. But not the praise,
> Phoebus replied, and touched my trembling ears;
> Fame is no plant that grows on mortal soil.
>
> (67–78)

Now, suddenly, we see the depths of that ideal student, who does not belong to humanism alone. Fame is the spur, as in Petrarchism, compensating hardworking poets for denied love. But in Milton sexual success and poetic immortality have fallen into perfect opposition. Instead of pursuing the first and settling for the second, like the wooer of Saccharissa in Waller's "Story of Phoebus and Daphne, Applied," the clear spirits of "Lycidas" choose fame from the very beginning and do not woo anybody. The Petrarchan poet is compounded with the Petrarchan mistress in the figure of a fame-seeking male refusing the tempting seductions of Amaryllis and Neaera: this poetic identity can be observed in the Daphne-like Lady of *Comus,* resistor of Comus's poetry of seduction.[7] Furies that conventionally torment unrequited lovers now strike against the lust for fame; unrequited fame, not love, is the cruelty that must be interpreted in the first third of "Lycidas." With the lesson of Apollo, immortality in the hereafter saves the motivational structure of fame. This *translatio* even retains the key image of Petrarchism. For Milton's "fair guerdon" almost certainly means "laurel crown" ("Canzone"'s *L'immortal guiderdon*), an interpretation that links this passage to the opening line of the elegy, and makes good sense of the first words of Phoebus, whose frustrated desire produced the original laurel: "Fame is *no plant* that grows on mortal soil." There is more than one vision of heaven in "Lycidas." The first vision, however, is keyed to the attitudes of humanist fame-consciousness.

Love is by and large a postponed subject for the early Milton, in art as well as life. Yet if the fair singer celebrated in his Italian sonnets was not, after all, much of an inspiration, his brief Petrarchan fever signals the future—another of the youthful possibilities reworked intriguingly in *Paradise Lost.* We have a foretaste of his mature disposition toward the postponed subject in a mythological flight from *The Doctrine and Discipline of Divorce:*

> Love, if he be not twin-born, yet hath a brother wondrous like him, called Anteros: whom while he seeks all about, his chance is to meet with many false and faining desires that wander singly up and down in his likeness. By them in their borrowed garb, Love, though not wholly blind, as poets wrong him, yet having but one eye, as being born an archer aiming, and that eye not the quickest in this dark region here below, which is not Love's proper sphere, partly out of the simplicity and credulity which is native to him, often deceived, embraces and consorts him with these obvious and suborned striplings, as if they were his mother's own sons, for so he thinks them, while they subtly keep themselves most on his blind side. But after

a while, as his manner is, when soaring up into the high tower of his *apogaeum,* above the shadow of the earth, he darts out the direct rays of his then most piercing eyesight upon the impostures and trim disguises that were used with him, and discerns that this is not his genuine brother, as he imagined; he has no longer the power to hold fellowship with such a personated mate. For straight his arrows lose their golden heads, and shed their purple feathers; his silken braids untwine, and slip their knots; and that original and fiery virtue given him by Fate all on a sudden goes out and leaves him undeified, and despoiled of all his force: till finding Anteros at last, he kindles and repairs the almost faded ammunition of his deity by the reflection of a coequal and homogeneal fire. . . . this is a deep and serious verity, showing us that Love in marriage cannot live nor subsist, unless it be mutual; and where love cannot be, there can be left of wedlock nothing but the empty husk of an outside matrimony as undelightful and unpleasing to God as any other kind of hypocrisy. (*Prose Works,* 2:254–56)

Taking hints from classical sources, Milton crafts a myth similar to the ones in *Areopagitica* about moral epistemology, where Psyche culls the almost indistinguishable seeds of good and evil (*Prose Works,* 2:514) and Christians search like Isis for pieces of the dismembered body of Truth (2:549). In all three cases, someone confronts a large array of almost identical objects, within which, nonetheless, a tremendous difference exists. It is easy to make an error—in this instance, an error in courtship. Here the almost identical objects are all the people one might love enough to marry. The "deep and serious verity" concerns the tremendous difference: it is not just a matter of knowing who to love, but who loves you back; if love is not mutual, it is not love. In the highest love, married love, we seek Anteros, a brotherly companion or soul mate returning our own love "by the reflection of a coequal and homogeneal fire." Milton's emphasis on mutuality belongs to the tradition of Protestant literature (tracts, sermons, commentaries, casuistry, books of domestic advice) on married life.[8]

Marriage has internalized the theme of male friendship in the early poems. Like other seventeenth-century poets, Milton will programmatically turn aside from the anguish of unrequited love, and he will also pass through the barrier of nonconsummation. But on the other side of the barrier for Milton, uniquely (with the exception of Spenser) among the poets studied in the previous chapter, sexual love enters wholly into the sphere of marriage. In *Paradise Lost* adjectives like "matron," "nuptial," and "conjugal" control nouns like "lip," "embrace," and "kiss." Carew alludes to "Love's rites" in "A Rapture." Milton sanctifies the commonplace in "the rites / Mysterious of connubial love" (4.742–43). His epic captures the lust of Renaissance poetry for a Protestant conception of married life.

As in the companion myths about morality and truth, Eros commits errors. Milton has him fly up to the heavens to gain the clearsightedness that can tell Anteros from his many look-alikes; it seems more likely that he would discover the difference up close. How can one tell if he is loved back without first loving? It almost requires marriage to separate true love from false. Once Eros realizes his mistake, "he has no power to hold fellowship," and "that original and fiery virtue" dies out, leaving him "undeified and despoiled of all his force": the errors have sexual consequences. Adam and Eve are made for each other in *Paradise Lost*. Yet they suffer the disillusionment that is, for their author, the threat in any marriage. Some days before that, at the very beginning, they also have a brief but highly meaningful courtship.

Alexander Ross observed that Browne was wrong about the inherent foolishness of the sexual act, because God himself had sculpted the genitals of man and woman (in one stroke).[9] *Paradise Lost* is also happy, in the main, with the gift of sexuality: God made it right, following, with certain modifications, a design he had already worked out in the creation of the angels. Yet those loving angels also inform us that human sexuality is not perfect in the sense of final; a still more perfect sexual congress exists in heaven. Adam and Eve, had they not fallen, would gradually have acquired the spiritual bodies of the angels, and in this sense the Fall was an erotic loss as well. The epic sounds a faint echo of the disappointment with intercourse so widespread in seventeenth-century verse. It might be better to say that Milton interprets this disappointment.

At the end of book 8, Adam finally brings himself to ask Raphael how they do it, if they do it, in heaven. He nervously overexplains, wondering if maybe angels just look at each other, or mix the beams of their auras, or maybe really touch. The truth turns out to be deeper than this. Adam's sexual imagination is limited by *the* limit, the boundary that sexuality repeatedly explores: flesh. Sex as we know it is a friction of surfaces. During the vogue for Lucretius in the late seventeenth century, Dryden translated his powerful vision of the futility of sexual love:

> As he, who in a dream with drought is cursed,
> And finds no real drink to quench his thirst;
> Runs to imagined lakes his heat to steep,
> And vainly swills and labors in his sleep;

So Love with phantoms cheats our longing eyes,
Which hourly seeing never satisfies;
Our hands pull nothing from the parts they strain,
But wander o'er the lovely limbs in vain;
Nor when the youthful pair more closely join,
When hands in hands they lock, and thighs in thighs they twine,
Just in the raging foam of full desire,
When both press on, both murmur, both expire,
They grip, they squeeze, their humid tongues they dart,
As each would force their way to t'other's heart:
In vain; they only cruise about the coast,
For bodies cannot pierce, nor be in bodies lost:
As sure they strive to be, when both engage,
In that tumultuous momentary rage;
So 'tangled in the nets of love they lie,
Till man dissolves in that excess of joy.
Then, when the gathered bag has burst its way,
And ebbing tides the slackened nerves betray,
A pause ensues: and Nature nods a while,
Till with recruited rage new spirits boil;
And then the same vain violence returns;
With flames renewed the erected furnace burns,
Again they in each other would be lost,
But still by adamantine bars are crossed;
All ways they try, successless all they prove,
To cure the secret sore of lingering love.[10]

Erotic disposition may change somewhat from age to age. It is our impression that during the nineteenth century, with its interest in vampires and mesmerism, men characteristically feared the dissolution of individual boundary in sexual situations. The contrary fear predominates in the sexual literature of the Renaissance. In Lucretius, the central fantasy of the sexual act, the desire for bodily merger, turns out to be a cheat. The boundaries are impermeable. Similarly, one recurrent charge in the anti-orgasm poems of the seventeenth century is the feeling of depleted isolation that follows climax; the abrupt return from fantasies of transcendent union to customary distinctness appears to have been a source of melancholy. In this respect, if our speculations have merit, Milton's is a Renaissance heaven.

God has solved the problem Lucretius defined. Raphael reveals that when good angels copulate, they mingle all the way:

Whatever pure thou in the body enjoy'st
(And pure thou wert created) we enjoy
In eminence, and obstacle find none
Of membrane, joint, or limb, exclusive bars:
Easier than air with air, if spirits embrace,
Total they mix, union of pure with pure
Desiring; nor restrained conveyance need
As flesh to mix with flesh, or soul with soul.
                    (8.622–29)

For Milton, love radiates from spiritual companionship. The fantasy of perfect sexuality extends the soul-mating of Eros and Anteros to the body, allowing the desire for "union of pure with pure" to be fulfilled. Love as the angels know it is a mixture of depths, a relief from solitude. The loving angels become each other with no trace, suggestively, of a dread of lost autonomy.

The mutuality of human love receives sincere celebration in the poem. Adam and Eve are not tantalized or frustrated by their rites in the manner of the driven couple in Lucretius. However, like all writing about sexual love, Milton's has its own fantasy structure, a *way* in which sex is right. The crux of Adam and Eve's sexual connection is a cunningly and poetically imagined version of the dominant sexual fantasy of the Renaissance or, if that is too provincial, of the dominant sexual fantasy of Western culture from the Romans to this day, so pervasive and so enmeshed in cultural symbols that to many people it has looked like nature, with little or nothing of the fantastic about it. Moreover, Milton presents this fantasy so as to guard his garden sexuality, not only from hypocrites who feel that this particular beast should not be there, but also from the libertine melancholy that fell so heavily on the love poetry of his day.[11]

In rough and ready form the fantasy, as well as its major metaphors, is already there in Ovid. It is slowed down into a ritual, given rules and a code of minute gestures, by the Christian tradition of courtly love. It is central to Petrarch, who dwells on myths of dangerous chase—the ill fates of Daphne and Actaeon. The fantasy passed down through the centuries is venery, the love hunt. Men chase, women flee. Men aggressively manifest their interest. Women are coy, demur, hard-to-get, which is to say, undeclared, ambiguous. When the fantasy is successfully realized, there comes a turning, a sign from the woman that she will yield by gradual degrees and the two desires will be as one, declared equally and simultaneously in sexual activity—the moment dramatized with such pungency in *Hero and Leander*, where the turning coincides with the sexualization of resistance. The fantasy has its inverse, as when Corinna comes at noon to Ovid or the special lady stalks Wyatt in his chambers. But the impressed male's thankfulness implies that such gifts are, indeed, breaks with routine.

This is the erotic scenario Milton activates when, outdoing his predecessors, he narrates in the person of Eve the first first time. The threshold-crossing act is, of course, a simultaneous double loss of virginity, still considered in many quarters the ideal initiation. Milton's may be the most reflective, even philosophical account of courtship in all of Renaissance literature. For the story of how Eve lost her virginity turns upon the psychological and metaphysical status of her own image. Beginning in primitive form as the captivating shape that pleases in the pool, Eve's image of herself goes through an astonishing series of intellectual metamorphoses, as if Milton were creating a new genre for this occasion—Ovidian wisdom literature. Here is the voice of God breaking into Eve's vain rapture:

> What thou seest,
> What there thou seest fair creature is thyself,
> With thee it came and goes: but follow me
> And I will bring thee where no shadow stays
> Thy coming, and thy soft embraces, he
> Whose image thou art, him thou shalt enjoy
> Inseparably thine, and to him shalt bear
> Multitudes like thyself, and thence be called
> Mother of human race.
>
> (4.467–75)

God ends Eve's ignorant and therefore innocent romance with her image by first imparting to her the unmistakably Platonic concept of the mirror image. From this primal idea others are born. The future opens. Eve is led by imaginative foreshadowing to him whose image *she* is, different from the mirror image in that this one can be embraced as a sexual and spiritual partner: Anteros. The embrace, the dialectic of the flesh, will disseminate her image in "Multitudes like thyself." In dilating the concept of the image, God has moved from mirror to mother, arriving thereby at the concept of Eve: the voice is reflecting her in a mirror of knowledge. God's speech concludes with the most sophisticated of the images of Eve—what she will be called, "Mother of human race," the definitive epithet forever to be coupled with her proper name. The final promise is her fame. As Milton, in creating Adam and Eve, places the lust of Renaissance love poetry within marriage, he locates the twin subject of Renaissance fame-consciousness within the family.[12]

"Invisibly thus led," self-knowledge being the route to sexual knowledge, Eve sees Adam and the love hunt is off and running. She turns and flees. Adam gives chase. The narrative itself is now mirroring the romance at the pool, where Eve also "started back" and "soon returned." Adam calls out to his skittish mate, mirroring the voice of God. But whereas the divine speaker reflected in his invisible mirror the image of Eve, the voice of the male, "he / Whose image thou art," reflects himself:

> Return fair Eve,
> Whom fly'st thou? Whom thou fly'st, of him thou art,
> His flesh, his bone; to give thee being I lent
> Out of my side to thee, nearest my heart
> Substantial life, to have thee by my side
> Henceforth an individual solace dear;
> Part of my soul I seek thee, and thee claim
> My other half.
>
> (4.481–88)

"Me" is the answer to his initial question, but a "me" whose essence is relatedness to "thee," his "other half." Whereupon her hand is gently seized, and the transition from repulsion to welcome that Marlowe represented in rocking bodies Milton renders in a play of hands. Seizure becomes clasp: "with that thy gentle hand / Seized mine, I yielded" (4.488–89). We are not told much about the reasons for her flight, only her sudden fear in the presence of Adam's angular body, "Less winning soft, less amiably mild, / Than that smooth watery image" (4.479–80). Because she must know at this point that the image was of her own form, Adam's rival in the courtship of Eve is Eve herself.

The narrative ends with a passage commonly subjected to misinterpretation:

> I yielded, and from that time see
> How beauty is excelled by manly grace
> And wisdom, which alone is truly fair.
>
> (4.489–91)

She is telling us just what she has been enabled to "see" after all these image lessons, and there is nothing in her conclusions that need disturb a modern liberal mind. "Manly" modifies "grace," but not "wisdom." Wisdom is something separate from manly grace, though joined with it in their shared superiority to physical beauty; the true fairness of wisdom summarizes all the substitutions for the image in the pool. Beauty is excelled by manly grace. Eve is simply noting what her yielding meant, telling Adam that he is preferable as a love object to his rival, that she is, in other words, heterosexual. And beauty, once again, is also excelled by wisdom, as in the intellectual sense given to the verb "see" in this very passage. Wisdom led her from the beautiful image in the pool, and again detached her from that image, thus bringing her story to "I yielded," when reborn in the invisible voice of Adam calling out behind her. Wisdom, which is linguistic and invisible, conceptual rather than perceptible, is a higher-order beauty, alone *truly* fair, because truth is not an image but a knowing and, for the speaker of these words, was first of all a knowing *of* a beautiful image.

Having told her tale and summed her wisdom, Eve proceeds to act out its happy ending, replaying her courtship:

So spake our general mother, and with eyes
Of conjugal attraction unreproved,
And meek surrender, half embracing leaned
On our first father, half her swelling breast
Naked met his under the flowing gold
Of her loose tresses hid: he in delight
Both of her beauty and submissive charms
Smiled with superior love, as Jupiter
On Juno smiles, when he impregns the clouds
That shed May flowers; and pressed her matron lip
With kisses pure.

(4.492–502)

The passage is strongly marked by the love poetry of the seventeenth century. Eve's "loose tresses" reflect the usual taste among his contemporaries, most famously declared in Lovelace's "To Amarantha. That she would dishevel her hair" and the picture in Marvell's "The Gallery" that "likes me best": "A tender shepherdess, whose hair / Hangs loosely playing in the air." Milton is competing with the verse of "Bacchus and his revellers" (7.33): the enticement of loose tresses has never before, to our knowledge, been heightened by the invisible promise of a swelling breast.

Above all there is Milton's contribution to his century's pronounced obsession with lyrical kisses. How will our great-grandparents kiss? What will a kiss be so close to our creator, and so in tune with his designs? Milton, possibly alone among English Renaissance poets, who are of course known for their extraordinary ingenuity in metaphor, unearths the conceit of a kiss that impregnates. Drawn from the *Georgics,* the simile of Jove and Juno is stitched in between smiling and kissing. Because "matron" signifies "a married woman considered as having expert knowledge in matters of childbirth, pregnancy, etc." (*OED*), the schema of the simile is realized or brought to fruition in Eve's matronly reception of Adam's mouth, accepting his print as the paper does the press. The kiss anticipates us, posterity, by symbolizing the act through which they will win their forthcoming fame as mother and father of all mankind. Sexuality in Eden has been enjoined as fruitfulness, and this commandment inheres, as pleasure, in the very nerve ends of eroticism. In libertine literature, the sexual act is isolated or decontextualized; poets assess the relative merits of forepleasure and endpleasure. Milton's portrait of Adam and Eve links forepleasure to endpleasure, and endpleasure to the fame of making a family, founding a race. The ambition sanctified in *Paradise Lost* is the Renaissance fusion of parenthood with the humanist cult of literary immortality.

Man chases, woman yields. Throughout book 4 we find variations on the dynamic of their courtship. When Satan first glimpses Eve "with native honor clad" (289), she has adopted the erotic attitude she learned in the beginning—subjection, submission, yielding. Drawing out his syntax, Milton seems driven to become more and more precise about the logic of their erotic bond:

> Subjection, but required with gentle sway,
> And by her yielded, by him best received,
> Yielded with coy submission, modest pride,
> And sweet reluctant amorous delay.
>
> (4.308–11)

Coy submission—a red-flag word in seventeenth-century poetry, and we are reading, it is appropriate to remember here, Andrew Marvell's employer. Eve has learned something from those moments in the libertine tradition that unexpectedly affirm the erotic value of modesty and withholding. In her yielding, there is a pretense of refusal, an evocation of the Platonic Lady. A fluid coupling of three perfect adjectives charges the word "delay" with considerable libidinal power.[13] Reluctant to be amorous? Reluctant to delay? In either case it is sweet. Apparently they play this slowpoke game of chasing and yielding, sweetening the day, but postpone consummation until the night: as at the end of book 4, sex is the last thing they do, the pleasure that crowns the working day and discharges the energy built up through sweet reluctant amorous delaying.

A naked man and woman arise in the morning, intermix the duties of the day with flirtatious venery, then consummate their love at night with a real capture, a real yielding, and go to sleep. This is paradise. It depends upon the wise management of temptation. In Milton's literature of temptation, an offer, if successfully resisted, will eventually be given as a reward in a higher and transmuted form.[14] His sexual imagination was of a piece with his moral vision—patient resistance in the service of ideal consummation. In the rhythm of paradisal eroticism, as in the rhythm of sacred history, all is "ever best found in the close" (*Samson Agonistes*, l. 1748). At our entrance into Eden in *Paradise Lost* we are introduced to an established sexual relationship, as in Carew's "A Rapture." But in place of the voluptuous décor that surrounds sexual renewal in Carew's poem we find instead a drama of delay in which Adam and Eve restage each day, as reliable foreplay, the chase-capture-yielding of the first time. Sexuality is integrated into life, delight to labor joined. And as in Milton generally, origins are conclusive. In his representation of the ideal sexual life on earth, virginity is symbolically always being lost, and every time is as the first time. Eve will not, at day's end, turn away, coyer than she is submissive:

> nor turned I ween
> Adam from his fair spouse, nor Eve the rites
> Mysterious of connubial love refused.
>
> (4.741–43)

The text says that Adam did not turn from Eve, and Eve did not refuse, but it may be lawful to speculate that she might have turned away, as she did in the beginning, only to return in answerable style.

"Sweet reluctant amorous delay" is Milton's excellent contribution to the problem of how to enjoy another sexually and not, afterward, suffer the rebound of degradation—a bulwark against boredom, disinterest, depletion, depression, lovelessness, all of the curses and deprivations that, in Renaissance lyrics, constitute sexuality's brush with the Fall. Milton understood the erotic importance of the barrier. In his

Eden, coyness and delay protect love by incorporating an obstacle into a sexual life of satisfied consummation. Antifruition sets up happy fruition.

This surely was Milton's goal, as can be learned from observing what he has done with the three major myths of the Petrarchan tradition—the love chase of Apollo and Daphne, the disastrous love-at-first-sight of Actaeon and Diana, and the suicidal love of Narcissus: all three myths of nonconsummation, of unfulfilled love and thwarted chase.

Milton subsumes Narcissus and Apollo/Daphne into the narrative of love's genesis, giving even the myths of the barrier a place in his representation of fulfillment. There were two threats to the primal mating. Eve might have fixed her eyes forever on the image, but God intervenes to the break the Narcissus spell; like Daphne, she might never have consented to capture, but the voice of Adam intervenes to break the Daphne spell. Furthermore, as we have, along with many other critics, suggested, Eve's birth narrative is bound in several ways to Sin's, where the Narcissus myth appears *in malo*. Like Eve, Satan first recoiled from his "perfect image" (2.764), then "Becamest enamored." Eventually Sin conceived, "such joy" he took with her "in secret" (765–66). We are not told how many times this secret joy was taken, but the most imaginative guess would be only once. For Sin is the prototype of the degraded love object. The next time Satan sees her she is literally debased, as if she were the archetype of Lear's woman, her nether parts a hellish kennel, and he cannot bear to recognize her. Myths implode upon this victim of decay. Her unchaste, monstrously fertile womb suffers the fate of Actaeon, hounded by his own dogs. Irksome disappointment, pining always with vain desire, is the demonic fate in *Paradise Lost*. Satan, we are told in the hymn to wedded love, "bids abstain" (4.748). Inverting the usual vision of the Christian cosmos, the poem shows us sex in Heaven and its deprivation in Hell.

The rebel angels, then, have been cursed with the frustration of Petrarchan love. Indeed, exclusion from sexuality has become one of the engines of their ambition. Satan, who turns aside in rage at the sight of Adam and Eve kissing, is stunned by her beauty in book 9. For one abstracted moment, he is in love with her. The "terror . . . in love" (490) he names in his ensuing soliloquy is the desire to serve and adore; love threatens to undermine autarchic selfhood when "not approached by stronger hate" (491). The emotional alchemy through which he distills the "fierce hate" to remake himself begins with the catalyst of frustration; by the end of the process, the sexual excitement denied relief has been transferred to the destructive plots of his hatred:

> But the hot hell that always in him burns,
> Though in mid heaven, soon ended his delight,
> And tortures him now more, the more he sees
> Of pleasure not for him ordained: then soon
> Fierce hate he recollects, and all his thoughts
> Of mischief, gratulating, thus excites.
>
>   (9.467–72)

Implicit in the way Milton has apportioned Petrarchan myths and motifs lies a redemptive polemic against frustration.

Human sexuality does not result in Eve's degradation in the eyes of her husband, but rather the opposite, as he informs Raphael when seeking counsel on this matter in book 8. Adam's problem bears upon the social meaning of the chase and capture fantasy.

There is a charming and suggestive episode reminiscent of Spenser's "Like as a huntsman after weary chase" (*Amoretti* 67) in the *Lusiads* of Camoens. At last the long-wandered Portuguese receive a reward from Venus, their divine champion. She peoples an island with her nymphs and instructs them in how to please these storm-tossed sailors. And the game on this Belle Isle, at the wise decree of Venus, is the dominant sexual fantasy of Western culture: the nymphs flee, the sailors run them down. But one sailor, a man notoriously unlucky in love, draws a perverse nymph. She will not be caught. After the other sailors have captured their partners and they have consented to more stationary delights, the unlucky sailor is still in pursuit. "Who told you it was me?" he cries out in despair, and quotes Petrarch in Italian—"Tra la spica e la man, qual muro è messo" (What a wall is set between the grain and my hand) (*Canzoniere* 56)—as he is swept to a vision of his fate as a calculus of endless frustration: even if she were to stop now, he would be too tired to touch her (book 9, stanzas 77–78). But he is completing the nymph's erotic playlet; at the sound of his lament she returns to prove him memorably wrong. She is the pupil of Venus, attuned to complaints, that Petrarchans dreamed of finding. She is also, according to Camoens, desirous of selling at a greater price than the others (stanza 76)—a nymph with a high opinion of her worth.[15]

Why must there be a chase? Why must woman run and man pursue, even on the Isle of Venus, even in Eden? We have suggested in psychoanalytic terms that obstacles may help to save desire and its object from decay. There is a social side as well to this preservation of value. Venery has a lot to do with dearness, which is how Adam, speaking with his angelic counselor, interprets the ambiguous gesture of Eve's original flight:

> Yet innocence and virgin modesty,
> Her virtue and the conscience of her worth,
> That would be wooed, and not unsought be won,
> Not obvious, not obtrusive, but retired,
> The more desirable, or to say all,
> Nature her self, though pure of sinful thought,
> Wrought in her so, that seeing me, she turned.
>
> (8.501–7)

Her flight was "more desirable" than overt invitation would have been, but that was not, in Adam's view, its purpose. As women will tend to do in a society in which they flee and men pursue (making the common mistake, Adam confuses her behavior with "Nature her self"), Eve was expressing "the conscience of her worth." By her elusiveness, by the precise degree of her coyness, by exactly how hard she is to get, a woman measures her worth, and by his pursuit, by the precise degree of his tenacity, by exactly the effort he expends, a man acknowledges this worth: a match. When a period of delay and not an end in itself, Petrarchan devotion is a couple's way of reckoning or settling female worth. Male worth remains secondary as the game was usually played in Renaissance poetry, determined primarily by the poet-lover's willing consent to his mistress's demand. Self-interest— male worth—keeps resurfacing in the characteristic conflicts between reason and passion, or the chiding friends and the heedless heart, but must be put aside in obedience to the fundamental rule of idealization. The rule, in this sense, is submission to the female's assessment of her value—the chase at all costs. Compensations in fame and artistic achievement recuperate the value forfeited by the love itself.

After proposing an infinite courtship in the first section of "To His Coy Mistress," Marvell surprisingly adds, contrary to his ironic hyperbole,

> For Lady you deserve this state;
> Nor would I love at lower rate.

Prolonged Petrarchan devotion, about to be repudiated by mortal necessity, retains its imaginative truth. The impossibly lengthy chase required by her coyness is indeed the ideal measure of her value: though in a subjunctive world contrary to fact, the woman is loved at her own rate. Even in the best of the *carpe diem* poems a social transaction, an agreed reckoning of female worth, lies at the heart of the chase and capture fantasy. In *Paradise Lost* this game is fraught with moral danger.

Because sweet reluctant amorous delay will provide a daily reaffirmation of "the conscience of her worth," Adam will inevitably be vulnerable to uxoriousness, the opposite of object-debasement. The game that preserves Eve's value from depreciation works all too well, and the consequence is a tendency in the first husband to abase himself before the idol of his mate. When she strikes off, he is prone to follow. It is no surprise when he falls "Fondly overcome with female charm" (9.999). The sexual fantasy Milton embedded at the origins of human love simply has to, by its very logic, buck against the ordained hierarchy that sets the man over the woman. It makes the Fall explicable.

Eve also falls when fondly overcome with female charm: "nor was godhead from her thought" (9.790). It is not until the fatal temptation of book 9 that we can appreciate why Milton married the origin of love to so many lessons about the image of Eve. At the moral center of the epic stands an acute diagnosis of Renaissance love poetry.

The deadly *uenator* in this love hunt is Satan, eavesdropper at the intimate revelations of book 4. He paid special attention, it is clear, to the images clustered about the loss of virginity. Adam's first words to Eve ("Return fair Eve, / Whom fly'st thou?") appear to have inspired the dream of flight Satan designs for her in order to strengthen that initial mysterious impulse toward solitude; adopting the voice of Adam, which spoke against her romance with the image, Satan tells her that stars exist to gaze upon her beauty. Something in Eve, independent of his insinuation, takes the bait. She leaves the symposium in book 8 to look after her garden, knowing Adam will mix his account of the discussion with "conjugal kisses" (8.56); at this point she still plays the Edenic game of erotic delay. Yet in book 9 she feels distracted and diverted by such behavior, their inefficient looking and smiling (9.222); though she does not mention kisses, we know whereto those smiles tend. The game of sweet flirtation, "so near each other thus all day" (9.220), has soured for her. "With thee conversing I forget all time," her love lyric once began (4.639); now she wants to remember it.

Perhaps she feels anxious over undone work. Perhaps the closeness of Adam in their imparadising arms engulfs her. Perhaps the anticipated glory of being "Mother of human race" is not enough to content her when she is, as yet, mother of nothing; certainly an intensification of her proto-maternal interest in gardening is her professed reason for requesting solitude. Perhaps it is a requirement of Milton's moral vision that real temptation take place in solitude, because the constraint of external observation makes it impossible to tell someone who is good because they do not wish to be seen from someone who truly chooses the good. Technically, it is no sin. But the question of what she can do by herself has supplanted the question of what they can do together, and this turning away rhymes ominously with her initial flight from Adam, more ominously with Satan's revulsion at the "sight hateful" (4.505) of their embrace. The devil gets his wish, "Eve separate" (9.422).

As the voice of the snake, Satan leads Eve symbolically back to the image in the pool, Adam's rival, and uncreates her wisdom. The successor to that image is the tree of prohibition in book 9. Satan assures her that its fruits pleased as "the teats / Of ewe or goat dropping with milk at even, / Unsucked of lamb or kid" (581–83). Like Eve, or like the image of Eve he intends to reflect, the tree is an ignored mother, a provider whose worthy goods have not been allowed their due fruition; it is subordinate, underappreciated, cursed. In her first fallen musings, Eve addresses the tree as "hitherto obscured, infamed, / And thy fair fruit let hang, as to no end / Created" (797–99): this, clearly, is the projection of a self, a self justified in having upgraded her value. As the snake leaves her, her eyes are once again fixed in self-worship on her own enchanting image. To have eaten the fruit is to have realized or unfolded her true worth. And once again, as at the beginning, she has no awareness that the tree she thinks she knows is her own image. Gone is the wisdom. Gone is the sweet reluctant amorous delay: a rash hand plucks and eats. As it turns out, delay is one thing, absence another. For the absence of Adam gives Eve over to his rival— the solitude and singularity of her image.

Satan accomplishes his design by exploiting something very close to what seventeenth-century poets learned about the character of Petrarchism:

> Fairest resemblance of thy maker fair,
> Thee all things living gaze on, all things thine
> By gift, and thy celestial beauty adore
> With ravishment beheld, there best beheld
> Where universally admired; but here
> In this enclosure wild, these beasts among,
> Beholders rude, and shallow to discern

Half what in thee is fair, one man except,
Who sees thee? (And what is one?) Who shouldst be seen
A goddess among gods, adored and served
By angels numberless, thy daily train.

(9.538–48)

And what is one? Why not multiply Anteros into an empire of subservient admirers? Waller's Apollo found in "unsought praise," an
armful of bays, a good trade-off for the lost Daphne. Eve should be
adored by many, an empress at a civilized court, crowned and on display; Satan returns to the lure of idolatrous singularity overcome—
folded, that is, into mutual love—during her courtship. The imperial
destiny now laid before Eve extricates her image from the exclusive
mutual devotion of her marriage and positions it as the centerpiece in
a court of gazers, guiding her desire onto the same track that made
fame an agreeable substitute for love in the Petrarchan tradition. Fame
extricated from God's designs is the first infirmity of fallen mind; Satan fell when he could not bear to be eclipsed by the crowned Son.
The Cavalier poets spoke for erotic satisfaction, which was the usual
motive for the imperial compliments they paid to women. Satan, a
specialist in the pleasures left to the frustrated, draws rather on the
imperial yearning, the wish for the crown, found in Petrarchan love.

Once again, her vulnerability to this lethal gambit springs from the
way Milton has represented ideal love. The image in the pool was
never abandoned. Adam fell in love with it. Eve, still thinking about
it, ran away. Adam chased after her, willing to love at whatever rate
she priced her worth. Eve yielded, fixing the value of her image, and
each day the game has been replayed. Because Miltonic love is ultimately about the determination of female worth, one can readily see
how Satan is able to convert Eve from the fixed value agreed upon in
her marriage to the inflation of an imperial reckoning. What is one?
Love is a fragile knot woven of narcissism—the consummate pleasure
of paradise, but equally the precondition of paradise lost. As Eve falls,
Adam is weaving "Of choicest flowers a garland to adorn / Her
tresses, and her rural labors crown, / As reapers oft are wont their
harvest queen" (9.840–42). The bridge between this innocent rural
token woven by a husband for his harvest queen and the pomposities
of Satan's Hell, where he sits crowned like a king of kings, in Godlike
imitated state—the bridge actually built in the poem by Sin and
Death—measures exactly the extent to which Eve's image has fallen.

The temptation Eve designs for Adam is a love trial. He must again
reckon her worth. And again, eating, he pays the price, choosing

against another Eve. Courtly love was charged early on with idolatry, and Adam's Fall is in this sense a medieval one. Eve's is the more modern. In the Petrarchan poetry of the Renaissance, the old threat of idolatrous love gave way to a reflexive idolatry of the self in the newly expansive and resourceful ego of the suitor-poet; the rejected male began to try out new and extravagant compensations, the most durable of these being poetic immortality, a widening empire of admirers. The female Fall has this distinctly Renaissance flavor.

Hell in *Paradise Lost,* built like the Renaissance itself in imitation of a lost magnificence, smacks of Burckhardt's territory, with its great building remembered from Milton's Italian travels and its many reminders of the culture of imperial Rome. Satan opens wide the gates of this secondhand *imperium* to entertain the image of Eve, and her dizzy imagination welcomes the Hell disguised in her tempter's rhetoric. She flies away from her rustic garden to thrones and pillared halls where power, the chief delight of the frustrated, is displayed and adored, and the delay of loving sexual gratification may become, as it is for Hell's monarch, infinite. One of the secrets of Milton's artistic creations lies in the way he entitled himself to fulfill his soaring ambitions by sacrificing, in the works themselves, versions of these desires.[16] It is difficult to believe that the Renaissance Fall of Eve in *Paradise Lost* does not derive in part from a purgation of intimate wishes consummated in the creation of the epic: the Lady of Christ's, the Lady of *Comus,* and in the end the Lady Eve of *Paradise Lost.*

After his medieval Fall, however, Adam becomes wonderfully evocative of the seventeenth century. Once intoxicated on the fruit, he expresses some new libertine anxieties: he wishes that there were ten forbidden trees in what seems a not altogether jocular concern with making provision for his erotic future;[17] the fires, his little joke implies, may never be this intense again. The game of sweet reluctant amorous delaying now seems to him, as it did to Eve at the beginning of this book, a failure:

> But come, so well refreshed, now let us play,
> As meet is, after such delicious fare;
> For never did thy beauty since the day
> I saw thee first and wedded thee, adorned
> With all perfections, so inflame my sense
> With ardor to enjoy thee, fairer now
> Than ever, bounty of this virtuous tree.
>
> (9.1027–33)

The Renaissance left us hundreds of these lyrics of sexual invitation in which the man says to the woman, in so many words, "But come . . . now let us play." But this one is rich with the meaning of a long and lofty poem. It seems at first that Adam might simply be saying that he is as excited now as he was the first time—that only the days of sweet reluctant amorous play now seem impoverished, not that the rites mysterious of connubial love have themselves been intensified. Alas, Eve is "fairer now / Than ever," and we must hear in sorrow that Adam has never before been so excited. The Fall has indeed charged her image with heightened fairness. Between "come" and "let us play" lies "so well refreshed," which is to say, the Fall. In fallen sexuality, the barrier that sweetens and secures desire is no longer delay, the mastered temptation of erotic postponement. The new excitement is moral transgression; the new barrier, the law that forbids, taboo itself. God, in other words, now takes his place among those erotic barriers whose presence, when defied, paradoxically serves to protect desire against fatigue. Throughout the poem Milton has striven unto heresy to avoid the usual conflicts between God and sexuality. But that ideal is finally compromised. The last act of intercourse in paradise sets the urgent flesh against the deity, and that, in fact, is its pleasure, "bounty of this virtuous tree." Like the appetite for food, sexual desire becomes capable of heightened satisfaction with the Fall, and this heightening has a name: "in lust they burn" (9.1015).

Adam seizes Eve's hand, not gently, and leads her to "a shady bank." It is still daylight, as at their first coupling, and they will seize this day, too, before it fades. There are no prayers, no delays. They fall upon each other like amorous birds of prey: "There they their fill of love and love's disport / Took largely, of their mutual guilt the seal, / The solace of their sin" (9.1042–44). The gustatory metaphor reminds us that this sex act is the first in an unended series of repetitions of the Fall. Fallen sex, "their fill" taken largely, is a carnivorous meal; as Adam put it when punning in his invitation lyric, their dalliance "meet is." Milton ends garden eroticism with a sinister transformation of the love hunt.

The course of sexual fruition in the poem may be viewed as a pointed expansion of "To His Coy Mistress." When, before the Fall, there is world enough and time, coyness is no crime, and delay in the game of love is both the government of desire and its major inducement. But as soon as they hear what they are the first to hear, Time's winged chariot, Adam and Eve rather at once their time devour. Time has been hurrying near us human beings for some while now, and modern lovers may no longer hear it as clearly as these do. To this pair the impending catastrophe is not simply or even primarily death, which these sinful lovers have no experience of, but punishing justice. Their defiance of justice through fugitive intercourse stamps the "seal" of legitimacy on a confession of "mutual guilt." Their act declares: we have sinned, us, the ones made to multiply your image and likeness. Their "solace" is to convert sin into pleasure.

Sexual pleasure is one of the first victims of this guilt. The next morning, shame sits on their genitals. The spiritual fallout moves from the quarrelsome "mutual accusation" of 9.1187 to the self-accusations of book 10, where each of them wishes that the judgment might light "on me, me only" (832; 935–36). Their dynastic fame has of course been poisoned. Yet Eve, when she regrets her legacy to the future, mentions only the sorrow of her children's mortal lot (979–88). Adam, however, is acutely sensitive to his place in history, and this theme initiates his long tormented soliloquy:

> O miserable of happy! Is this the end
> Of this new glorious world, and me so late
> The glory of that glory, who now become
> Accurst of blessed, hide me from the face
> Of God, whom to behold was then my highth
> Of happiness: yet well, if here would end
> The misery, I deserved it, and would bear
> My own deservings; but this will not serve;
> All that I eat or drink, or shall beget,
> Is propagated curse. O voice once heard
> Delightfully, *Increase and multiply,*
> Now death to hear! For what can I increase
> Or multiply, but curses on my head?
> Who of all ages to succeed, but feeling
> The evil on him brought by me, will curse
> My head, Ill fare our ancestor impure,
> For this we may thank Adam; but his thanks
> Shall be the execration; so besides
> Mine own that bide upon me, all from me
> Shall with a fierce reflux on me redound,
> On me as on their natural center light
> Heavy, though in their place. O fleeting joys
> Of Paradise, dear bought with lasting woes!
>
> (10.720–42)

This is not the Herostratic topos. Being cursed through all of history was surely not Adam's express motive. But was it not implicit in his motive, though unrecognized? What else could it have meant to join in fallenness the mother of the human race? With a profound attunement to infamy that he himself takes as the reflex of his original attunement to glory, Adam feels the weight of the curses, even pronounces the first of them himself. "Heavy, though in their place" refers to the Aristotelian notion that the elements in their proper stations—water in water, air in air—are suspended weightlessly; but in the soul of Adam a different physics rules, as the curses of aftertimes light upon him, their proper "place," yet continue to bear down upon him.[18] They amplify the shaming self-indictment of his predicament. The commandment enjoining marriage and sexuality, "Increase and multiply," which was originally coincident with the fame promised our first progenitors, now entails for Adam the unlimited propagation of his infamy—every new child another new curse. He is the origin for everyone of all that is wrong. In the long tradition of Renaissance Petrarchism, frustration, nonconsummation, a love that for one reason or another does not obey the commandment to increase and multiply, became fundamentally associated with artistic success, the increasing multiplication of fame. Not fathering a family would be no fame; but at least it would not be infamy. Before the Fall, the happy pair could anticipate a success rare in Renaissance love poetry, the issue of their consummation increasing and multiplying their fame. About the lamentations of our fallen father, however, the disjunction of fame and family looms. Like some of the later poets in the Petrarchan tradition, Adam is being led away from a woman by considerations of fame.

As the speech progresses, he projects (and tries to escape) God's infinite wrath, gives voice to misogyny, questions the wisdom of sexuality as a means of generation, and laments the many sorts of nuptial distress his sons would endure.[19] He will be thanked for every bit of their pain: his ever-heavier crown of infamy. The mind of the father of the human race is sickened with loathing for marriage and family. This is the moment Eros reaches in *The Doctrine and Discipline of Divorce* when, seeing the falseness of his mate, he becomes undeified, his fire gone out.

Adam and Eve will of course be reconciled, united in their loss, their guilt, their enmity toward Satan, their "faith unanimous" (12.603). They will mother and father. Eventually, toward the end of the Renaissance, one of their children will write an epic to forgive them for all of us. The potentially endless quarrel announced at the

end of book 9 stems from the common blindness in the moral sense
of fallen human beings. Both hurl "accusation," but neither is "self
condemning." A guilty mind sees faults in the other, yet ignores its
own. How might this new failure in men be made productive? The
first to achieve self-condemnation, Eve also discovers one of the perennial secrets for inspiring self-knowledge in a person suffering from
benighted introspection: reflect for him an external image, in art or
conversation, of his own spiritual state on the assumption that what
he cannot grasp directly within himself, he may catch on the rebound
from another's enactment of it.

Claiming that she is divulging "thoughts in my unquiet breast"
(10.975), Eve shows Adam the meaning of his despair:

> Childless thou art, childless remain:
> So death shall be deceived his glut, and with us two
> Be forced to satisfy his ravenous maw.
> But if thou judge it hard and difficult,
> Conversing, looking, loving, to abstain
> From love's due rights, nuptial embraces sweet,
> And with desire to languish without hope,
> Before the present object languishing
> With like desire, which would be misery
> And torment less than none of what we dread,
> Then both our selves and seed at once to free
> From what we fear for both, let us make short,
> Let us seek death, or he not found, supply
> With our own hands his office on our selves.
>
> (10.989–1002)

If the thought of their posterity is, on any grounds, unbearable, if the
first commandment cannot be tolerated, then two choices confront
them: frustration and suicide. Eve has heard his lament, caught the
drift, and exposed the pragmatic consequences.

This wifely intervention is deft beyond praise. We have studied
many frustrations in this and the preceding chapter, and all of them,
save one, have arisen from asymmetrical desire. The sole exception is
Astrophil and Stella, where love and desire turn out to be reciprocal.[20]
There, however, Stella's honor (and Astrophil's respect for it) mutes
desire. In the frustration Eve projects for the edification of her husband, both would face "the present object" in a state of "like desire,"
and both would have to deny themselves, over and over, "nuptial embraces sweet": her proposed frustration, the sharpest in Renaissance

literature, has unobtrusively restored sweetness to the thought of their sexuality. No flight, no chase, no capture, no yielding, but a static tableau of perfect frustration, waiting for death. Delay and reluctance that could not become sweetly amorous—this would be "no less" than any of God's sentences, death included. The clear implication, of course, is that death would come as a welcome relief from this irksome discipline.

Eve's second alternative addresses the egotism latent in Adam's hysterical vision of infamy spreading with his family tree. The bond between "our selves and seed" must allow their children their life, their choice, their chance to bruise the head of the enemy. It is no gift of freedom not to let them live. Eve has Adam behold the maniacal sour grapes of an apocalyptic suicide obliterating all of history beyond themselves. The aim of this brilliantly calculated anterotic speech is to restore in Adam the "homogeneal fire" of paternal ambition, bringing his tormented soul back within the sphere of the family.

Adam, whose appetite for severity has become alarming, initially finds Eve's willingness to forego pleasure or commit suicide high-minded. But ultimately he realizes what, it seems to us, Eve all along expected him to see. The two alternatives come to the same thing, a deliberate destruction of the image of God that they are, a self-damnation.

Eve's therapy succeeds. The image of acute sexual frustration, which presupposes sexual desire, appears to have stirred Adam's unconscious. For suddenly he remembers something, something that signals renewed flames from the bitter ashes of his paternal ambition. In the very terms of God's judgment, an obscure victory has been foretold for her seed; there will a second, and victorious, encounter with their foe. From an intimate angle Adam has stumbled onto the full dilation of Eve's narcissism in *Paradise Lost*. God's first trope on the image in the pool was marriage and children. Satan's dire revision was the interdicted tree, the fall into self-centered ambition. As the lessons of Michael will have revealed by the end of the poem, God's second trope on her image is Christ's mission of redemption: when the eyes of the newborn Eve found the entrancing creature in the pool, she was staring in embryonic form at our half of *theanthropos,* the humanity that the second Eve will contribute to the Christ.

Adam then begins to justify God's ways to men, turning into the great argument of the epic by purging himself of his own initial response to the thought of their lifelong sexual frustration, which is now morally equivalent to suicide:

No more be mentioned then of violence
Against our selves, and wilful barrenness,
That cuts us off from hope, and savors only
Rancor and pride, impatience and despite,
Reluctance against God and his just yoke
Laid on our necks.

(1041–46)

The Edenic fusion of sexuality, marriage, and fame has now been converted to Christianity, infused with Christian hope, and joined to the
glory of Christ, which is joined to the glory of the Father. Their curses
are not so hard. To Eve "Pains only in child-bearing were foretold,"
and these are "soon recompensed with joy" (1051–52). He himself
"with labor . . . must earn" his bread: "what harm?" (1054–55).
Adam has found the way again.

He rebukes Eve for voicing bitter reluctant unloving delay against
God. Yet this is more profoundly Adam's voice, the hopeless voice we
have heard complaining through the night. At the beginning of the
reconciliation scene in book 10 Eve must seek out an Adam who has
turned away from her, fall down at his feet, embrace and implore him.
But after Eve has been accepted, her technique remakes the origin:
running past her husband, presenting images opposite to her desire,
in the confidence that Adam, coming to his senses, will chase after
her, seize her hand, and lead her back. We begin to understand how
the process of mirroring images of each other will evolve in the history of marriage, as the Renaissance myths at the origins of their love
are refitted to shelter the prospects of their family in the rain of new
circumstances. The idea will endure.

Notes

Unless otherwise indicated, translations are by the authors. We have silently modernized spelling and punctuation for Renaissance texts. Shakespeare is cited from *The Riverside Shakespeare,* ed. G. Blakemore Evans et al. (Boston: Houghton Mifflin, 1974). Milton's poetry is from *The Poems of John Milton,* ed. John Carey and Alastair Fowler (London: Longmans, 1968), and his prose from *The Complete Works of John Milton,* ed. Don M. Wolfe et al., 8 vols. (New Haven: Yale University Press, 1953–82).

PREFACE

1. E.M.W. Tillyard, *The English Renaissance: Fact or Fiction?* (Baltimore: Johns Hopkins Press, 1952), p. 15.

2. The debate has already begun, of course. Polemics against extreme versions of individualism are a regular feature of the criticism loosely termed "new historicist," although certain scholars associated with this movement, such as Richard Helgerson and Leah Marcus, seem fairly comfortable with the traditional concept of the individual author. Renaissance scholars have begun to address the subject in terms of broad interest to contemporary intellectuals; see, for example, the essays of Stephen Greenblatt and Natalie Zemon Davis in *Reconstructing Individualism: Autonomy, Individuality, and the Self in Western Thought,* ed. Thomas C. Heller et al. (Stanford: Stanford University Press, 1986), pp. 30–63.

3. Period concepts are an obvious instance of the hermeneutic circle. See Wilhelm Dilthey's classic, "The Rise of Hermeneutics," trans. Frederic Jameson, *New Literary History* 3 (1972): 229–44. So long as they are subject to

revision, so long as they are not underwritten, that is, by metaphysical absolutes, such circles are not vicious.

1: BURCKHARDT'S RENAISSANCE

1. *Die Baukunst der Renaissance in Italien,* vol. 2 in Jacob Burckhardt, *Gesammelte Werke,* 10 vols. (Basel: Schwabe, 1970), translated by James Palmes and Peter Murray as *The Architecture of the Italian Renaissance* (Chicago: University of Chicago Press, 1985). A few fragments on painting and painters have also survived.

2. Heinrich Wölfflin, *Renaissance and Baroque,* trans. Kathrin Simon (Ithaca: Cornell University Press, 1966), p. 77.

3. *The Letters of Jacob Burckhardt,* ed. and trans. Alexander Dru (New York: Pantheon, 1955), p. 187 (to Nietzsche, 1879).

4. Wölfflin, *Renaissance and Baroque,* pp. 76–77 (Simon translates *Stimmung* as "a temper or a mood").

5. See the *Einleitung* to *Griechische Kulturgeschichte,* in *Gesammelte Werke,* 5:3–12—not included in the abridged version of the work available in English.

6. E. H. Gombrich, "In Search of Cultural History" (1967), in *Ideals and Idols* (Oxford: Phaidon, 1979), p. 43.

7. Heinrich Plett, "Aesthetic Constituents in the Courtly Culture of Renaissance England," *New Literary History* 14 (1983): 597.

8. Frank Kermode, *The Classic* (New York: Viking, 1975), pp. 28–38. This longer view supplements the otherwise standard discussion of Wallace Ferguson, *The Renaissance in Historical Thought* (Cambridge, Mass.: Harvard University Press, 1948), on which the following account relies heavily.

9. Moduin, *Egloga* (composed 804–10); text and translation from *Poetry of the Carolingian Renaissance,* ed. Peter Godman (Norman: University of Oklahoma Press, 1985), pp. 192–93. The conceit itself has poignant precedents in the waning of antiquity. See Rutilius Namatianus, addressing fifth-century Rome in *De reditu suo:* "illud te reparat quod cetera regna resoluit: / ordo renascendi est crescere posse malis" (1.139–40; what ruins other kingdoms restores you; the rule of rebirth is to grow with your misfortunes).

10. See Percy Ernst Schramm, *Hitler: The Man and the Military Leader,* ed. and trans. Donald S. Detwiler (Chicago: Quadrangle, 1971). Schramm's *Kaiser, Rom und Renovatio,* 2nd ed. (Darmstadt: Gentner, 1957), is still standard.

11. *A Renaissance Entertainment: Festivities for the Marriage of Cosimo I, Duke of Florence, in 1539,* ed. and trans. Andrew C. Minor and Bonner Mitchell (Columbia: University of Missouri Press, 1968), p. 121. The inscription adapts *Aeneid* 6.792–93. On the imperial symbolism of Charles and others, see Frances Yates, *Astraea* (London: Routledge & Kegan Paul, 1975). In her pursuit of the often occult forms of this dream, Yates is, in this book and others, the subtlest modern historian of this aspect of Renaissance self-consciousness.

12. B. L. Ullman locates the first instance of the ruling metaphor of rebirth just prior to Petrarch, in Benvenuto Campesani's verses "de resurrectione Catulli" (composed 1303–7); see "Renaissance: The Word and the Underlying Concept" (1952), in *Studies in the Italian Renaissance,* 2nd ed. (Rome: Storia e Letteratura, 1973), p. 13.

13. *Praefatio* to book 1 of the *Elegantiae,* in Lorenzo Valla, *Opera omnia,* 2 vols., ed. Eugenio Garin (Turin: Bottega d'Erasmo, 1962), 1:1–3.

14. Erasmus, *Adages* 2.1.1; trans. Margaret Mann Phillips, *Erasmus on His Times* (Cambridge: Cambridge University Press, 1967), p. 10 (the quotation immediately following is from the same page). A picture of Titus's coin may be found in Harold Mattingly et al., *The Roman Imperial Coinage* (London: Spink, 1923–), 2, plate 3, no. 49. The emblem in this unreversed form— though without explicit imperial associations—circulated widely as an illustration in Francesco Colonna's *Hypnerotomachia Poliphili,* first printed by the Aldine Press in 1499; see the edition of Giovanni Pozzi and Lucia A. Ciapponi, 2nd ed. (Padua: Antenore, 1980), 1:61 and (on the genealogy of the device) 2:91–93.

15. Trans. Ferguson, *Renaissance in Historical Thought,* p. 56, from Théodore de Bèze, *Histoire ecclésiastique,* ed. G. Baum and E. Cunitz, 3 vols. (Paris: Fischbacher, 1883–89), 1:v–vi.

16. See Barrie Bullen, "The Source and Development of the Idea of the Renaissance in Early Nineteenth-Century French Criticism," *Modern Language Review* 76 (1981): 311–22.

17. Erwin Panofsky, *Renaissance and Renascences in Western Art* (New York: Harper & Row, 1969), pp. 18–35.

18. Leon Battista Alberti, *On Painting,* trans. John R. Spencer, 2nd ed. (New Haven: Yale University Press, 1966), p. 40.

19. Jacob Burckhardt, *The Civilization of the Renaissance in Italy,* trans. S.G.C. Middlemore and intro. Benjamin Nelson and Charles Trinkaus (New York: Harper & Row, 1958). Quotations and page numbers in the text are from this edition, except as noted. Occasional German references are from the text in Burckhardt, *Gesammelte Werke,* vol. 3. Irene Gordon's revision of Middlemore's translation (New York: New American Library, 1960) is in many particulars preferable, but it is out of print and also omits most of Burckhardt's notes.

20. Shakespeare, *Julius Caesar* 5.4.25; Lope de Vega, *Peribáñez* 119–20 (You look like yourself, since you have no equal); Antoine de Montchrestien, *La Reine d'Écosse* 900 (I am myself self-assured of myself); John Marston, *Sophonisba* 2.2.72; Shakespeare, *Sonnets* 121.9–10; Lope de Vega, *La Estrella de Sevilla* 2340–42 (I am who I am, and being who I am I contain myself in silence); Mathurin Régnier, *Satire* 5 (Everyone holds to his purpose in accord with his own taste); John Webster, *The Duchess of Malfi* 1.1.319–21; Milton, *Samson Agonistes,* ll. 1709–10. See Hereward Price, "Like Himself," *Review of English Studies* 16 (1940): 178–81; Leo Spitzer, "Soy Quien Soy," *Nueva Revista de Filología Hispánica* 1 (1947): 113–27, and 2 (1948): 275; and José Antonio Maravall, *Teatro y literatura en la sociedad barroca* (Madrid: Seminarios y

Ediciones, 1972), pp. 97–104. Maravall emphasizes the social assertiveness of such formulae, perhaps most evident in Spanish examples: "soy quien soy, / y aquí reino en lo que mando, / como el Rey en su Castilla" (I am who I am, and I reign here where I command as the king does in Castille; Lope de Vega, *El mejor alcalde, el Rey* 1581–83). The bluntest proclamation is perhaps the aristocratic motto that long appeared on Bearnaise currency, GRATIA DEI SVM ID QVOD SVM (By the grace of God I am what I am); see Adrien Blanchet and Adolphe Dieudonné, *Manuel numismatique française,* 4 vols. (Paris: Picard, 1912–36), 2:140 and plate 8. The phrasing is from Saint Paul (1 Cor. 15.10), but the emphasis has shifted perceptibly from the first phrase to the second. We may measure its bravura by its morosely collective survival on the town crest of Lake Wobegon, Minnesota: *Sumus quod sumus* (We are what we are); Garrison Keillor, *Lake Wobegon Days* (New York: Viking, 1985), p. 6.

21. G.W.F. Hegel, *The Philosophy of History,* trans. J. Sibree and intro. C. J. Friedrich (New York: Dover, 1956), p. 225. Citations of Hegel's German are from *Sämtliche Werke,* ed. Hermann Glockner et al., 26 vols. (Stuttgart: Frommann, 1927–39), vol. 11.

22. Hegel, *Philosophy of History,* pp. 238–39. Burckhardt may well have been thinking also of Hegel on Greek sculpture: "Greece is not to be understood at its heart unless we bring with us as a key to our comprehension an insight into the ideals of sculpture and unless we consider from the point of view of their plasticity not only the heroic figures in epic and drama but also the actual statesmen and philosophers. After all, in the beautiful days of Greece men of action, like poets and thinkers, had this same plastic and universal yet individual character both inwardly and outwardly. . . . The Periclean age was especially rich in such characters . . . each of them of his own sort, unimpaired by another's: all of them are out-and-out artists by nature, ideal artists shaping themselves, individuals of a single case, works of art standing there like immortal and deathless images of the gods" (*Aesthetics,* trans. T. M. Knox [Oxford: Clarendon Press, 1975], p. 719). The filiation of the metaphor reaches back through Giovanni Pico to Plotinus; see chap. 7, n.6, below.

23. See Richard Koebner, *Empire* (Cambridge: Cambridge University Press, 1961), pp. 18–60.

24. John Addington Symonds, *Renaissance in Italy,* 7 vols. (New York: Scribner's, 1888), 1:142. For specifics on this point, see Francesco Cognasso, "Istituzioni comunali e signorili di Milano sotto i Visconti," in *Storia di Milano,* 17 vols. (Milan: Fondazione Treccani degli Alfieri, 1953–66), 6:451–544.

25. Hans Baron, *The Crisis of the Early Italian Renaissance,* rev. ed. (Princeton: Princeton University Press, 1966). Baron revives the pre-Burckhardtian emphasis of another Swiss historian, Simonde de Sismondi, whose eighteen-volume *Histoire des républiques italiennes du moyen âge* (1807–18) is firmly partisan in its opposition to monarchy. For a significant scholarly continuation, see J.G.A. Pocock, *The Machiavellian Moment: Florentine Political Thought and the Atlantic Republican Tradition* (Princeton: Princeton University Press, 1975). A vigorous new case for removing at least Machiavelli from this tradition has

recently been made by Mark Hulliung, *Citizen Machiavelli* (Princeton: Princeton University Press, 1983).

26. Cognasso, "Istituzioni communali e signorili," p. 537.

27. That lineage is not always fully acknowledged, to sometimes distorting effect. Stephen Greenblatt gives Burckhardt credit for his "crucial perception . . . that the political upheavals in Italy . . . fostered a radical change in consciousness," but warns that "his related assertion that, in the process, these men emerged at last as free individuals must be sharply qualified" (*Renaissance Self-Fashioning* [Chicago: University of Chicago Press, 1980], pp. 161–62). It is part of the burden of our argument that many of these qualifications are already there in Burckhardt, implicit in his conception when not in his book. The qualifications Greenblatt has in mind mostly concern the role of social determinants in personal identity; the major thrust of his argument, summed up in his now famous epilogue, is that awareness of these determinants exposes the fraudulence of that "pure unfettered subjectivity" that he had sought in Renaissance culture: "the human subject itself began to seem remarkably unfree, the ideological product of the relations of power in a particular society. Whenever I focused sharply upon a moment of apparently autonomous self-fashioning, I found not an epiphany of identity freely chosen but a cultural artifact" (p. 256). Recent British critics, on what they take to be a political imperative, have worked similar arguments into a concerted attack on Burckhardtian selfhood—variously identified as "Christian-Stoic essentialism" or "the liberal humanist subject"—as a corrupt heritage to be discarded; see Jonathan Dollimore, *Radical Tragedy: Religion, Ideology, and Power in the Drama of Shakespeare and His Contemporaries* (Chicago: University of Chicago Press, 1984), and Catherine Belsey, *The Subject of Tragedy* (London: Methuen, 1985). Our own discussion parallels these in many regards; the paradoxes of selfhood which they highlight are real and important. But we are unconvinced that what is called for in the end is some kind of choice between the oppositions involved. Greenblatt in particular seems to posit an ideal of independent self-fashioning far purer than anything ever seriously proposed for Renaissance individualism—something close indeed to Hegel's *unendende Subjectivität*—so that the concluding revelation of its insupportability is something of a set-up. Society and the rest of the outside world are already involved in Renaissance individualism from its conception (indeed, as Edward Tayler has shown in an unpublished lecture, "Essences and New Historicists," in the philosophical definition of the individual's essence), and we follow the resulting negotiations to a less brutal and disillusioned conclusion. We find ourselves in sympathy with Edward Pechter's suggestions that the new historicism relies rather uncritically on the regnant cliché "It's a jungle out there" when "Love makes the world go round" (see part 3 of this book) is sometimes the one to look to for guidance; see "The New Historicism and Its Discontents: Politicizing Renaissance Drama," *PMLA* 102 (1987): 292–303.

28. Baldassare Castiglione, *The Book of the Courtier*, trans. Charles S. Singleton (Garden City, N.Y.: Doubleday, 1959), pp. 37, 70, 74, 77, 43, 32.

29. See especially Frank Whigham, *Ambition and Privilege: The Social*

Tropes of Elizabethan Courtesy Theory (Berkeley and Los Angeles: University of California Press, 1984).

30. Thomas G. Bergin, ed., in Petrarch, *Selected Sonnets, Odes and Letters* (Northbrook, Ill.: AHM, 1966), p. xi.

31. *The Letters of Dante*, ed. and trans. Paget Toynbee, 2nd ed. (Oxford: Clarendon Press, 1966), p. 159.

32. Gioviano Pontano, *De fortitudine* 2.4, in *Opera omnia* (Venice, 1518), p. 76.

33. Lorenzo Ghiberti, *I commentari*, ed. Ottavio Morisani (Naples: Ricciardi, 1947), p. 41.

34. From the *Vita* by Bartolomeo Blanchini in Codro (Antonio) Urceo's collected works, ed. Filippo Beroaldo (Bologna, 1502), sig. αiir.

35. Leon Battista Alberti, "Self-Portrait of a Universal Man," trans. James Bruce Ross, in *The Portable Renaissance Reader*, ed. James Bruce Ross and Mary Martin McLaughlin, 2nd ed. (New York: Viking, 1968), pp. 480, 491, 483, 484, 480. If the work is Alberti's, it has inept precedent in the autobiographical section of Ghiberti's *Commentari*, which begins in the third person and then slides into the first—an inattentiveness noted with disapproval by Vasari.

36. The *longue durée* on this subject is now treated in rich detail by Leo Braudy in *The Frenzy of Renown: Fame and Its History* (New York: Oxford University Press, 1986). The emergence of the cult in its Renaissance form is traced as a progression from Saint Francis—self-conscious about his sainthood in an innovative way—through Dante and Chaucer to Petrarch (pp. 219–64).

37. Giorgio Vasari, *Artists of the Renaissance*, ed. and trans. George Bull (New York: Viking, 1978), p. 129 (on Alberti).

38. Trans. Ernest Hatch Wilkins in his *Studies in the Life and Works of Petrarch* (Cambridge, Mass.: Medieval Academy of America, 1955), p. 309.

39. Petrarca, *Rerum Familiarium Libri I-VIII*, trans. Aldo S. Bernardo (Albany: State University of New York Press, 1975), pp. 15–16, 21.

40. Pius II, *Memoirs of a Renaissance Pope*, trans. Florence A. Gragg, ed. Leona C. Gabel (New York: Putnam, 1959), p. 27.

41. *Petrarch's Secret*, trans. William H. Draper (London: Chatto & Windus, 1911), p. 166.

42. Jerome Cardan (Girolamo Cardano), *The Book of My Life*, trans. Jean Stoner (New York: Dutton, 1930), p. 33.

43. Reported by Valerius Maximus in his book of illustrative examples for orators, 8.14, example 5. Cf. Plutarch, *Alexander* 55.3, where Callisthenes incites a conspiracy against Alexander by saying that the way to become very famous is to kill someone very famous.

44. Burckhardt, *Letters*, p. 147 (on a threatened burning of the Louvre in 1871).

45. Preface to *The History of Florence*, in Machiavelli, *The Chief Works and Others*, trans. Allan Gilbert (Durham, N.C.: Duke University Press, 1965), pp. 1032–33.

46. *The Letters of Pietro Aretino,* ed. and trans. Thomas Caldecot Chubb (Hamden, Conn.: Archon, 1967), p. 205.

47. Ibid., p. 194.

48. Ibid., p. 256.

49. *Pasquinate di Pietro Aretino,* ed. Vittorio Rossi (Palermo: Clausen, 1891), p. 161; from a pastoral satire that appeared anonymously but that is almost certainly by Aretino.

50. *Capitolo secondo,* in *Poesie di Pietro Aretino,* ed. G. Sborselli, 2 vols. (Lanciano: Carabba, 1930), 1:103; against Gian Alberto Albicante.

51. Symonds, *Renaissance in Italy,* 2:235–36.

52. Charles Nisard, *Les Gladiateurs de la république des lettres aux xve, xvie et xviie siècles* (1860; reprint, Geneva: Slatkine, 1970); some particularly interesting perversions of laureation are noted on pp. 130, 183, 232. For recent commentary on the phenomenon, see Anthony Grafton and Lisa Jardine, *From Humanism to the Humanities* (Cambridge, Mass.: Harvard University Press, 1986), pp. 62–82, who relate it specifically to the rise of the University of Rome. It is, interestingly, in discussing the theory of the *ad hominem* insult that Guicciardini anticipates Burckhardt's definition of the Renaissance individual: "If you want to insult a particular person, do not speak ill of his country, his family, or his relatives. It is great folly to offend many if you only want to insult one man" (*Ricordi* C8, in *Maxims and Reflections of a Renaissance Statesman,* trans. Mario Domandi [New York: Harper & Row, 1965]).

53. *Letters of Pietro Aretino,* pp. 149–51, 154.

54. Francesco Guicciardini, *The History of Italy,* ed. and trans. Sidney Alexander (New York: Collier, 1969), p. 8.

55. We quote the *Ricordi* in Domandi's translation of *Maxims and Reflections.* On *il particulare* in Guicciardini's political thought, see Pocock, *Machiavellian Moment,* pp. 121–38.

56. Michael Ann Holly, *Panofsky and the Foundations of Art History* (Ithaca: Cornell University Press, 1984), p. 31.

57. *Satire 6,* in *The Satires of Ludovico Ariosto,* trans. Peter DeSa Wiggins (Athens: Ohio University Press, 1976), pp. 152–53.

58. The quoted phrase (not identified in English editions) is from Filippo Villani's life of Zanobi da Strada: "Nesciret, ex innata nobilitate, inferiora uiliaque prospicere" (*Philippi Villani liber de ciuitatis Florentiae famosis ciuibus,* ed. Gustav Camillo Galletti [Florence: Mazzoni, 1847], p. 16). Middlemore translates "pride" rather than "nobility" (Burckhardt has "Hochsinn"), but, for reasons we shall discuss later, the social innuendo seems particularly worth preserving.

59. Jacob Burckhardt, *Force and Freedom,* ed. James Hastings Nichols (New York: Pantheon, 1943), p. 184; from Burckhardt's *Weltgeschichtliche Betrachtungen* (vol. 4 in *Gesammelte Werke*).

60. Middlemore translates "excessive," but the German is "entwickelte," echoing the title of section 2, "Entwicklung des Individuums."

61. François Rabelais, *The Histories of Gargantua and Pantagruel,* trans. J. M. Cohen (Harmondsworth, Eng.: Penguin, 1955), p. 159.

62. "The Freedom of a Christian," trans. W. A. Lambert and Harold J. Gramm, in Martin Luther, *Selections from His Writings,* ed. John Dillenberger (Garden City, N.Y.: Doubleday, 1961), pp. 53, 55–56, 64.

2: BEYOND BURCKHARDT

1. Jean Bodin, *Les Six Livres de la république* (Paris, 1583; fac. reprint, Aalen: Scientia, 1977), p. 122—from the definition of *souveraineté.*

2. Ibid., pp. 132–33, 131, 142. For the Latin phrase, see Justinian's *Institutes* 1.2.6.

3. José Antonio Maravall, *Culture of the Baroque: Analysis of a Historical Structure,* trans. Terry Cochran (Minneapolis: University of Minnesota Press, 1986), pp. 159ff. Maravall's own term, lifted from the picaresque novelist Mateo Aléman, is "the waylaying human being" (p. 162; *el hombre en acecho*). The wolf proverb (which derives ultimately from Plautus) is cited by Erasmus, who pairs it with *Homo homini deus* (Man is a god to man) (*Adages* 1.1.69–70).

4. Richard Overton, *An Arrow against All Tyrants* (1646); *The Levellers in the English Revolution,* ed. G. E. Aylmer (Ithaca: Cornell University Press, 1975), p. 69.

5. Quoted by Fernand Braudel, *Civilization and Capitalism: Fifteenth to Eighteenth Century,* trans. Siân Reynolds, 3 vols. (New York: Harper & Row, 1981–84), 2:256.

6. To be fair, Burckhardt elsewhere offers the model of a trinity of historical forces, of which the state is only one, along with religion and culture. The core of his *Weltgeschichtliche Betrachtungen* (translated as *Force and Freedom,* ed. James Hastings Nichols [New York: Pantheon, 1943]) is a series of analyses of how each force can in turn determine the others. The results, however, are not memorable; the most impressive concern the state (see chap. 1, n.59, above).

7. Braudel, *Civilization and Capitalism,* 2:515. Braudel usefully summarizes his argument in *Afterthoughts on Material Civilization and Capitalism,* trans. Patricia Ranum (Baltimore: Johns Hopkins University Press, 1977).

8. See Iris Origo, *The Merchant of Prato* (New York: Knopf, 1957), from which most of the information in this paragraph is taken.

9. Ibid., p. 78.

10. We alter Mario Domandi's translation of the *Ricordi,* in *Maxims and Reflections of a Renaissance Statesman* (New York: Harper & Row, 1965), to bring out the bracketed phrase. On the fortunes of *capitale* and related words in the Renaissance, see Braudel, *Civilization and Capitalism,* 2:232ff.

11. Robert Weimann, "'Appropriation' and Modern History in Renaissance Prose Narrative," *New Literary History* 14 (1983): 468–69.

12. The equation reaches back at least to Isaiah 23, where it attracted the attention of Calvin and other moralists. Unusually complex symbolism is afforded by the liaison of Agostino Chigi, the Sienese banker who cultivated

the classical aura of his first name, with the Roman courtesan whose name apparently really was Imperia. A Roman wit did not miss the opportunity: "Illa tua Imperia, Auguste, est non illa, sed illa / Nomine mutato dicitur Emporium" (Your Imperia, Augustus, she is no empire, but she with her name altered is called Emporium). Ingrid D. Rowland, "Render unto Caesar the Things Which Are Caesar's: Humanism and the Arts in the Patronage of Agostino Chigi," *Renaissance Quarterly* 39 (1986): 693.

13. Thomas Nashe, *Christ's Tears over Jerusalem* (1593), in *Life in Shakespeare's England,* ed. John Dover Wilson (Harmondsworth, Eng.: Penguin, 1944), p. 25.

14. See W. Calvin Dickinson, *James Harrington's Republic* (Washington, D.C.: University Press of America, 1983), p. 54.

15. "Poor fellow never joy'd since the price of oats rose, it was the death of him" (Shakespeare, *1 Henry IV* 2.1.12–13).

16. Neapolitan proverb, in Braudel, *Civilization and Capitalism,* 2:249.

17. Poggio Bracciolini, "On Nobility," in *Humanism and Liberty: Writings on Freedom from Fifteenth-Century Florence,* trans. Renée Neu Watkins (Columbia: University of South Carolina Press, 1978), pp. 142, 124, 138, 132.

18. Leon Battista Alberti, *The Family in Renaissance Florence (= I libri della famiglia),* trans. Renée Neu Watkins (Columbia: University of South Carolina Press, 1969), p. 174: "Do you, by any chance, use the word honor [*onore*] as some of our fellow citizens do, to signify holding public office and being in the government?" "Far from it, my dear Lionardo, far from it, my dear children."

19. Ibid., p. 149.

20. Baldassare Castiglione, *The Book of the Courtier,* trans. Charles S. Singleton (Garden City, N.Y.: Doubleday, 1959), p. 117.

21. A common proverb, cited in this context by Sir Thomas Smith, *De republica Anglorum,* ed. Mary Dewar (Cambridge: Cambridge University Press, 1982), p. 72: "For whosoever . . . will bear the port, charge, and countenance of a gentleman, he shall be called master . . . and shall be taken for a gentleman."

22. We choose our words carefully, trying to walk common ground in the often intense current controversy on this subject. A helpful survey of recent work is provided by Barbara B. Diefendorf, "Family Culture, Renaissance Culture," *Renaissance Quarterly* 40 (1987): 661–81. For two important diverging statements, see Lawrence Stone, *The Family, Sex, and Marriage in England, 1500–1800* (New York: Harper & Row, 1977), pp. 151–218; and Stephen Ozment, *When Fathers Ruled: Family Life in Reformation Europe* (Cambridge, Mass.: Harvard University Press, 1983). Debate is less over the patriarchal character of the early modern family than over its emotional content. Stone cites "affective individualism" and "companionate marriage" as contrasting later developments, whereas Ozment insists that warmth and mutuality were fully present in both paternalist theory and practice. The debate here seems to us one with no real answer, as irresistible but hopeless as all discussions about how other people raise their children. We agree with Ozment that con-

temporary polemics are probably too quick to insist that the subservient members of a patriarchal household could not have felt happy or free in the modern sense. Specific case histories often show middle-class wives exercising considerable power in the management of the household, and even the family business. Individual examples, of course, do not prove that the opposite was not usually the case. We doubt that particular social structures entail specific affective arrangements in this regard. People accommodate themselves in widely varying ways to the rules of any particular game; the human capacity for happiness and misery is uncontrollably inventive.

Along another axis, debate frequently concerns the degree to which the early modern family was "lineal" (aristocratic) or "nuclear" (bourgeois). We wish to draw attention to the imaginative intersection of those two categories.

23. James Graham, Marquis of Montrose, "My dear and only love, I pray," in *Ben Jonson and the Cavalier Poets,* ed. Hugh Maclean (New York: Norton, 1974), pp. 290–91. There is controversy as to whether the poem is "really" a love poem or a royalist polemic (lines not quoted mention synods and committees). The possibility of the latter being written in the guise of the former suffices for our point. We touch here on another rich area of recent controversy, one in which all generalizations are to an unusual degree up for discussion. The issues involved are usefully on display in the essays in *Rewriting the Renaissance: The Discourses of Sexual Difference in Early Modern Europe,* ed. Margaret W. Ferguson, Maureen Quilligan, and Nancy J. Vickers (Chicago: University of Chicago Press, 1986). To the question as posed in an particularly influential essay by Joan Kelly, "Did Women Have a Renaissance?" (1977)—in her *Women, History and Theory* (Chicago: University of Chicago Press, 1984), pp. 19–50—the answer appears to be, individual exceptions aside, no (though there is much debate as to what constitutes exceptions and what their significance, if they exist, is). In an especially strong statement, Catherine Belsey devotes the second half of *The Subject of Tragedy* (London: Methuen, 1985) to an account of Renaissance woman as the systematic inverse of the liberal humanist subject, the negation on which that subject relies in order to persist, but which also exposes its fraudulence. We emphasize a specific sense in which women served the ends of male ambition, but draw less drastic conclusions.

24. Alberti, *Family,* p. 177.

25. Torquato Tasso, "The Father of the Family," in *Tasso's Dialogues,* trans. Carnes Lord and Dain A. Trafton (Berkeley and Los Angeles: University of California Press, 1982), p. 55.

26. François Rabelais, *The Histories of Gargantua and Pantagruel,* trans. J. M. Cohen (Harmondsworth, Eng.: Penguin, 1955), p. 193.

27. Abel Lefranc, *Rabelais* (Paris: Michel, 1953), p. 136.

28. Rabelais, *Histories of Gargantua and Pantagruel,* p. 193.

29. In the classical account of the alliance between love and procreation, Plato's *Symposium,* the urge to procreate rapidly becomes metaphorical. Medieval Christianity invests this impulse with a new sanctity. The Renaissance, fitting out procreation in the humanist style, makes it answerable to

individualistic ambitions on a secular plane. For the "doctrine of increase" in Renaissance epithalamia, see Virginia Tufte, *The Poetry of Marriage: The Epithalamium in Europe and Its Development in England* (Los Angeles: Tinnon-Brown, 1970). The topic is there in Catullus (61.204ff.), but Renaissance literature gives it special emphasis. Spenser, for example, in celebrating the marriage of the Thames and the Medway, takes some of Catullus's neighboring metaphors of numerosity (61.199–203) and applies them not to the joys of love but to "the sea's progeny" (*Faerie Queene* 4.11.53–12.1). Robert Herrick is even more memorable: "Blest is the bride on whom the sun doth shine; / And thousands gladly wish / You multiply, as doth a fish" ("A Nuptial Song, or Epithalamy, on Sir Clipseby Crew and his Lady," ll. 48–50).

30. Alan Macfarlane, *The Family Life of Ralph Josselin* (Cambridge: Cambridge University Press, 1970), p. 119.

31. John Stephens, *Essays and Characters* (1615), in Wilson, *Life in Shakespeare's England*, p. 31.

32. Smith, *De republica Anglorum*, p. 74.

33. Shakespeare's succession ended with the death in 1670 of a childless granddaughter named Elizabeth. She was some four years old when *Henry VIII* was first performed; the play ends with a paean to the golden age to come through her royal namesake.

34. Rabelais, *Histories of Gargantua and Pantagruel*, pp. 312, 311.

35. The restless wife in Antonio Barzizza's neo-Plautine *Cauteraria* makes this point to her husband with particular force: "Men like you—and there are a lot of them—are crazy to think that by taking enough trouble you can keep your wives from doing what they want. Let me tell you how clever women are. If they've decided to keep their chastity, they can't be corrupted with silver or gold or anything else; but if they've got it in them to sin, it would be easier to keep an army of flies in the sun from moving than to keep a woman who wants to sin from doing it" (Ernst Beutler, ed., *Forschungen und Texte zur frühhumanistischen Komödie* [Hamburg: Staats- und Universitäts-Bibliothek, 1927], p. 164). The wife pays harrowingly for her eventual adultery with a priest—her husband brands her on "the sinning part" (*errantem locum*, p. 175; hence the play's title)—but she eventually wins her right to keep her lover on a regular basis.

3 : THE PRINCE AND THE PLAYHOUSE: A FABLE

1. Niccolò Machiavelli's *The Prince* is quoted from the translation of Mark Musa, with interpolations from the Italian in his bilingual edition (New York: St. Martin's, 1964).

2. Earlier approximations of Machiavelli's formula here are canvassed by Hanna Fenichel Pitkin, *Fortune Is a Woman: Gender and Politics in the Thought of Niccolò Machiavelli* (Berkeley and Los Angeles: University of California Press, 1984), pp. 142–43. The closer the parallel, the clearer the boldness of Machiavelli's claim. Marsilio Ficino, for instance, writes that *ingenium* and

fortune have a *diuisum imperium* over our lives; by this he means that fortune can rule only over external affairs, while *ingenium* has power in matters of the spirit (Ficino, *Epistolae* 11, in *Opera omnia*, 2 vols. [Basel, 1576; fac. reprint, Turin: Bottega d'Erasmo, 1962], 1:973). Machiavelli is making an un-Stoic assertion that *virtù* holds divided sway over things outside the mind as well.

3. Claudian, *Epithalamium de nuptiis Honorii Augusti*, l. 332. For the classical aphorisms that were almost certainly on Machiavelli's mind here, see Gordon Braden, *Renaissance Tragedy and the Senecan Tradition: Anger's Privilege* (New Haven: Yale University Press, 1985), p. 31.

4. See Anne Righter (later Barton), *Shakespeare and the Idea of the Play* (London: Chatto & Windus, 1962). The earlier history of the metaphor is reviewed on pp. 64–68; among the more interesting examples is one from the deathbed utterances of the Emperor Augustus (Suetonius, *Augustus* 99.1). Recent commentators have been particularly interested in the connections between the theater and absolutism; see, to very different effect, Walter Cohen, *Drama of a Nation: Public Theater in Renaissance England and Spain* (Ithaca: Cornell University Press, 1985); and Jonathan Goldberg, *James I and the Politics of Literature: Jonson, Shakespeare, Donne, and Their Contemporaries* (Baltimore: Johns Hopkins University Press, 1983).

5. Juan Luis Vives, "A Fable about Man," trans. Nancy Lenkeith, in *The Renaissance Philosophy of Man*, ed. Ernst Cassirer, Paul Oskar Kristeller, and John Herman Randall, Jr. (Chicago: University of Chicago Press, 1948), p. 389.

6. Kenneth Burke, *A Rhetoric of Motives* (1950; reprint, Berkeley and Los Angeles: University of California Press, 1969), p. 286.

7. Frank Whigham has some particularly acute pages on these dynamics—"the performative life as *predicament*"—as manifested within the court society, where image is even more fully everything: "The typical courtier's dominant Other will be the embodiment of an nonexistent 'public opinion,' readable in the mirroring responses of witnesses but dangerously evanescent. In fact, no one is in charge here" (*Ambition and Privilege: The Social Tropes of Elizabethan Courtesy Theory* [Berkeley and Los Angeles: University of California Press, 1984], p. 39).

8. Niccolò Machiavelli, letter 116 (to Piero Soderini), in *The Chief Works and Others*, trans. Allan Gilbert (Durham, N.C.: Duke University Press, 1965), p. 897. This version of the philosopher-king is, here and in *The Prince*, immediately hedged with pragmatic pessimism: "there never are such wise men, since men in the first place are shortsighted and in the second place cannot command their natures." What impresses us, though, is the force of the imagination that strains, in pursuit of extraordinary power over contingency, to transcend the stubbornness of individual character. The argument is played out to similar effect in Machiavelli's *Capitolo di Fortuna*, where we are offered the image of the individual defeating Fortune by jumping from wheel to wheel in her palace so as to stay always on top (ll. 115–17; in Gilbert, p. 747). In a comparable meditation in the *Discorsi* (3.9), respect for the practical limits on princely versatility leads Machiavelli to an argument for the

strength of republicanism: a variety of individuals in positions of power makes the needed variety of state action easier and more likely.

9. Abraham Cowley, translating Seneca, *Thyestes* 402–3 ("qui, notus nimis omnibus, / ignotus moritur sibi"). The chorus (on political ambition) from which these lines come was a particular favorite with English Renaissance and eighteenth-century translators, including Wyatt and Marvell. See G. K. Hunter, "Seneca and English Tragedy," in *Seneca*, ed. C.D.N. Costa (London: Routledge & Kegan Paul, 1974), pp. 197–201.

10. There is more to be said about this conflict in Machiavelli's own work; see Pitkin, *Fortune Is a Woman*, especially pp. 109–69.

11. Richard seems to imagine his own possible children only late, when attempting to win over Queen Elizabeth in his courtship of her daughter (4.4). We may take their appearance here as tactically motivated; in what may be an instance of his frequently cryptic honesty, Richard consistently refers to the prospective dynastic pleasure as Elizabeth's rather than his (296–306, 423–25). His own announced purpose in the courtship is merely to forestall Richmond's similar purpose (4.3.40–43).

12. Leon Battista Alberti, *The Family in Renaissance Florence*, trans. Renée Neu Watkins (Columbia: University of South Carolina Press, 1969), p. 136.

13. Milton's Satan seems to remember Richard in various specifics: "Which way shall I fly / Infinite wrath, and infinite despair? / Which way I fly is hell; my self am hell" (*Paradise Lost* 4.73–75). Satan's whole speech here is a Ricardian moment, because he is *rededicating* himself to his ambition.

4: CASSIRER'S LEGACY TO THE BURCKHARDT TRADITION

1. Fritz Saxl, "Ernst Cassirer," in *The Philosophy of Ernst Cassirer*, ed. Paul Arthur Schilpp (La Salle, Ill.: Open Court, 1949), p. 48. Saxl also recounts the story, which Renaissance scholars may find heartwarming, of Cassirer visiting Warburg at a sanitarium in Switzerland. Warburg told him that "modern thought was born when Kepler broke the traditional supremacy of the circle," which was the sort of thing that made his doctors shake their heads in dismay. Cassirer enthusiastically agreed and quoted from memory the relevant passage. This cheered Warburg.

2. Ernst Cassirer, *The Individual and the Cosmos in Renaissance Philosophy*, appeared in English in 1963, trans. Mario Domandi (New York: Harper & Row); we use the paperback edition published in 1972 by the University of Pennsylvania Press. Page numbers in the text are to this edition. *Die platonische Renaissance* was translated by James B. Pettegrove as *The Platonic Renaissance in England* (Austin: University of Texas Press, 1953). In his last years Cassirer wrote "Giovanni Pico della Mirandola: A Study in the History of Renaissance Ideas," *Journal of the History of Ideas* 3 (1942): 123–44, 319–46; "Force and Freedom: Remarks on the English Edition of Jacob Burckhardt's 'Reflections on History,'" *American Scholar* 13 (1944): 407–17; and new studies of Galileo, Descartes, and Vesalius. His review of Paul Oskar Kristeller's *The*

Philosophy of Marsilio Ficino appeared posthumously as "Ficino's Place in Intellectual History," *Journal of the History of Ideas* 6 (1945): 483–501.

3. Translated by Pettegrove in Cassirer, *The Platonic Renaissance in England,* p. 154. We shall see in chapter 6 how aptly Leibniz paired Ficino and Plotinus.

4. A major gap has recently been filled by the appearance of *The Cambridge History of Renaissance Philosophy,* ed. C. B. Schmitt et al. (Cambridge: Cambridge University Press, 1988), which promises all of us an easier access to this immense and difficult field.

5. John Herman Randall, "Cassirer's Theory of History as Illustrated in His Treatment of Renaissance Thought," in *Philosophy of Ernst Cassirer,* pp. 712–15; also *The Career of Philosophy,* 2 vols. (New York: Columbia University Press, 1962), 1:256–307.

6. Francis Macdonald Cornford, *The Unwritten Philosophy and Other Essays* (Cambridge: Cambridge University Press, 1967), p. 28. We have not done much in this book to recapture the life of Renaissance Stoicism; but see Gordon Braden, *Renaissance Tragedy and the Senecan Tradition: Anger's Privilege* (New Haven: Yale University Press, 1985).

7. For obvious reasons, Cassirer's work did take on moral urgency in the decade after *The Individual and the Cosmos* was published. See the essays collected in *Symbol, Myth, and Culture,* ed. Donald Philip Verene (New Haven: Yale University Press, 1979), especially "The Concept of Philosophy as a Philosophical Problem," pp. 49–63; "The Crisis in Man's Knowledge of Himself," in *An Essay on Man* (New Haven: Yale University Press, 1969), pp. 1–23; and the sections on Renaissance political thought in *The Myth of the State* (New Haven: Yale University Press, 1946), pp. 116–75, which are marked, as *The Individual and the Cosmos* is not, by an interest in Stoicism.

8. We take "postmodernism" to refer to the work of people who are trying to escape the traditions of Enlightenment rationalism. Some of the directions that postmodernism might go in the historiography of Renaissance thought can be sampled in Timothy J. Reiss's *The Discourse of Modernism* (Ithaca: Cornell University Press, 1982) and the historical sections of Richard Rorty's *Philosophy and the Mirror of Nature* (Princeton: Princeton University Press, 1979).

9. Hans Blumenberg's *Die Legitimität der Neuzeit* first appeared in 1966 and was revised when printed in three paperback volumes (1973, 1974, 1976); these revised texts have been translated into English as *The Legitimacy of the Modern Age,* by Robert M. Wallace (Cambridge, Mass.: MIT Press, 1983). Page numbers in the text are to this edition.

10. On Burckhardt's view of the Middle Ages, see Blumenberg, *Legitimacy of the Modern Age,* pp. 468–69.

11. Ernst Cassirer, "Some Remarks on the Question of the Originality of the Renaissance," *Journal of the History of Ideas* 4 (1943): 55. Cf. Blumenberg's metaphor of "reoccupied positions" (*Legitimacy of the Modern Age,* p. 466).

12. In the preface to *De sapientia ueterum,* which some scholars have taken rather solemnly, Bacon gives the best arguments he can concoct for the intendedness of the meanings he will attribute to the old fables, but throughout he concedes that people have always read their own truths into them. "Upon

the whole I conclude with this: the wisdom of the primitive ages was either great or lucky; great, if they knew what they were doing and invented the figure to shadow the meaning; lucky, if without meaning or intending it they fell upon matter which gives occasion to such worthy contemplation. My own pains, if there be any help in them, I shall think well bestowed either way: I shall be throwing light either upon antiquity or upon nature itself." Intended or not, he goes on, at least the meanings he has found are new. (*The Works of Francis Bacon,* ed. James Spedding, Robert Ellis, and Douglas Heath, 15 vols. [reprint, Saint Clair Shores, Mich.: Scholarly, 1976], 13:80–81.)

5: NICOLAS OF CUSA'S SYMBOLIC RENAISSANCE

1. Paul Sigmund, *Nicholas of Cusa and Medieval Political Thought* (Cambridge, Mass.: Harvard University Press, 1963), pp. 249–51; also Jasper Hopkins, *A Concise Introduction to the Philosophy of Nicholas of Cusa* (Minneapolis: University of Minnesota Press, 1978), pp. 6–7. (To prevent confusion, we note that *Concise Introduction* also contains the Latin text and an English translation of *Trialogus de possest,* cited later in this chapter.) The connection to Thierry of Chartres was first noted by Pierre Duhem, "Thierry of Chartres et Nicolas de Cues," *Revue des sciences philosophiques et théologiques* 3 (1909): 525–31.

2. From the introduction to Pauline Moffitt Watts's translation, with facing facsimile from the 1514 *Opera omnia,* of *De ludo globi (The Game of Spheres)* (New York: Abaris, 1986), p. 41. Jasper Hopkins, having attacked the work of Blumenberg for over forty pages of the introduction to his edition and translation of *De uisione dei* entitled *Nicholas of Cusa's Dialectical Mysticism* (Minneapolis: Banning, 1985), concedes that Nicolas "opens the door to Modernity by developing concepts and motifs which, had they been carried further, had they been more influential, had they been detached from their traditional associations, would have ushered in the Modern Age, instead of signaling its possibility" (p. 93). We will settle for, and we think Blumenberg would settle for, signaling its possibility, which must entail a certain degree of detachment from traditional associations.

3. Hans Blumenberg, *The Legitimacy of the Modern Age,* trans. Robert M. Wallace (Cambridge, Mass.: MIT Press, 1983), pp. 483–549; and on Gadamer, p. 476.

4. See n.2 above. Blumenberg's unfortunately melodramatic passage about Nicolas as would-be savior of his era appears in *Legitimacy of the Modern Age,* p. 483.

5. Perhaps the final paragraphs of Johan Huizinga's *Homo Ludens* (New York: Beacon, 1955) about religion as the "fixed, unmoving point" (p. 213) transcending the opposition of play and seriousness fit Nicolas better than Erasmus.

6. A learned philosopher seeking reassurance on the question of human immortality visits the wise craftsman of *Idiota de mente.*

7. *The Works of Francis Bacon,* ed. James Spedding, Robert Ellis, and Douglas Heath, 15 vols. (reprint, Saint Clair Shores, Mich.: Scholarly, 1976), 5:163–64.

8. Nicolas of Cusa, *The Vision of God (De visione dei)*, trans. Emma G. Salter (New York: Ungar, 1978), p. 44. In *De li non aliud,* chap. 14, Nicolas deems Pseudo-Dionysius "the greatest of the theologians," and quotes copiously from his works; see Jasper Hopkins, *Nicholas of Cusa on God as Not-other* (Minneapolis: University of Minnesota Press, 1979), p. 83. Nicolas suggests that his opponent, John Wenck, should read Erigena in *Apologia doctae ignorantiae;* Hopkins, *Nicholas of Cusa's Debate with John Wenck* (Minneapolis: Banning, 1981), p. 56.

9. Phillip Damon has noted the mistake in taking passages from Nicolas to give philosophical weight to a highly subjectivist account of perspective in Renaissance art; see his anthology *Literary Criticism and Historical Understanding* (New York: Columbia University Press, 1967), pp. 29–30. The most confident rationalism of our century, Husserl's phenomenology, finds in perspective its favorite example; different views of an object are views of the selfsame object, which could not be known apart from perspectival viewing—see E. D. Hirsch, Jr., *The Aims of Interpretation* (Chicago: University of Chicago Press, 1976), pp. 36–49.

10. Nicolas of Cusa, *Vision of God,* p. 25.

11. Ibid., p. 24.

12. Jorge Luis Borges, *Labyrinths,* ed. Donald A. Yates and James E. Irby (New York: New Directions, 1964), p. 208.

13. Sigmund, *Nicholas of Cusa and Medieval Political Thought,* p. 280.

14. Ernst Cassirer, *The Individual and the Cosmos in Renaissance Philosophy,* trans. Mario Domandi (Philadelphia: University of Pennsylvania Press, 1972), p. 35.

15. *De docta ignorantia* 1.3, in Jasper Hopkins, *Nicholas of Cusa on Learned Ignorance,* 2nd. ed. (Minneapolis: Banning, 1985), p. 52. On the question of the infinity of this world, see Alexandre Koyré, *From the Closed World to the Infinite Universe* (Baltimore: Johns Hopkins Press, 1957), pp. 5–28.

16. See Watts, in her introduction to *Game of Spheres,* p. 28.

17. Nicolas of Cusa, *Vision of God,* pp. 50–51.

18. On this theme in Nicolas, see Pauline Moffitt Watts, *Nicolaus Cusanus: A Fifteenth-Century Vision of Man* (Leiden: E. J. Brill, 1982), pp. 109–39. Man's deiformity in Renaissance thought has been studied by Charles Trinkaus in *"In Our Image and Likeness,"* 2 vols. (London: Constable, 1970). Trinkaus has defined his project, in terms evocative of Feuerbach, as a history of the gradual absorption of the concept of God into man's concept of himself, sacralizing the secular and secularizing the sacred, in *The Scope of Renaissance Humanism* (Ann Arbor: University of Michigan Press, 1983), p. xx.

19. Cassirer, *Individual and the Cosmos,* p. 23.

20. The possession of correct method was claimed by, and against, the humanists. Magicians and alchemists had method. Protestants had method, and by the eighteenth century had produced a sect calling itself Methodism.

Counter-Reformation Catholicism had method. Ramists had method. Jean Bodin's work on history was entitled *Methodus ad facilem historiarum cognitionem* (1566). Almost every intellectual reformer was certain that he had the right method. Often the only thing disputants agreed upon was that the previous age and its surviving traditions lacked method. Commentators have suggested that Nicolas presents his *docta ignorantia* as a *uia*, or "way," of the devotional life; by the seventeenth century, "way" was synonymous with "method," as in John Smith's "The True Way or Method of Attaining to Divine Knowledge." See Neal Ward Gilbert, *Renaissance Concepts of Method* (New York: Columbia University Press, 1967); and Walter J. Ong, *Ramus, Method, and the Decay of Dialogue* (Cambridge, Mass.: Harvard University Press, 1958).

This tradition still survives among contemporary humanists. After the theory blitz of the 1970s and 1980s, which seems to have made us fear public disagreement, as if the explosive new theories were analogous to nuclear weapons, it has become conventional for one intellectual to criticize the shortcomings of another by observing that his or her "methodology"—a euphemism, apparently, for stupidity and mistakenness—must be at fault.

The idea of progress has been the subject of many excellent studies. A recent discussion may be found in Achsah Guibbory, *The Map of Time: Seventeenth-Century English Literature and Ideas of Pattern in History* (Urbana: University of Illinois Press, 1986).

21. Leopold Damrosch, Jr., *Symbol and Truth in Blake's Myth* (Princeton: Princeton University Press, 1980), p. 242. Damrosch's discussion of this point contains interesting parallels with Nicolas.

22. See, for example, *De dato patris luminum* 5, in Jasper Hopkins, *Nicholas of Cusa's Metaphysic of Contraction* (Minneapolis: Banning, 1983), pp. 126–31; in *De docta ignorantia* 2.3, Nicolas asserts that "rest is oneness which enfolds motion, and motion is rest ordered serially" (Hopkins, p. 93).

23. From the translation of *De possest*, in Hopkins, *Concise Introduction*, p. 85.

24. Hopkins, *Nicholas of Cusa on Learned Ignorance*, pp. 155–56.

25. See Gordon Braden, "Nonnos' Typhoon: *Dionysiaca*, Books I and II," *Texas Studies in Literature and Language* 15 (1974): 873, where a Dantean analogue (*Purgatorio* 31.129) is also cited. The presence of the motif in Dante indicates that, by calling it "unmedieval," we are indeed dealing in gross generalizations. Still, a more full-blown development of the topos of prolonged appetite in Christian literature appears in *Paradise Lost* 5.493–505, where Milton incorporates the principle of motion into paradise by having Raphael declare that the bodies of Adam and Eve, through the mere process of digestion, "may at last turn all to spirit" and "wing'd ascend" to heaven. On the contrast between the clarified cosmos of Dante, pivoting on a chained Lucifer, and the dynamic universe of Milton, see William Kerrigan, *The Sacred Complex: On the Psychogenesis of Paradise Lost* (Cambridge, Mass.: Harvard University Press, 1983), pp. 152–53.

26. See Paul Schrader, *Transcendental Style in Cinema: Ozu, Bresson, Dreyer*

(Berkeley and Los Angeles: University of California Press, 1972).

27. Hopkins, *Concise Introduction,* p. 63.

28. It is no small part of the excellence of *Paradise Lost* among the verse narratives of the Renaissance that its entirety has been imaginatively compressed into moments of summary radiance. Kerrigan, thinking of Nicolas, calls this effect "the enfolded sublime" in *Sacred Complex,* pp. 230–35.

29. William Rossky, "Imagination in the English Renaissance: Psychology and Poetic," *Studies in the Renaissance* 5 (1958): 49–71.

30. Harry A. Wolfson, *Studies in the History of Philosophy and Religion* (Cambridge, Mass.: Harvard University Press, 1973), pp. 250–314. See also the historical chart in Edward S. Casey, *Imagining: A Phenomenological Study* (Bloomington: Indiana University Press, 1976), p. 130.

Cusanus figures centrally in Edgar Wind's well-known study of Renaissance symbolism, *Pagan Mysteries in the Renaissance* (New York: Norton, 1968).

31. Nicolas distinguishes between *ratio,* a discursive faculty linked to the senses, and *intellectus,* which is attuned to the eternal. Yet the intellectual faculty contains, in a more perfect way, the senses, and this is also true of the divine intellect: "Just as in the intellectual nature all degrees of perfection of the senses are implied, so in the divine are implied all degrees of perfection, alike of the intellect and of the senses" (*Vision of God,* p. 111).

32. Dan Sperber, *Rethinking Symbolism,* trans. Alice L. Morton (Cambridge: Cambridge University Press, 1975), p. 123. See also Paul Ricoeur's theory (derived from Benveniste) of symbolism as "semantic impertinence," in *The Rule of Metaphor: Multidisciplinary Studies of the Creation of Meaning in Language,* trans. Robert Czerny, Kathleen McLaughlin, and John Costello (Toronto: University of Toronto Press, 1977).

33. Nicolas of Cusa, *Idiota de mente,* 1–2, trans. Clyde Lee Miller as *The Layman, about Mind* (New York: Abaris, 1979); Cassirer appended this dialogue to the German edition of *Individuum und Kosmos.*

34. On manual labor, see Paolo Rossi, *Philosophy, Technology, and the Arts in the Early Modern Era,* ed. Benjamin Nelson and trans. Salvator Attanasio (New York: Harper & Row, 1970); on Puritanism and Baconianism in the mid-seventeenth century, Charles Webster, *The Great Instauration: Science, Medicine, and Reform, 1626–1660* (New York: Holmes & Meier, 1975). The American reprint is *The Idiot,* preface by W. R. Dennes (San Francisco: California State Library Occasional Papers, Reprint Series no. 19, 1940).

35. Ronald Levao, *Renaissance Minds and Their Fictions* (Berkeley and Los Angeles: University of California Press, 1985), p. 132.

36. Ibid., pp. 294–305.

37. Hopkins, *Concise Introduction,* p. 133.

38. Hopkins, *Nicolas of Cusa on Learned Ignorance,* p. 49.

39. Immanuel Kant, *Critique of Pure Reason,* trans. Norman Kemp Smith (New York: St. Martin's, 1965), p. 665.

40. Nicolas of Cusa, *Vision of God,* p. 36. See also p. 107, for the idea that God's knowledge of our minds is analogous to our reading of texts.

41. Nicolas of Cusa, *Vision of God*, p. 84. The Augustinian analogue would be book 8 of the *De trinitate*, where he meditates on the Trinity in terms of love and righteousness. But he assumes throughout that we love righteousness even though we are not righteous; when he arrives at the Trinity as lover, beloved, and the bond between (8.10.14), the linked loving is not reflected in the self.

6: THE NEOPLATONIC INDIVIDUALISM OF MARSILIO FICINO

1. *The Letters of Marsilio Ficino*, intro. Paul Oskar Kristeller, 3 vols. (London: Shepheard-Walwyn, 1975–), 1:136 (letter 86).

2. Frances Yates, *Giordano Bruno and the Hermetic Tradition* (New York: Random House, 1969), pp. 20–43.

3. D. P. Walker, *The Ancient Theology* (London: Warburg Institute, 1972).

4. Yates, *Giordano Bruno*, pp. 62–83; D. P. Walker, *Spiritual and Demonic Magic from Ficino to Campanella* (Notre Dame: University of Notre Dame Press, 1975); Robert Klein, *Form and Meaning: Essays on Renaissance and Modern Art*, trans. Madeline Jay and Leon Wieseltier (New York: Viking, 1979), pp. 62–88.

5. See Michael J. B. Allen, "Marsilio Ficino on Plato, the Neoplatonists and the Christian Doctrine of the Trinity," *Renaissance Quarterly* 37 (1984): 555–84. Allen thinks that it is important to stress that Ficino did *not* find all of Christian doctrine encoded in the Platonists. What strikes us, however, is that he found nothing in the Platonists abhorrent to Christian doctrine.

6. Michael J. B. Allen, *Marsilio Ficino and the Phaedran Charioteer* (Berkeley and Los Angeles: University of California Press, 1981), p. 110.

7. At one point in this work John Smith tellingly cites Plotinus when he thinks he is quoting Plato: see *The Cambridge Platonists*, ed. C. A. Patrides (Cambridge, Mass.: Harvard University Press, 1970), p. 141n.54.

8. A. O. Lovejoy, "The Dialectic of Bruno and Spinoza," *University of California Publications in Philosophy* 1 (1904): 150.

9. When writing against the Gnostics, Plotinus asserted the goodness of the flesh (though many stretches in his work imply otherwise); Ficino's pronounced tendency to equate flesh with evil and error is closer to Plato himself, as well as representing the reflex of centuries of Christian moralizing. Though both of them have large affection for unity, Ficino thinks of beauty as the harmony among parts, whereas Plotinus offers unanalyzable oneness as its highest form. But such differences pale beside their shared emphasis on contemplative ascent. In *John Colet and the Platonic Tradition* (London: Allen & Unwin, 1962), p. xiv, Leland Miles quotes the entertaining formulation of a German scholar: when Ficino declares in his *Enneads* translation that Plotinus should be read as Plato speaking in the person of his pupil, it is as if Plato had said, "This is my beloved son, hear ye him."

10. Jacques Derrida, "Form and Meaning," note 14, in *Speech and Phenomena*, trans. David B. Allison (Evanston: Northwestern University Press,

1973), pp. 127–28. This essay has been translated again by Alan Bass in his rendering of Derrida's *Margins of Philosophy* (Chicago: University of Chicago Press, 1982). In the Bass version the remarks about Plotinus, which are crucial for anyone who wants to understand Derrida's relation to the history of metaphysics, appear as note 16. One would think that for Derrida to grant an exemption to Plotinus would be tantamount to granting an exemption to Renaissance Neoplatonism, and thus to its historical heir, German idealism. It might seem unlikely that Derrida would make such a deep concession in a footnote, but of course that is exactly the sort of fissure he has taught us to seek in the "margins" of other ambitious philosophers. These questions should be investigated in detail. We note in passing that some of the criticisms traditionally leveled against Plotinus—his inert fixation on the absent One, for example—reappear in commentaries on Derrida. There are conceptual resemblances: "différance," the hidden act of differing deferred in every way we register differences, seems notably less unprecedented in light of Plotinus's One.

11. Plotinus, *Enneads* 4.3.30. On time and the hypostases, see Helena Weiss, "An Interpretative Note on a Passage in Plotinus' *On Eternity and Time*," *Classical Philology* 36 (1941): 230–39.

12. H. J. Blumenthal, "Did Plotinus Believe in Ideas of Individuals?" *Phronesis* 11 (1966): 61–80.

13. Émile Bréhier, *The Philosophy of Plotinus*, trans. Joseph Thomas (Chicago: University of Chicago Press, 1958), p. 6.

14. Sometimes Ficino wrote in more scholastic terms of gradations of substances, as Paul Oskar Kristeller notes in *The Philosophy of Marsilio Ficino*, trans. Virginia Conant (Gloucester, Mass.: Peter Smith, 1964), pp. 84–87.

15. Marsilio Ficino, *The Philebus Commentary*, trans. Michael J. B. Allen (Berkeley and Los Angeles: University of California Press, 1975), p. 46.

16. Their early prototype would be Proclus: Pseudo-Dionysius (whom Ficino also wrote a treatise on) did not change his "Archons" much in creating the rudiments of Christian angelology.

17. *Marsilio Ficino's Commentary on Plato's Symposium*, ed. and trans. Sears Reynolds Jayne, University of Missouri Studies, vol. 19, no. 1 (Columbia: University of Missouri, 1944), pp. 49–52, 143–46.

18. For an expanded discussion of Donne in these terms, see William Kerrigan, "What Was Donne Doing?" *South Central Review* 4 (1987): 9–11.

19. Marsilio Ficino, *Platonic Theology*, trans. Josephine Burroughs, "Ficino and Pomponazzi on Man," *Journal of the History of Ideas* 5 (1944): 237–38. The entire Latin text has been edited and translated into French in a three-volume edition, *Théologie platonicienne de l'immortalité des âmes*, by Raymond Marcel (Paris: Société d'Edition "Les Belles Lettres," 1964); for this passage, see 2:258–59. See also Allen, *Marsilio Ficino and the Phaedran Charioteer*, p. 76.

20. On the problem of intellect and will in Ficino, consult Kristeller's *Philosophy of Marsilio Ficino*, pp. 256–88, and Allen's introduction to *Philebus Commentary*, pp. 35–48. Allen gives text and translation of the letter in question, pp. 486–89.

21. Ficino, *Philebus Commentary,* p. 310.

22. Ibid., p. 47.

23. Ovid tells the tale in *Metamorphoses* 3.173–252; for the moral readings, see George Sandys, *Ovid's Metamorphosis Englished,* ed. Karl Hulley and Stanley Vandersall (Lincoln: University of Nebraska Press, 1970), pp. 150–52.

24. Giordano Bruno, *The Heroic Frenzies,* trans. Paul Eugene Memmo (Chapel Hill: University of North Carolina Press, 1960), p. 125.

25. Devotional literature offers some confirmation for this idea. In the seventeenth century, the German Jesuit Jacobus Masenius presented the usual negative readings of the myth, but then suggested that Narcissus in love with his image was like God in love with the human form; Pierre Marbeuf found Narcissus in God beholding the Virgin Mary; and Sor Juana Inés de la Cruz wrote a sacred drama, *El divino Narciso,* about the life of Christ. See Louise Vinge, *The Narcissus Theme* (Lund: Gleerups, 1967), pp. 189–91, 226–27, 244–48.

26. *Averrois Cordubensis Commentarium Magnum in Aristotelis de Anima Libros,* ed. F. Stuart Crawford (Cambridge, Mass.: Medieval Academy of America, 1953), pp. 406–7. Cassirer treats the influence of Averroës on Italian Renaissance doctrines of the soul in *The Individual and the Cosmos,* trans. Mario Domandi (New York: Harper & Row, 1963), pp. 127–30.

27. See Julius Weinberg, *A Short History of Medieval Philosophy* (Princeton: Princeton University Press, 1964), pp. 169–72, and Beatrice Zedler, "Averroës and Immortality," *New Scholasticism* 28 (1954): 453.

28. Ralph Waldo Emerson, "The Over-Soul," in *Essays and Lectures* (New York: Library of America, 1983), p. 386.

29. Ralph Waldo Emerson, "History," in ibid., p. 237.

30. Paul Oskar Kristeller, *Renaissance Concepts of Man* (New York: Harper & Row, 1972), p. 33; Aquinas, *Summa contra gentiles* 2.73. Petrarch also condemned Averroës; see Charles Trinkaus, *The Poet as Philosopher* (New Haven: Yale University Press, 1979), p. 97.

31. Kristeller, *Renaissance Concepts of Man,* p. 30.

32. Ibid., pp. 24–25; see also Paul Oskar Kristeller's *Eight Philosophers of the Italian Renaissance* (Stanford: Stanford University Press, 1964), p. 46.

33. From letter 40 in *Letters of Marsilio Ficino,* 1:82.

34. Ibid., pp. 82–83.

35. As Ficino wrote, "the entire effort of our soul is to become God" (*Platonic Theology* 14.1; trans. Kristeller, in *Philosophy of Marsilio Ficino,* p. 337). The arguments for immortality that follow in our text derive, unless otherwise noted, from Ficino's "Five Questions Concerning the Mind," in *Renaissance Philosophy of Man,* ed. Ernst Cassirer, Paul Oskar Kristeller, and John Herman Randall, Jr. (Chicago: University of Chicago Press, 1948), pp. 193–214. Antecedents to Ficino's "proof"—that because we want it, we will have it—include Dante's *Convivio* 2.9; see Richard Waswo, *Language and Meaning in the Renaissance* (Princeton: Princeton University Press, 1987), pp. 48–51.

36. Ficino, *Platonic Theology* 14.4, trans. Josephine Burroughs, in "Ficino

and Pomponazzi on Man," pp. 238–39. The source for the Alexander anecdote is in Plutarch's *Moralia,* "De tranquillitate animi" 466D; we are grateful
to G. W. Pigman III for this reference. Aquinas also knows that all things
strive to become godlike (*Summa contra gentiles* 3.19–21) and argues that the
beatific vision will satisfy, as no worldly object can, our appetites for honor,
pleasure, wealth, and renown (3.63). But his subdued language does not exalt
and deify such human desires.

37. A close analogue in English poetry is Edmund Waller's "Pride" (*Poems,*
ed. G. Thorn Drury, 2 vols. [London: Routledge, 1901], 2:114):

Not the brave Macedonian youth alone,
But base Caligula, when on the throne,
Boundless in power, would make himself a god,
As if the world depended on his nod.
The Syrian King to beasts was headlong thrown,
Ere to himself he could be mortal known.
The meanest wretch, if Heaven should give him line,
Would never stop till he were thought divine.

38. Ficino, "Five Questions," p. 208. See also Jerome Cardan (Girolamo
Cardano), *The Book of My Life,* trans. Jean Stoner (New York: Dutton, 1930),
p. 231: "There never has been, nor will there be, any rest for mortal man."
Fame is the main source of his restlessness (pp. 32, 35, 171, and passim).

39. Ficino, "Five Questions," p. 208.

40. Ficino, *Platonic Theology* 14.7, trans. Kristeller, in *Philosophy of Marsilio
Ficino,* p. 208. Cf., among other Shakespearean parallels, the opening speech
of *Twelfth Night.* Ben Jonson, too, had a melancholy streak: "What a deal of
cold business doth a man misspend the better part of life in! in scattering
compliments, tendering visits, gathering and venting news, following feasts
and plays, making a little winter love in a dark corner" (*Ben Jonson,* ed. C. H.
Herford, Percy Simpson, and Evelyn Simpson, 11 vols. [Oxford: Clarendon
Press, 1932–47], 8:565). See William Kerrigan, "Ben Jonson Full of Shame
and Scorn," *Studies in the Literary Imagination* 6 (1973): 199–217.

41. The phrases may be found in Ficino, "Five Questions," p. 209, and in
Kristeller's *Philosophy of Marsilio Ficino,* p. 340.

42. Erwin Panofsky, Fritz Saxl, and Raymond Klibansky, *Saturn and Melancholy* (Cambridge: Cambridge University Press, 1964). See also Rudolf
Wittkower and Margot Wittkower, *Born under Saturn* (New York: Norton,
1969). Classical antecedents include Plato's theory of divine frenzy and Aristotle's *Problemata* 30.1. Agrippa's revision of Ficino in *De occulta philosophia*
1.60 was influential.

It seems to us that Ficino's founding association of melancholy with denied
or unobtainable birthright, our severance from the "celestial fatherland,"
holds good throughout the cultural life of this psychology, appearing in the
secular frustrations of Shakespeare's Hamlet, the despairing exile of Milton's

Satan, the "sweet and potent voice" of the soul's "own birth" that Coleridge cannot retrieve in "Dejection: An Ode," and the melancholy fit that falls "sudden from heaven" in Keats's "Ode on Melancholy."

43. Ficino, "Five Questions," p. 212.

44. Ibid.

7: PICO DELLA MIRANDOLA AND RENAISSANCE AMBITION

1. See the Averroistic section of the *Conclusiones,* in Giovanni Pico della Mirandola and Gianfrancesco Pico della Mirandola, *Opera omnia,* 2 vols. (Basel, 1557; fac. reprint, Hildesheim: Olms, 1969), 1:67–68.

2. See Frances Yates, *Giordano Bruno and the Hermetic Tradition* (New York: Random House, 1969), pp. 84–116, and also her book *The Occult Philosophy in the Elizabethan Age* (London: Routledge & Kegan Paul, 1979), pp. 17–71.

3. We quote Pico's *Oration* in the translation by Charles Wallis, with page references to Giovanni Pico della Mirandola, *On the Dignity of Man, On Being and the One, Heptaplus,* trans. Charles Wallis, Paul Miller, and Douglas Carmichael (New York: Bobbs-Merrill, 1965). Pico's use of the Osiris myth to evoke the double motion of enfolding and unfolding in the act of interpreting texts is suggestively close to Milton's language in *Areopagitica* about reforming the scattered body of Truth (*Prose Works,* 2:549–51, 554–55).

4. Here we are indebted to the excellent discussion of Harry Berger, Jr., in "Pico and Neoplatonist Idealism: Philosophy as Escape," *Centennial Review* 13 (1969): 38–83. Berger adduces two particularly apt passages from Augustine warning against the spiritual pride that often accompanies a fascination with our misty angelic betters (p. 47).

5. In his early *Commentary on a Canzone of Benivieni* (trans. Sears Jayne, American University Studies, series 2, vol. 19 [New York: Peter Lang, 1984]), Pico follows the hypostases of Plotinus. God (the One) thus created one time only, making a First Mind or First Angel who must then have been the creator of Genesis (pp. 81, 86)—hence, in the allegorical fables of classical myth, the birth of Venus from the castration of Uranus (p. 115). This cosmogony is not obviously defended in *Heptaplus,* and does not intrude into the *Oration.* But the transaction between a finished creator and Adam retains a similar pattern: creativity is passed on through completion; after allness or perfection, there is an initiation of moreness.

6. The sculpting metaphor probably derives from Plotinus, *Enneads* 1.6.9: "Withdraw into yourself and look. If you do not as yet see beauty within you, do as does the sculptor of a statue that is to be beautified: he cuts away here, he smooths it there, he makes this line lighter, this other one purer, until he disengages beautiful lineaments in the marble. Do you this, too. Cut away all that is excessive, straighten all that is crooked, bring light to all that is overcast, labor to make all one radiance of beauty. Never cease 'working at the statue' until there shines out upon you from it the divine sheen of virtue, until you see perfect 'goodness firmly established in stainless shrine'" (*The Essential*

Plotinus, ed. Elmer O'Brien [Indianapolis: Hackett, 1964], p. 42). For Hegel's appropriation of the trope, see chap. 1, n.22, above. A Piconian element survives in Kant's rationalization of Genesis, but pushed ahead from the creation of man to the Fall, where man "discovered in himself an ability to choose his own way of life and thus not to be bound like the other animals to only a single one" ("Speculative Beginning of Human History," in *Perpetual Peace and Other Essays,* trans. Ted Humphrey [Indianapolis: Hackett, 1983], p. 51).

7. Berger, "Pico and Neoplatonist Idealism," p. 45.

8. Ibid., p. 63.

9. Jonathan Dollimore, in *Radical Tragedy: Religion, Ideology, and Power in the Drama of Shakespeare and His Contemporaries* (Chicago: University of Chicago Press, 1984), compliments Pico's vision of human identity for being "anti-essentialist" (p. 179), which is not, in his view, the prevailing opinion of the age. He indicates elsewhere (pp. 162–63) that by "anti-essentialist" he means in part the separation of mankind from God. However, because this apparent independence stems in Pico from the gift to man of God's own unboundedness, the separation can also be characterized as an affinity.

10. George B. Parks, "Pico della Mirandola in Tudor Translation," in *Philosophy and Humanism: Renaissance Essays in Honor of Paul Oskar Kristeller,* ed. Edward P. Mahoney (New York: Columbia University Press, 1976), pp. 352–69.

11. Translation and page references for Montaigne are from *The Complete Essays of Montaigne,* trans. Donald M. Frame (Stanford: Stanford University Press, 1965). By "human," Montaigne means that we mortals are vulnerable to the folly of aspiring beyond our limits.

12. Sir Philip Sidney, *An Apology for Poetry,* in *Elizabethan Critical Essays,* ed. G. Gregory Smith, 2 vols. (London: Oxford University Press, 1904), 1:155–56.

13. *The Works of Francis Bacon,* ed. James Spedding, Robert Ellis, and Douglas Heath, 15 vols. (reprint, Saint Clair Shores, Mich.: Scholarly, 1976), 12:187–88; Bacon inserted a Latin version of this essay into the *De augmentis* (9:297–311). A Spanish engraving of 1599, reproduced as the frontispiece to J. H. Elliott, *The Old World and the New, 1432–1650* (Cambridge: Cambridge University Press, 1972), chillingly illustrates the would-be infinity of imperial power. A conquistador, his left hand on the hilt of his sword, reaches toward a globe with his right hand, which holds surveyor's compasses. "Mas y mas y mas y mas," the inscription reads. Spain, incidentally, is Bacon's example of imperial overextension.

14. Torquato Tasso, "The Father of the Family," in *Tasso's Dialogues,* trans. Carnes Lord and Dain A. Trafton (Berkeley and Los Angeles: University of California Press, 1982), p. 141; for a version in Renaissance English, see *The Works of Thomas Kyd,* ed. F. S. Boas (Oxford: Clarendon Press, 1901), p. 279. Piconian man, ever surpassing himself, is like a money-market fund. On the eventual alliance of virtue, land, and anticommercialism, see J.G.A. Pocock, *The Machiavellian Moment: Florentine Political Thought and the Atlantic Republican Tradition* (Princeton: Princeton University Press, 1975), pp. 401–505.

15. Hobbes, and to some extent Browne, belong to the tradition defined by George Williamson in "The Restoration Revolt against Enthusiasm," *Studies in Philology* 30 (1933): 571–603.

16. For quotations from Sir Thomas Browne, we give page references to *Religio Medici and Other Works*, ed. L. C. Martin (Oxford: Oxford University Press, 1964). Neither of Browne's contemporary critics may have been especially perceptive about the details of his *Religio Medici*, but they nonetheless registered important currents in his work. Kenelm Digby was appalled that Browne once courted the mortalist heresy, and proceeded, in high Renaissance fashion, to supply his soul with some newfangled Cartesian arguments for its immortality. But at least Digby sensed, however confusedly, that Browne was a Christian remarkably at ease with the thought of oblivion. Alexander Ross thought Browne's attack on zeal was impious, and produced arguments against tolerance. But at least Ross sensed, however confusedly, that Browne was a new kind of belonger, one who had broken free from blind confinement by the "general categories," as Burckhardt called them, of country, class, and church. (Browne is acute as usual about the prejudices of patriotism—see p. 60.) On Digby and Ross, see James N. Wise, *Sir Thomas Browne's Religio Medici and Two Seventeenth-Century Critics* (Columbia: University of Missouri Press, 1973). The young Milton, suggestively, refuted Browne-like arguments against ambition in prolusion 7 (*Prose Works*, 1:288–306).

17. Justus Lipsius might be an apt example here. The most powerful opponent of constancy is sorrow, especially sorrow for the ills of one's country, which is the infinite instance among human passions: "For all the other affections have some final cause and scope to which they tend (as the lover enjoys his desire, the angry man to be revenged, the covetous churl to acquire, and so on), while only sorrow has no end" (*De constantia*, in *Renaissance Philosophy*, ed. and trans. Herman Shapiro and Arthur Fallico, 2 vols. [New York: Random House, 1969], 2:125–26). To defeat this mighty opponent, the stoic sage goes to the extreme of seeking to obliterate national identification altogether, methodically reproducing the interior homelessness of Burckhardt's exiles (pp. 113–16, 119–23).

18. T. S. Eliot, "Andrew Marvell," in *Selected Essays* (New York: Harcourt, 1960), p. 262.

19. Bacon, *The Advancement of Learning*, in *Works*, 6:120.

8: Descartes's Beginning

1. Catherine Belsey, *The Subject of Tragedy* (London: Methuen, 1985): "Following Descartes, Locke [proposes a new] metaphysics of the human essence" (p. 83); Jonathan Dollimore, *Radical Tragedy: Religion, Ideology, and Power in the Drama of Shakespeare and His Contemporaries* (Chicago: University of Chicago Press, 1984): "In Descartes we can see a crucial stage in the history of

metaphysics, one whereby essence takes on a new importance in the schema" (p. 254).

2. Richard Popkin, *The History of Skepticism from Erasmus to Spinoza,* 2nd ed. (Berkeley and Los Angeles: University of California Press, 1979).

3. We quote *The Search for Truth,* in *The Philosophical Works of Descartes,* trans. Elizabeth Haldane and G.R.T. Ross, 2 vols. (Cambridge: Cambridge University Press, 1911), 1:324. We prefer this translation of the work to the one in the revised Cambridge Descartes, *The Philosophical Writings,* ed. John Cottingham, Robert Stoothoff, and Dugald Murdoch, 2 vols. (Cambridge: Cambridge University Press, 1984). However, all the other Cartesian texts are cited in our text by volume and page of the later edition. We shall use notes to identify quotations from *The Search for Truth,* which are all from Haldane and Ross.

4. It goes forward at least as far as Samuel Beckett's *Fallor, ergo sum* in "Whoroscope"; see his *Poems in English* (New York: Grove, 1961), p. 14.

5. John Dryden, *The Dramatic Works,* ed. Montague Summers, 6 vols. (London: Nonesuch, 1932), 3:431.

6. *The Collected Poems of Wallace Stevens* (New York: Knopf, 1962), p. 383.

7. Ralph Waldo Emerson, "Self-Reliance," in *Essays and Lectures* (New York: Library of America, 1983), p. 270.

8. Martin Heidegger, *Being and Time,* trans. John Macquarrie and Edward Robinson (New York: Harper & Row, 1962), p. 254. Heidegger believed that Descartes left unexamined "the kind of Being that belongs to the *res cogitans,* or—more precisely—the *meaning of the Being of the 'sum'*" (p. 46).

9. Paul Ricoeur, *Freud and Philosophy,* trans. Denis Savage (New Haven: Yale University Press, 1970), pp. 42–56.

10. Jacques Lacan, "The Agency of the Letter in the Unconscious or Reason since Freud," in *Ecrits,* trans. Alan Sheridan (New York: Norton, 1977), p. 166.

11. A. J. Ayer, "'I Think, Therefore I Am,'" in *Descartes: A Collection of Critical Essays,* ed. Willis Doney (Notre Dame: University of Notre Dame Press, 1968), p. 85. Probably the most influential attack on Descartes in twentieth-century British philosophy was Gilbert Ryle's *The Concept of Mind* (New York: Barnes & Noble, 1949); see especially the opening chapter, "Descartes' Myth."

12. Edmund Husserl, *Cartesian Meditations,* trans. Dorion Cairns (The Hague: Nijhoff, 1973), p. 2; see also (same page) an appended passage on the objection that science is already a communal enterprise.

13. Descartes, *Search for Truth,* 1:305. See also *Discourse on Method,* in *Philosophical Writings,* 1:117.

14. Quoted in *Cartesian Studies,* ed. R. J. Butler (Oxford: Basil Blackwell, 1972), pp. 80, 38.

15. Descartes, *Search for Truth,* 1:323.

16. Jacques Derrida, "Cogito and the History of Madness," in *Writing and Difference,* trans. Alan Bass (Chicago: University of Chicago Press, 1978), p. 56.

17. Ibid., p. 60.

18. Martin Heidegger, "The Age of the World Picture," in *The Question Concerning Technology and Other Essays,* trans. William Lovitt (New York: Harper & Row, 1977), pp. 115–54, and on Descartes's "co-agitatio," pp. 151–53; John Dewey, *Reconstruction in Philosophy* (Boston: Beacon, 1948), pp. 111–12.

19. Émile Bréhier, "The Creation of the Eternal Truths in Descartes's System," in *Descartes: A Collection of Critical Essays,* ed. Doney, pp. 192–208. On voluntarism, see also *Descartes' Conversation with Burman,* ed. and trans. John Cottingham (Oxford: Clarendon Press, 1976), p. 22.

20. Descartes, *Search for Truth,* 1:322.

21. Ibid., 1:308.

22. See also Descartes's letter to the doctors of the Sorbonne (*Philosophical Writings,* 2:3–6), where he argues that he has fulfilled the injunction of the Lateran Council of 1513, which established the dogma of immortality in condemning Averroës.

23. Here we are again indebted to Bréhier's essay "Creation of the Eternal Truths."

24. Anthony Kenny, "Descartes on the Will," in *Cartesian Studies,* ed. Butler, p. 6. See also Hiram Caton, "Will and Reason in Descartes's Theory of Error," *Journal of Philosophy* 4 (1975): 87–104.

25. See Immanuel Kant, *The Critique of Judgement,* trans. J. H. Bernard (New York: Hafner, 1951), pp. 85–100.

26. Ralph Waldo Emerson, *Nature,* in *Essays and Lectures,* p. 15.

27. Richard Rorty, "Freud and Moral Reflection," in *Pragmatism's Freud: The Moral Disposition of Psychoanalysis,* ed. Joseph Smith and William Kerrigan (Baltimore: Johns Hopkins University Press, 1986), p. 15.

28. *The Standard Edition of the Complete Psychological Works of Sigmund Freud,* ed. and trans. James Strachey, 24 vols. (London: Hogarth, 1953–64), 9:210–11. Hereafter, this edition is cited as *SE.*

On Freud's imaginative affinity with the Renaissance, see William Kerrigan, "Atoms Again: The Deaths of Individualism," in *Taking Chances: Derrida, Psychoanalysis, and Literature,* ed. Joseph H. Smith and William Kerrigan (Baltimore: Johns Hopkins University Press, 1984), pp. 86–106; and "What Freud Forgot: A Parable for Intellectuals," in *Pragmatism's Freud,* pp. 159–73; also Gordon Braden, "Love and Fame: The Petrarchan Career," in *Pragmatism's Freud,* pp. 129–58.

29. Sigmund Freud, "Creative Writers and Day-Dreams," in *SE,* 9:153.

9: PETRARCH REFRACTED: THE EVOLUTION OF THE ENGLISH LOVE LYRIC

1. We use the text and translation in *Petrarch's Lyric Poems,* ed. and trans. Robert M. Durling (Cambridge, Mass.: Harvard University Press, 1976).

2. See James V. Mirollo, *Mannerism and Renaissance Poetry: Concept, Mode,*

Inner Design (New Haven: Yale University Press, 1984), pp. 99–159.

3. Petrarch himself defensively insisted to Giacomo Colonna that Laura was not merely a literary character. See *Rerum Familiarum Libri I–VIII,* trans. Aldo S. Bernardo (Albany: State University of New York Press, 1975), p. 102.

4. Maurice Valency, *In Praise of Love: An Introduction to the Love Poetry of the Renaissance,* 2nd. ed. (New York: Schocken, 1982), p. 160.

5. Baldassare Castiglione, *The Book of the Courtier,* trans. Charles S. Singleton (Garden City, N.Y.: Doubleday, 1959), p. 351.

6. The fullest source on the mythography of Narcissus is Louise Vinge's *The Narcissus Theme* (Lund: Gleerups, 1967). An important tradition of late medieval moral thought makes much of the lover's *immoderata cogitatio;* see D. W. Robertson, *A Preface to Chaucer* (Princeton: Princeton University Press, 1962), pp. 65–113; also, with regard to Petrarch, John Freccero, "The Fig Tree and the Laurel: Petrarch's Poetics," *Diacritics* 5 (1975): 34–40.

7. Petrarch, *De remediis utriusque fortunae* 1.10, in *Opera quae extant omnia* (Basel, 1554; fac. reprint in 3 vols., Ridgewood, N.J.: Gregg, 1965), 1:14–15.

8. We quote the translation by Henry Bettenson: Augustine, *Concerning the City of God against the Pagans* (Harmondsworth, Eng.: Penguin, 1984).

9. *Petrarch's Secret,* trans. William H. Draper (London: Chatto & Windus, 1911), pp. 55, 165–66, 192.

10. Petrarca, *Letters on Familiar Matters: Rerum Familiarium Libri IX–XVI,* trans. Aldo S. Bernardo (Baltimore: Johns Hopkins University Press, 1982), p. 199.

11. Petrarch, *Epistolae seniles,* book 17, epistle 2, quoted from Ernest Hatch Wilkins, *Petrarch's Later Years* (Cambridge, Mass.: Medieval Academy of America, 1959), p. 248; on the persistence of Petrarch's *desiderium gloriae,* see Hans Baron, "Petrarch: His Inner Struggles and the Humanistic Discovery of Man's Nature," in *Florilegium Historiale: Essays Presented to Wallace K. Ferguson,* ed. J. G. Rowe and W. H. Stockdale (Toronto: University of Toronto Press, 1971).

12. Thomas M. Greene, "The Flexibility of the Self in Renaissance Literature," in *The Disciplines of Criticism: Essays in Literary Theory, Interpretation, and History,* ed. Peter Demetz, Thomas M. Greene, and Lowry Nelson, Jr. (New Haven: Yale University Press, 1968), p. 247.

13. Here we have modified Durling's translation.

14. On the absent presence of the Narcissus myth in *Canzoniere* 23, see Durling's perceptive remarks in *Petrarch's Lyric Poems,* p. 28.

15. Durling treats the appearance of the myth in *Canzoniere* 23 as an inversion of the myth of Daphne (*Petrarch's Lyric Poems,* pp. 28–29); we go on to suggest a positive likeness.

16. Nicholas Kilmer's translation is felicitous in *Songs and Sonnets from Laura's Lifetime* (San Francisco: North Point, 1981): "I can hear the dogs while I write this."

17. For Wyatt, we use the text and poem numbers in *Sir Thomas Wyatt: The Complete Poems,* ed. R. A. Rebholz (New Haven: Yale University Press,

1981). The Italian of the last line of this poem reads "Ché bel fin fa chi ben amando more" (For he makes a good end who dies loving well).

18. Petrarch, *Triumphus mortis* 2.76ff.; see Aldo S. Bernardo, *Petrarch, Laura, and the Triumphs* (Albany: State University of New York Press, 1974), pp. 123–27.

19. *The Works of Michael Drayton*, ed. J. William Hebel, 5 vols. (Oxford: Shakespeare Head, 1932), 2:332. The frontispiece to the *Poems* (1619), reproduced in volume 2 of this edition, shows Drayton wearing the laurel crown.

20. In the seventeenth century, Thomas Stanley summarized Spenser's marriage of narcissisms in a single poem, "To Chariessa, beholding herself in a Glass"; in *Minor Poets of the Caroline Period*, ed. George Saintsbury, 3 vols. (Oxford: Clarendon Press, 1905), 3:102.

21. We realize that the appetite for female resistance in Renaissance love poetry may provoke suspicion and outrage today, with our new alertness to what Susan Brownmiller calls "The Myth of the Heroic Rapist," in *Against Our Will* (New York: Simon & Schuster, 1975). The concern is a real one, especially in view of the repeated centrality of rape in the classical myths that adorn Renaissance love lyrics—most notably, of course, the key Petrarchan myth of Apollo and Daphne; see Froma Zeitlin's "Configurations of Rape in Greek Myth," in *Rape*, ed. Sylvana Tomaselli and Roy Porter (Oxford: Basil Blackwell, 1986), pp. 122–51. We do not, however, think such myths reducible to their crudest application, a gesture that would render almost any source of erotic excitement appalling.

Society has to make distinctions between sexual advance and attempted rape, and some of the distinctions are bound to be difficult. We do not think any of the love poems discussed in this final section really urge a dishonorable coercion of the woman. Marlowe does imagine Hero discovering physical excitement in physical resistance, which calls to mind the classic excuse for rape, but Marlowe (ever a specialist in conquest) is an extreme. There are marked variations in the extent to which the male's physical engagement of the resistance, a full sexualization of Petrarchan courtship, is desired. A notch below Marlowe stands William Cartwright's "Song of Dalliance," where the male wants to be resisted, but wants the woman to agree beforehand that her refusal will be a pretense; *The Plays and Poems of William Cartwright*, ed. G. Blakemore Evans (Madison: University of Wisconsin Press, 1951), pp. 467–68. Writing of the London Fire in *Annus Mirabilis*, Dryden imagines the nascent blaze pent up in an enclosure, trying, against (apparent) resistance from the winds, to break out. This friction of the elements reminds him of the male libido:

The winds, like crafty courtesans, withheld
His flames from burning, but to blow them more:
And, every fresh attempt, he is repell'd
With faint denials, weaker than before.

(Ll. 881–84)

Here, as "crafty" indicates, the scenario of eroticized female resistance is a mutual strategy for fanning the flames. In *Paradise Lost,* as we shall see in the next chapter, the daily game of eroticized resistance is just a matter of delay and modesty, not of pretending to exert force upon the woman.

22. Collop's work remains largely unknown even among specialists, despite the convenient edition of Conrad Hilberry, *The Poems of John Collop* (Madison: University of Wisconsin Press, 1962).

23. Drayton, *Works,* 2:372.

24. In his autobiography, Edward Herbert tells of his fascination with a certain Monsieur Balagny, who combined a reputation for honor with sexual magnetism. Finally, as was the habit of this rivalrous spirit, Herbert approached the Frenchman with a challenge, saying "I heard he had a fair mistress, and that the scarf he wore was her gift, and that I would maintain I had a worthier mistress than he, and that I would do as much for her sake as he or any else durst do for his. Balagny hereupon looking merrily upon me, said, 'If we shall try who is the abler man to serve his mistress, let both of us get two wenches, and he that does his business best, let him be the braver'; and that for his part, he had no mind to fight on that quarrel. I looking hereupon somewhat disdainfully on him, said he spoke more like a palliard than a cavalier; to which he answered nothing" (*The Life of Lord Herbert of Cherbury* [London: Cassell, 1893], p. 87). Like some of the seventeenth-century poets, Balagny had made the transition from Petrarchism to libertinism. It is interesting that the second should be associated with male camaraderie and the first with stiff contentiousness. A dark version of the same contrast is dramatized in *Titus Andronicus* 2.1.

25. For the spirit of rivalry in Marvell's own temperament, see William Kerrigan, "Marvell and Nymphets," *Greyfriar* 27 (1986): 12–16.

26. Edmund Waller, *Poems,* ed. G. Thorn Drury, 2 vols. (London: Bullen, 1901), 1:52. In a similar poem translated from Giambattista Marino, Thomas Stanley has the laurel watered by Apollo's tears until he plucks a branch to kiss: "Thus this disdainful maid his aim deceives: / Where he expected fruit he gathers leaves" (in Saintsbury, *Minor Poets of the Caroline Period,* 3:128–29). But here emphasis falls on the continued success of Daphne's refusal, and not, as in Waller, on the excellence of the substitution.

27. Donne's "The Cross," l. 58, and Herrick's "His Age, Dedicated to His Peculiar Friend, Master John Wickes, under the Name of Posthumous," l. 112.

28. "If we are one, dear friend!" (answering William Fairfax's "The Union"), in Saintsbury, *Minor Poets of the Caroline Period,* 3:155.

29. See the discussion of the authorship of this lyric in *The Life, Letters, and Writings of John Hoskyns, 1566–1638,* ed. Louise Brown Osborn (Hamden, Conn.: Archon, 1973), pp. 285–87. H.J.C. Grierson printed the poem among the *dubia* in *The Poems of John Donne,* 2 vols. (Oxford: Clarendon Press, 1912). Donne rejects mental images as substitute gratification in his elegy "The Dream," but his poems often exploit dichotomies ("The Storm," "The

Calm"), and that fact alone does not mean much one way or the other in determining the authorship of "Absence, hear thou my protestation." Because Osborn prints inferior variants in her edition of Hoskyns, we have quoted the version found in Francis Davison's *Poetic Rhapsody,* as it appears in *Poetry of the English Renaissance, 1509–1660,* ed. J. William Hebel and Hoyt H. Hudson (New York: Appleton-Century-Crofts, 1957), pp. 203–4.

30. In "To Althea, from Prison," Lovelace almost seems to prefer to Althea's presence the companionship of her image in the loneliness of his cell. Mariann Sanders Regan discusses the Petrarchan preference for images in *Love Words: The Self and the Text in Medieval and Renaissance Poetry* (Ithaca: Cornell University Press, 1982). On the theme of inwardness in love poetry, see Anne Ferry, *The "Inward Language": Sonnets of Wyatt, Sidney, Shakespeare, Donne* (Chicago: University of Chicago Press, 1984). The conception of the individual implicit in our book does not rest, as Ferry's seems to, on the supposition that all of us have a private selfhood given outside of language and announced in the breakdown of language. People may learn to cultivate such a selfhood, but they do not, in our view, recognize one that is already there, ready-made.

31. On the theme of deliberate male discourtesy in Renaissance verse, see Louis B. Salomon, *The Devil Take Her! A Study of the Rebellious Lover in English Poetry* (New York: A. S. Barnes, 1961).

32. Robert Burton, *The Anatomy of Melancholy,* ed. Floyd Dell and Paul Jordan-Smith (New York: Farrar & Rinehart, 1927), p. 786. Both the sentiment and the phrasing here recall the refrain of George Wither's "Shall I be wasting in despair" (Hebel and Hudson, p. 592).

33. *The Poems and Amyntas of Thomas Randolph,* ed. John Jay Parry (New Haven: Yale University Press, 1917), p. 167. See Gordon Braden's *"Viuamus, mea Lesbia* in the English Renaissance," *English Literary Renaissance* 9 (1979): 199–224. The classical precedent for infinite kisses is Martial 6.34. See n.39 below.

34. "Paradox. That Fruition Destroys Love," in *The Poems of Henry King,* ed. Margaret Crum (Oxford: Clarendon Press, 1969), p. 184. King touches on the same theme in "The Surrender." Even in "The Short Wooing" he speaks of his "chaste desire." In "Paradox. That Fruition Destroys Love" he notes that Adam, had he confined himself to looking, would not have lost his innocence. The association of orgasm with the Fall is a regular feature of the antifruition poems: it may be that one component of postcoital sadness is the male's mourning for his fallen erection. Doing, as Jonson and Pseudo-Petronius say, is *short.* This is also among Donne's complaints in "Farewell to Love."

Other lyrics on the fruition question may be found in *Speculum Amantis: Love-Poems from Rare Song-Books and Miscellanies of the Seventeenth Century,* ed. A. H. Bullen (Privately printed, 1895), pp. 5, 20, 71, 78–79. Stanley writes against frustrating delay in lyrics such as "Expectation" and "Delay," but elsewhere favors it; the conflict comes to a head in the two "answer" poems "Wert thou yet fairer than thou art" (pro-fruition) and "Wert thou by all affections sought" (antifruition). Along with the poems by Shakespeare, Donne, and Jonson, Nashe's "The Merry Ballad of Nashe His Dildo," sometimes entitled "A Choice of Valentines," is a main precursor of the genre. Its prolonged contest between the prick and a dildo turns on the shortness of the sexual act, in which "blissful hope" is always defeated. It may at least be wondered whether some of the poems in this minor seventeenth-century lyric genre expressly set out to answer the "fruition" sonnets that open Shakespeare's sequence.

35. Sir Thomas Browne, *Religio Medici and Other Works,* ed. L. C. Martin (Oxford: Oxford University Press, 1964), p. 67.

36. See Gordon Braden, *The Classics and English Renaissance Poetry: Three Case Studies* (New Haven: Yale University Press, 1978), pp. 217ff.

37. Printed in *The Works of Sir John Suckling: The Non-Dramatic Works,* ed. Thomas Clayton (Oxford: Clarendon Press, 1971), pp. 181–85.

38. See *Aglaura* 1.4.57–59, 1.5.1–7, 3.2.62–65, 3.2.106–12, and *The Goblins* 3.7.114–17, in *The Works of Sir John Suckling: The Plays,* ed. L. A. Beaurline (Oxford: Clarendon Press, 1971). This is the poet termed in the headnotes of the fourth edition of *The Norton Anthology of English Literature,* ed. M. H. Abrams et al., 2 vols. (New York: Norton, 1979), "the prototype of the Cavalier playboy" (1:1604).

39. The end of the poem, "He's only rich that cannot tell his store," echoes the concluding passage of Ralegh's imitation of *Viuamus, mea Lesbia,* "Now, Serena, be not coy," in *The Poems of Sir Walter Ralegh,* ed. Agnes Latham (Cambridge, Mass.: Harvard University Press, 1951), p. 20. Both the kiss lyric and the antifruition poem have origins in Martial 6.34, where the poet competes with the numbered kisses of Catullus and Lesbia: "pauca cupit qui numerare potest" (he wishes few who is able to count). See also *Antony and Cleopatra* 1.1.15, "There's beggary in the love that can be reckon'd."

40. Browne, *Religio Medici and Other Works,* p. 67.

41. *The Complete Poems of John Wilmot, Earl of Rochester,* ed. David Vieth (New Haven: Yale University Press, 1968), pp. 25–26.

42. See Ernest Jones, "The Early Development of Female Sexuality," in *Papers on Psychoanalysis* (London: Bailliere, Tindall & Cox, 1950), pp. 438–51. Jones contended that the dread of aphanisis was deeper than the castration complex, though it is difficult to see how the two could be separated.

43. A. J. Smith has argued that the famous line at the center of "The Canonization" is not, as often alleged, Donne flaunting any old orgasm as a religious mystery; he is rather celebrating orgasm without decay, without the appendage of *post coitum triste* so memorably (and seriously) evoked in "Farewell to Love." See "The Dismissal of Love," in *John Donne: Essays in Celebration,* ed. A. J. Smith (London: Methuen, 1972), p. 127.

44. In the *Standard Edition* the essay is given its less common English title, "On the Universal Tendency to Debasement in the Sphere of Love." A quotation from this essay prefaces the memorable account of fruitional complications in Philip Roth's *Portnoy's Complaint.*

10: Lust Captured: *Paradise Lost* and
Renaissance Love Poetry

1. See also prolusion 3, where the human mind enjoys the Renaissance liberty of ranging "beyond the confines of the world" (*Prose Works*, 1:247). The sentiment reappears in *Areopagitica*'s "minds that can wander beyond all limit and satiety" (*Prose Works*, 2:528), and most famously in Belial's desire to preserve at all costs "this intellectual being, / Those thoughts that wander through eternity" (*Paradise Lost* 2.147–48). In his introduction to Milton's *Private Correspondence and Academic Exercises* (Cambridge: Cambridge University Press, 1932), E. M. W. Tillyard speculated that this theme might owe something to Milton's unconscious memory of Marlowe's Tamburlaine (pp. xxix-xxx).

2. See the almost comic narrative by Thomas M. Greene in *The Descent from Heaven: A Study in Epic Continuity* (New Haven: Yale University Press, 1963), pp. 1–7.

3. In prolusion 7, the need for a humanist Renaissance to cure the stultified education of the Middle Ages is inseparable from the need for a Reformation to cure its spiritual ills: "Throughout this continent a few hundred years ago all the noble arts had perished and the Muses had deserted all the universities of the day, over which they had long presided; blind illiteracy had penetrated and entrenched itself everywhere, nothing was heard in the schools but the absurd doctrines of drivelling monks, and that profane and hideous monster, Ignorance, assumed the gown and lorded it on our empty platforms and pulpits and in our deserted professorial chairs. Then Piety went in mourning, and Religion sickened and flagged, so that only after prolonged suffering, and hardly even to this very day, has she recovered from her grievous wound" (*Prose Works*, 1:293).

4. The book most on our minds here is Barbara Kiefer Lewalski's *Paradise Lost and the Rhetoric of Literary Forms* (Princeton: Princeton University Press, 1985). We favor, and hope to extend, her study of the epic through its incorporation of shorter forms, especially the lyric. Our one cavil is that Lewalski's sense of genre, which is biblical and classical, seems too remote. At least with regard to love poetry, we find the genres more various and more inhabited than they appear to be in Lewalski.

5. Dynasticism is of course the generic form of lust in epic, but whereas Ariosto, Tasso, and Spenser featured a pair of lovers from the ancestry of their patrons, Milton gives us the first pairing in the tree of all family trees, democratizing the convention. At the end of *Poets Historical: Dynastic Epic in the Renaissance* (New Haven: Yale University Press, 1982), Andrew Fichter mistakenly argues that Milton wholly repudiates epic dynasticism and "brings a literary tradition to full closure" (p. 209). He rather (as usual) biblicizes the tradition.

6. Carey's translation, adjusted slightly.

7. See William Kerrigan, *The Sacred Complex: On the Psychogenesis of Paradise Lost* (Cambridge, Mass.: Harvard University Press, 1983), pp. 37–67.

Comus, in the first speech of the temptation scene, threatens to make the Lady "as Daphne was, / Root-bound, that fled Apollo" (660–61). He speaks in other words as Apollo, in the voice of the tradition of male love poetry that had spoken as Apollo for over two centuries. Milton forges his first sense of artistic identity out of the recurrent enemy of this tradition: the woman's resistance. (As he tells us in *An Apology,* male honor is not distinct from the conventional conception of female honor, but is rather an intensification of it.) When Comus makes good on his threat, the Attendant Spirit and Sabrina combine their magic to release her. In terms of the key myth of the Petrarchan tradition, Milton's youthful allegory centers on Daphne, her spiritual resources and her ultimate redemption. Love in *Paradise Lost* begins, we shall see, with the acceptance of the Apollo/Daphne myth, and its transformation into a myth of successful mutual love.

8. See, for example, John G. Halkett, *Milton and the Idea of Matrimony: A Study of the Divorce Tracts and Paradise Lost* (New Haven: Yale University Press, 1970), and Diane Kelsey McColley, *Milton's Eve* (Urbana: University of Illinois Press, 1983), pp. 22–62.

9. Alexander Ross, *Medicus Medicatus* (London, 1645), pp. 76–78; the sculpting metaphor is ours.

10. *The Poems of John Dryden,* ed. James Kinsley (Oxford: Clarendon Press, 1958), p. 415, translating Lucretius 4.1097–1120.

11. In "Milton, Freud, St. Augustine: *Paradise Lost* and the History of Sexuality" (*Mosaic* 15 [1982]: 109–21) and "Milton's *Paradise Lost:* Augustinian Theology and Fantasy" (*American Imago* 42 [1985]: 293–313), Wolfgang Rudat argues that Milton's representation of garden sexuality follows Augustine in leaving the male erection wholly voluntary and the hymen of prelapsarian Eve magically intact. Presumably there would be no foreplay in such a situation. But labor has been joined with delight; a day's work includes looks, embraces, kisses, advances and coy reluctances. There is nothing supernatural about Edenic sexuality in *Paradise Lost*. Milton declares that it would be hypocrisy to think that Adam and Eve did not enjoy sexuality as we enjoy sexuality, and Raphael himself asserts that the act Adam values so much is common to the beasts.

12. One thinks of the final lines of "On the Death of a Fair Infant," where the mother is promised "an offspring . . . / That till the world's last end shall make thy name to live." In Eve's situation this assurance is not, as it may be in the early poem, metaphorical.

13. Edward LeComte quotes *Ars amatoria* 2.717–18 on erotic delay in *Milton and Sex* (New York: Columbia University Press, 1978), p. 91. One of the profoundest explorations of the coyness prized by Milton and many other writers is Georg Simmel's "Flirtation," in *Georg Simmel: On Women, Sexuality, and Love,* ed. Guy Oakes (New Haven: Yale University Press, 1984), pp. 133–52. In flirtation, defined as "the alteration or simultaneity of accommodation and denial," Simmel finds the freedom of a woman in a system designed to favor male acquisitiveness, and, deeper than that, an expression of "the profound metaphysical loneliness of the individual" (p. 149). Perhaps Milton in-

tuited this bond between the autonomy of coyness and loneliness in giving the Eve of book 9 such a pronounced desire for solitude.

14. "Everything he has renounced in his own name is restored to him tenfold," Stanley Fish writes of *Paradise Regained*'s hero in "Inaction and Silence: The Reader in *Paradise Regained*" (in *Calm of Mind*, ed. Joseph Anthony Wittreich [Cleveland: Case Western Reserve University Press, 1971], p. 44). See also Kerrigan, *Sacred Complex*, p. 59 and passim.

15. A good deal of ethnography supports the ideas we are about to introduce concerning courtship and the determination of female worth. See Lucy Mair, *Marriage* (London: Scholar, 1977), especially pp. 48–73.

16. Kerrigan, *Sacred Complex*, pp. 256–59.

17. Not to worry, Adam: Fowler and other Miltonists (we are not sure who was the first) note that God would eventually fulfill this wish for ten taboos by delivering Moses the Ten Commandments.

18. The passage was censured by Richard Bentley for, among other things, the metaphysical nicety of "light / Heavy, though in their place," which he took as evidence that Adam was being drawn away from his situation by superficial prettinesses of expression; see Bentley's *Milton's Paradise Lost: A New Edition* (London, 1732; fac. reprint, New York: AMS, 1974), pp. 334–35. It seems to us that Milton has vested Adam with his own finely calibrated sensitivity to the opinions of aftertimes. The allusion to Aristotelian gravity registers infamy as a burden increasing without limit, which cannot be the case with spatial burdens, according to that (supposed) physical law. Gravity, heaviness, weight, burden: this is one of the major image-systems for the Fall. In old age, Michael tells Adam, "A melancholy damp of cold and dry" will "weigh thy spirits down, and last consume / The balm of life" (11.544–46), and the invocation to book 9 reveals the poet's vulnerability to this mortal depression (45–46). See also Paul Ricoeur, *The Symbolism of Evil*, trans. Emerson Buchanan (Boston: Beacon, 1969), pp. 101ff. Another trope in the passage, the idea of propagation recoiling back upon the propagator as curses, coincides with Milton's root figure for the condition of Satan (see 1.214–20; 3.84–86; 9.171–72; also *Comus*, ll. 592–96). At the end of the lamentations, we find an evocation of endlessly deeper engulfment (10.842–44) reminiscent of Satan's (4.73–78). The obvious implication is that Adam, in trying to understand his condition without the intuition of Christianity, falls into the satanic condition.

19. In her interesting discussion of the passage, McColley suggests that most of the complaints are associated with patristic rather than Protestant literature (*Milton's Eve*, pp. 24–34).

20. One also thinks of Paolo and Francesca in *Inferno* 5. But this was adulterous love, involving each of them with two sexual partners; and its frustration in hell seems diluted by the gusting winds. In the undistracted purity of its picture of sexual frustration, the imagination of Milton's Eve has no obvious peers.

Index

Actaeon, 109–10, 167, 175, 200, 206
Agathocles, 59
Agrippa, Cornelius, 240n.42
Alberti, Leon Battista, 9, 19, 23, 48, 50, 66, 224n.35, 227n.18
Albertus Magnus, 122
Albicante, Gian Alberto, 225n.50
Aldo Manuzio, 8
Alémán, Mateo, 226n.3
Alexander VI, Pope, 27
Alexander the Great, 18–19, 22, 50, 113–14, 117, 152, 192–93, 224n.43, 239n.36, 240n.37
Allen, Michael J. B., 108, 237n.5, 238nn. 19, 20
Anaxarchus, 113
Anselm of Canterbury, Saint, 136, 148
Aretino, Pietro, 23–26, 35
Ariosto, Lodovico, 29–30, 194, 251n.5
Aristophanes, 145
Aristotle, 10, 74–75, 78, 92, 95, 101, 105, 111, 117, 120, 130–31, 215, 240n.42, 253n.18
Augustine, Saint, 22, 79, 103, 107–8, 161–63, 167, 173, 237n.41, 241n.4, 252n.11
Austin, J. L., 150
Averroës (Ibn Rushd), 111–12, 117, 121, 239nn. 26, 30, 241n.1, 245n.22
Ayer, A. J., 139

Bacon, Francis, 74, 77, 81, 85–86, 97–98, 107, 122, 125, 130–31, 152, 191, 232n.12, 236n.34, 242n.13
Baron, Hans, 15, 222n.25, 246n.11
Barton, Anne Righter, 230n.4
Barzizza, Antonio, 229n.35
Beckett, Samuel, 244n.4
Belsey, Catherine, 223n.27, 228n.23, 243n.1
Bentley, Richard, 253n.18
Benveniste, Émile, 236n.32
Berger, Harry, Jr., 120, 241n.4
Bergin, Thomas G., 18
Bernardo, Aldo S., 247n.18
Bèze, Théodore de, 9
Bible, 35, 86, 103, 104, 111, 115, 117, 119–20, 122, 125, 128, 129, 161, 226n.12, 241nn. 5, 6
Blake, William, 91–92
Blanchini, Bartolomeo, 224n.34
Bloom, Harold, 118
Blumenberg, Hans, 78–80, 84–85, 232nn. 9, 10, 11, 233nn. 2, 4
Boccaccio, Giovanni, 163
Bodin, Jean, 37–38, 41, 234n.20
Boethius, 84
Bold, Henry, 185–86, 188
Borges, Jorge Luis, x, 87
Borgia, Cesare, 15, 58–60

Braudel, Fernand, 42, 226nn. 5, 7, 10, 227n.16
Braudy, Leo, 224n.36
Bréhier, Émile, 105, 146, 245n.23
Browne, Sir Thomas, 128–32, 175, 185–86, 198, 243nn. 15, 16
Brownmiller, Susan, 247n.21
Bruno, Giordano, 77–79, 86, 92, 109–10, 167
Bullen, Barrie, 22n.16
Burckhardt, Jacob
—*Civilization of the Renaissance in Italy,* ix, xi–xiii, 50–51, 58, 110, 112–14, 120, 127, 133, 135, 159, 212; and Cassirer, 73–74, 76, 79–81, 231n.2; on competitiveness, 24–27, 29–31; on fame, 19–24; and Hegel, 4–5, 11–13, 31, 222n.22; and idea of Renaissance (individualism), 9–13, 225n.52, 243n.16; and Marxism, 44–47; methodology of, 3–5; on morality, 31–35, 67; on political history, 13–16, 27–29, 37–38, 40–42; on politics and individualism, 16–19, 55–56, 64, 223n.27, 243n.17
—other works, 232n.10; *Architecture of the Italian Renaissance,* 3; *Force and Freedom,* 31, 226n.6; *Griechische Kulturgeschichte,* 4; letters, 4, 22
Burke, Kenneth, 59
Burton, Robert, 182–83
Bush, Douglas, ix-x

Caesar, Augustus, 8, 192–93, 226n.12, 230n.4
Caesar, Gaius Julius, 22
Caligula, 240n.37
Callisthenes, 224n.43
Calvin, John, 226n.12
Camoens, Luis Vaz de, 207
Campesani, Benvenuto, 221n.12
Cardano, Girolamo (Jerome Cardan), 22, 240n.38
Carew, Thomas, 175–76, 179–82, 187, 194, 197, 205
Cartwright, William, 247n.21
Casey, Edward S., 236n.30
Cassirer, Ernst, xii–xiii, 73–81, 83–85, 88–90, 97, 135, 159, 231nn. 1, 2, 232n.7, 236n.33, 239n.26

Castiglione, Baldassare, 16–17, 47–48, 161, 181
Caton, Hiram, 245n.24
Catullus, 157, 184, 228n.29, 250n.39
Cavell, Stanley, 136
Chapman, George, 53
Charlemagne, 6–7, 42
Charles I, King of England, 40
Charles V, Holy Roman Emperor, 7–8, 14, 24, 27, 42, 220n.11
Charles VIII, King of France, 27
Chaucer, Geoffrey, 224n.36
Chigi, Agostino, 226n.12
Chrysippus, 75
Ciapponi, Lucia A., 221n.14
Cicero, 101, 130–31, 163
Cimabue, Giovanni, 9
Claudian, 102, 230n.3
Cleveland, John, 194
Cognasso, Francesco, 222n.24
Cohen, Walter, 230n.4
Coleridge, Samuel Taylor, 240n.42
Collop, John, 175–76, 248n.22
Colonna, Francesco, 221n.14
Colonna, Giacomo, 246n.3
Columbus, Christopher, 10
Conrad, Joseph, 114
Constantine the Great, 5–7
Corneille, Pierre, 58
Cornford, F. M., 75
Cowley, Abraham, 61–62, 178–79, 184, 194
Crashaw, Richard, 194
Curtius, Quintus, 18–19
Cusanus, Nicolas. *See* Nicolas of Cusa

Damon, Philip, 234n.9
Damrosch, Leopold, Jr., 91, 235n.21
Daniel, Samuel, 178
Dante, 6, 14, 18, 195, 224n.36, 235n.25, 239n.35, 253n.20
Daphne, 163–64, 167, 179–81, 196, 200, 206, 211, 246n.15, 247n.21, 248n.26, 251n.7
Datini, Francesco di Marco, 42–43
Davenant, William, 194
Davis, Natalie Zemon, 219n.2
Davison, Francis, 248n.29
Democritus, 113, 117

Derrida, Jacques, 75, 77, 104, 142–43, 237n.10
Descartes, René, xii, 73–74, 77, 85, 90, 112, 122, 135–52, 163, 231n.2, 243n.16
Dewey, John, 144
Diefendorf, Barbara B., 227n.22
Digby, Kenelm, 243n.16
Dilthey, Wilhelm, 219n.3
Diodorus Siculus, 27
Dionysius, Pseudo-, 86, 234n.8, 238n.16
Dolce, Lodovico, 26
Dollimore, Jonathan, 223n.27, 242n.9, 243n.1
Donne, John, x, 76, 94, 107, 171, 175–77, 179, 181–83, 186–87, 194, 238n.18, 248n.29, 249n.34, 250n.43
Drayton, Michael, 173, 176, 178, 247n.19
Dryden, John, 137, 198–99, 247n.21
Duhem, Pierre, 233n.1
Duns Scotus, John, 107, 122
Durling, Robert M., 245n.1, 246nn.13, 14

Eliot, T. S., 131
Elizabeth I, 42, 94, 97, 158, 229n.33
Elliott, J. H., 242n.13
Emerson, Ralph Waldo, 111, 138, 151–52
Empedocles, 113
Erasmus, Desiderius, 8, 29, 44, 107, 226n.3, 233n.5
Erigena, John Scotus, 86, 234n.8
Euclid, 90–91

Fairfax, William, 248n.28
Ferguson, Margaret W., 228n.23
Ferguson, Wallace, 220nn.8, 15
Ferry, Anne, 249n.30
Feuerbach, Ludwig, 234n.18
Fichter, Andrew, 251n.5
Ficino, Marsilio, xii, 74, 85, 94–95, 101–15, 117, 119–22, 145, 148, 192, 229n.2, 232n.3, 237nn.5, 9, 238nn.14, 16, 20, 239n.35, 240nn.41, 42
Filelfo, Francesco, 25
Fish, Stanley, 253n.14
Foucault, Michel, 142–43
Fowler, Alastair, 253n.17
Francis of Assisi, Saint, 224n.36

Freccero, John, 246n.6
Frederick II, Holy Roman Emperor, 14
Freud, Sigmund, 138, 142, 151–53, 157, 188–89, 245n.28, 250n.44, 252n.11

Gadamer, Hans-Georg, 84–85
Galileo, 231n.2
Gassendi, Pierre, 140
George of Trebizond, 27
Ghiberti, Lorenzo, 18, 224n.35
Gilbert, Neal Ward, 234n.20
Giotto, 9
Giraldi Cinthio, Giambattista, 23
Goldberg, Jonathan, 230n.4
Gombrich, E. H., 4
Gordon, Irene, 221n.19
Grafton, Anthony, 225n.52
Graham, James, Marquis of Montrose, 50–51, 228n.23
Greenblatt, Stephen, 219n.2, 223n.27
Greene, Thomas M., 163, 251n.2
Grierson, H.J.C., 248n.29
Guibbory, Achsah, 234n.20
Guicciardini, Francesco, 27–28, 39, 44, 60, 225n.52

Halkett, John G., 252n.8
Harrington, James, 46
Hegel, G.W.F., xi, 4, 11–13, 28, 31, 35, 42, 74, 111, 147, 222n.22, 223n.27, 241n.6
Heidegger, Martin, 75, 77, 107, 119, 138–39, 144, 148, 244n.8
Helgerson, Richard, 219n.2
Helmont, Jean-Baptiste Van, 131
Henry VII, Holy Roman Emperor, 14
Henry VIII, King of England, 6, 52, 158–59, 168
Heracleitus, 75, 129
Herbert, George, 132–33, 151
Herbert of Cherbury, Edward, Lord, 248n.24
Hermes Trismegistus, 102
Herodotus, 22
Herostratus, 22–23, 33, 59–60, 215
Herrick, Robert, 176, 181, 184–85, 189, 194, 228n.29
Hirsch, E. D., Jr., 234n.9
Hitler, Adolf, 6

Hobbes, Thomas, 38–39, 41, 45, 59, 77, 90–92, 94, 127–30, 151–52, 243n.15
Holly, Michael Ann, 28
Homer, 93, 102, 121, 163, 193–94
Hopkins, Jasper, 85, 233nn. 1, 2, 234n.8, 235n.22
Horace, 102
Hoskyns, John, 182, 248n.29
Huizinga, Johan, 233n.5
Hull, Elizabeth, x
Hulliung, Mark, 222n.25
Hume, David, 90
Hunter, G. K., 231n.9
Husserl, Edmund, 107, 136, 139–40, 142–43, 234n.9

Imperia, 226n.12
Innocent VIII, Pope, 27, 118

Jardine, Lisa, 225n.52
Johnson, Samuel, 74
Jones, Ernest, 187, 250n.42
Jonson, Ben, 45, 51–52, 183–84, 194, 240n.40, 249n.34
Josselin, Ralph, 52
Juana Inés de la Cruz, Sor, 239n.25
Julius II, Pope, 62
Justinian, I, 226n.2

Kant, Immanuel, 73–78, 90, 98, 145, 148, 151, 241n.6
Keats, John, 240n.42
Keillor, Garrison, 221n.20
Kenny, Anthony, 150
Kepler, Johannes, 231n.1
Kermode, Frank, 5
Kierkegaard, Søren, 107
Kilmer, Nicholas, 246n.16
King, Henry, 184–85, 249n.34
Klibansky, Raymond, 115
Koebner, Richard, 222n.23
Koyré, Alexandre, 234n.15
Kristeller, Paul Oskar, 112, 231n.2, 238nn. 14, 20, 239n.32, 240n.41
Kyd, Thomas, 242n.14

Lacan, Jacques, 138–39
Laura, 158–67, 170–72, 174, 180–82, 195, 246n.3

LeComte, Edward, 252n.13
Lefranc, Abel, 228n.27
Leibniz, Gottfried Wilhelm von, 73–74, 232n.3
Levao, Ronald, 97
Lewalski, Barbara Kiefer, x, 251n.4
Lipsius, Justus, 243n.17
Livy, 55
Locke, John, 90, 243n.1
Lovejoy, A. O., 104
Lovelace, Richard, 175, 179, 182, 203, 249n.30
Lucretius, 198–200
Luther, Martin, 34–35, 46, 107

McColley, Diane Kelsey, 252n.8, 253n.19
Machiavelli, Niccolò, 22, 55–67, 77, 143, 222n.25, 230n.8
Mair, Lucy, 253n.15
Maravall, José Antonio, 38, 221n.20, 226n.3
Marbeuf, Pierre, 239n.25
Marcus, Leah, 219n.2
Marino, Giambattista, 248n.26
Marlowe, Christopher, 62–63, 126, 131, 175, 177, 187, 200–202, 247n.21, 251n.1
Marsilius of Inghen, 83
Marston, John, 221n.20
Martial, 185, 249n.33, 250n.39
Marvell, Andrew, 175, 179–80, 182, 187, 194, 203–4, 208–9, 213, 231n.9, 248n.25
Marx, Karl, xi, 44, 46–47
Masenius, Jacobus, 239n.25
Medici, Lorenzo de', 27
Medici, Lorenzo de', the younger, 56
Medici, Piero de', 27
Middlemore, S.G.C., 221n.19, 225nn. 58, 60
Miles, Leland, 237n.9
Milton, John, x, 37, 102, 127, 129, 149, 159, 175, 188; *Apology*, 193, 195, 251n.7; *Areopagitica*, 40, 197, 241n.3, 251n.1; "Canzone," 196; *Comus*, 196, 212, 251n.7, 253n.18; *Doctrine and Discipline of Divorce*, 196–98, 200–201, 211, 215; "L'Allegro," xii; "Lycidas," 194–96; "On the Death of a Fair Infant," 252n.12; *Paradise Lost*, xiii,

23, 35, 65, 100, 137, 183, 189, 192–
218, 231n.13, 235n.25, 236n.28,
240n.42, 247n.21, 251nn. 1, 5, 7,
252nn. 11, 12, 13, 253nn. 18, 20; *Paradise Regained*, 178, 253n.14; *Poems*
(1645), 195; prolusions, 191–93,
243n.16, 251nn. 1, 3; *Reason of Church
Government*, 93; *Samson Agonistes*,
143, 205, 221n.20; sonnets, 195
Mirollo, James V., 245n.2
Moduin, 220n.9
Montaigne, Michel de, 73, 77, 123, 125,
129, 167, 242n.11
Montchrestien, Antoine de, 221n.20
Montrose, Marquise of, 50–51, 228n.23
More, Thomas, 122
Musaeus, Pseudo-, 102

Namatianus, Rutilius, 220n.9
Napoleon I, 6
Narcissus, 110, 147, 160–63, 166, 174,
181, 206, 239n.25, 246nn. 6, 14
Nashe, Thomas, 46, 249n.34
Nicholas V, Pope, 25, 83
Nicolas of Cusa, xii, 73, 75, 77–78, 80–
81, 83–90, 92–100, 102, 109, 113–14,
118, 122, 137, 146, 153, 233nn. 2, 4,
5, 234nn. 8, 9, 20, 235nn. 21, 22,
236nn. 28, 30, 31
Nietzsche, Friedrich, 75, 107, 220n.3
Nisard, Charles, 225n.52
Nonnus of Panopolis, 93

Occam, William of, 89
Ong, Walter J., 234n.20
Origo, Iris, 226n.8
Orpheus, Pseudo-, 102
Osborn, Louise Brown, 248n.29
Ovid, 102–3, 109, 159, 164, 166, 172,
175–77, 183, 185–86, 188, 200–201,
239n.23
Ozment, Stephen, 227n.22

Panofsky, Erwin, 9, 115
Parks, George B., 242n.10
Paul, Saint, 103, 221n.20
Pechter, Edward, 223n.27
Petrarch, 5–6, 18, 24, 26, 37, 109, 153,
186–89, 194–96, 200, 206–8, 210–12,
215, 221n.12, 224n.36, 239n.30,
251n.7; *Africa*, 7–8, 35, 172, 193;
Canzoniere, xii–xiii, 78, 157–68, 170,
172, 174, 180–81, 187, 193, 207; *Coronation Oration*, 20; letters, 21, 163;
Secretum, 22, 162–63, 167, 172;
Trionfi, 171
Petronius, Pseudo-, 183–84, 249n.34
Petrucci, Pandolfo, 15
Pettegrove, James B., 231n.2
Philip II, King of Spain, 41
Philostratus, 183
Pico della Mirandola, Gianfrancesco,
122, 241n.1
Pico della Mirandola, Giovanni, xii, 48,
74, 77, 85, 93, 104, 117–29, 132–33,
149–51, 153, 191–93, 222n.22, 231n.2
Pigman, G. W., Jr., 239n.36
Pitkin, Hanna Fenichel, 229n.2, 231n.10
Pius II, Pope, 21
Plato, 74, 76, 78, 91–92, 94, 101–5, 107–
8, 112, 115, 117, 121–23, 145, 201,
204, 228n.29, 237nn. 5, 7, 9, 240n.42
Plautus, 83, 226n.3, 229n.35
Plett, Heinrich, 5
Plotinus, 74, 86, 94, 103–6, 110–11, 122,
222n.22, 232n.3, 237nn. 7, 9, 10,
241nn. 5, 6
Plutarch, 224n.43, 239n.36
Pocock, J.G.A., 222n.25, 225n.55,
242n.14
Poggio Bracciolini, 25, 27, 48
Poliziano, Angelo, 6
Pontano, Giovanni, 18
Popkin, Richard, 136
Pozzi, Giovanni, 221n.14
Price, Hereward, 221n.20
Proclus, 86, 238n.16
Pythagoras, 102

Quilligan, Maureen, 228n.23

Rabelais, François, 23, 32–33, 48, 51, 53
Ralegh, Sir Walter, 122, 250n.39
Randall, John Herman, xii, 75
Randolph, Thomas, 175, 184
Ranke, Leopold von, 41
Regan, Mariann Sanders, 249n.30
Régnier, Mathurin, 221n.20
Reiss, Timothy J., 232n.8

Ricoeur, Paul, 138, 236n.32, 253n.18
Rienzi, Cola di, 6
Righter, Anne. *See* Barton, Anne Righter
Robertson, D. W., 246n.6
Rochester, Earl of (John Wilmot), 186–87
Rorty, Richard, 77, 152, 232n.8
Ross, Alexander, 198, 243n.16
Rossi, Paolo, 236n.34
Rossky, William, 236n.29
Roth, Philip, 250n.44
Rousseau, Jean-Jacques, 151
Rowland, Ingrid D., 226n.12
Rudat, Wolfgang, 252n.11
Ryle, Gilbert, 244n.11

Salomon, Louis B., 249n.30
Sandys, George, 108, 239n.23
Saxl, Fritz, 73, 115, 231n.1
Schmitt, C. B., 232n.4
Schopenhauer, Arthur, 107
Schrader, Paul, 235n.26
Schramm, Percy Ernest, 220n.10
Seneca, Lucius Annaeus, 10, 23, 48, 102, 163, 231n.9
Seroux d'Agincourt, Jean-Baptiste, 9
Sforza, Lodovico, 27
Shakespeare, William, x, 73, 119, 194; *Antony and Cleopatra*, 250n.39; *As You Like It*, 143; *Coriolanus*, 193; *Hamlet*, 145, 170, 240n.42; *1 Henry IV*, 227n.15; *3 Henry VI*, 63–64; *Henry VIII*, 229n.33; *Julius Caesar*, 19, 221n.20; *King Lear*, 58, 206; *Macbeth*, 54, 69, 151; *A Midsummer Night's Dream*, 103; *Othello*, 33, 53–54, 97, 144; *Richard III*, 65–69, 97, 144, 231nn. 11, 13; sonnets, 52, 170, 173, 177–78, 183–84, 221n.20, 249n.34; *Taming of the Shrew*, 50; *Tempest*, 69; *Timon of Athens*, 109; *Titus Andronicus*, 248n.24; *Troilus and Cressida*, 45; *Twelfth Night*, 240n.40
Shirley, James, 20
Sidney, Sir Philip, 124–25, 170–73, 178, 194, 216
Sigmund, Paul, 88, 233n.1
Simmel, Georg, 252n.13
Simon, Kathrin, 220n.4
Sismondi, Simonde de, 222n.25

Smith, A. J., 250n.43
Smith, John, 104, 234n.20, 237n.7
Smith, Sir Thomas, 52, 227n.21
Socrates, 96–97, 101, 105, 110, 123
Soderini, Piero, 230n.8
Sophocles, 102
Spenser, Edmund, 94, 173–74, 178, 194, 197, 207, 228n.29, 247n.20, 251n.5
Sperber, Dan, 95–96
Spitzer, Leo, 221n.20
Stanley, Thomas, 181, 247n.20, 248n.26, 249n.34
Stephens, John, 52
Stevens, Wallace, x, 135, 137
Stone, Lawrence, 47, 227n.22
Strabo, 10
Suckling, Sir John, 175, 182–83, 185–87, 250n.38
Surrey, Earl of (Henry Howard), 158
Symonds, John Addington, 222n.24, 225n.51

Tacitus, 56
Tasso, Torquato, 51, 125, 194, 251n.5
Tayler, Edward, 223n.27
Thierry of Chartres, 84, 233n.1
Thomas Aquinas, Saint, 107–8, 112, 239n.36
Tillyard, E.M.W., ix–x, 251n.1
Titus Vespasianus, 8, 221n.14
Trinkaus, Charles, 234n.18, 239n.30
Tufte, Virginia, 228n.29

Ullman, B. L., 221n.12
Urceo, Codro, 18

Valency, Maurice, 159
Valerius Maximus, 224n.43
Valla, Lorenzo, 8, 25, 88
Vasari, Giorgio, 9, 20, 224n.35
Vaughan, Henry, 194
Vega Carpio, Lope de, 49, 58, 221n.20
Vergil (poet), 7, 20, 102, 193, 204, 220n.11
Vergil, Polydore, 6
Vesalius, Andreas, 106, 231n.2
Vickers, Nancy J., 228n.23
Villani, Filippo, 225n.58
Vinge, Louise, 239n.25, 246n.6

Visconti, Bernabò, 15
Vives, Juan Luis, 58, 120, 132, 230n.5
Voigt, Georg, 29
Voltaire, 25

Walker, D. P., 237n.3
Waller, Edmund, 179–81, 185–86, 196,
    211, 240n.37, 248n.26
Warburg, Aby, 231n.1
Waswo, Richard, 239n.35
Watts, Pauline Moffitt, 84, 234nn. 16, 18
Webster, Charles, 236n.34
Webster, John, 221n.20
Weimann, Robert, 44
Weinberg, Julius, 239n.27
Weiss, Helena, 238n.11
Wenck, John, 234n.8
Whigham, Frank, 223n.29, 230n.7
Williamson, George, 243n.15
Winckelmann, Johann, 4
Wind, Edgar, 236n.30

Winstanley, Gerrard, 129
Wise, James N., 243n.16
Wither, George, 249n.32
Wittgenstein, Ludwig, 139
Wittkower, Margot, 240n.42
Wittkower, Rudolf, 240n.42
Wölfflin, Heinrich, 3–4
Wolfson, Harry A., 236n.30
Wyatt, Sir Thomas, 158, 168–70, 177,
    201, 231n.9, 246n.17

Xenophon, 27

Yates, Frances, 220n.11, 237n.2, 241n.2
Yorkshire Tragedy, 23

Zamiatin, Eugene, 91
Zanobi da Strada, 225n.58
Zedler, Beatrice, 239n.27
Zeitlin, Froma, 247n.21
Zoroaster, 102